The Leadership Compass

Mapping Your Leadership Direction

Ben McDonald
Sidney McDonald

Benchmark Learning International

Bulk discounts available. Contact Benchmark Learning International.
Phone: 208-433-9093
Email: sales@benchmarkli.com

This publication is designed to provide accurate and authoritative information on the subject matter covered. The publisher and authors make no representations or warranties with respect to the content of this book and specifically disclaim any implied warranties of merchantability or fitness for a particular purpose. No warranty may be created or extended by sales representatives or written sales materials. The advice and strategies contained herein may not be suitable for your situation. You should consult with a professional where appropriate. Neither the publisher nor authors shall be liable for any loss of profit or any other commercial damages, including but not limited to special, incidental, consequential, or other damages. The example companies, organizations, products, people and events depicted herein are fictitious examples. No association with any real company, product, person, or events is intended or should be inferred.

ISBN: 0615812805
ISBN-13: 9780615812809

Benchmark Learning International
5239 Quarterpath Drive
Boise, ID 83716
USA

DEDICATION

To our future leaders:

Sean
Heather
Coreena
Luke
Jade
Kelcie
Blake
Rand
Daelyn
Caleb
Lydia

"May you always strive to be the best you can be...always humbly leading yourself and then others as you have opportunity while continuing to learn, knowing you can do even better and go even further."

ACKNOWLEDGMENTS

Leadership has always been our passion and throughout our careers we have had the opportunity to observe and work with many excellent leaders and more than a few poor ones. To those excellent leaders, we thank you for setting the bar high and for being an example for us and those around you. We would be amiss if we did not mention *some* of the great leaders we have experienced. Each would say they are not perfect, but we believe that they all strive to do their best.

Dominic Costa was a mentor who exhibits excellent leadership skills even today, in his retirement. Frank McSparren is a people leader with a strong heart for God, yet one who is not afraid to challenge others to be better. Pastor Paul Hatfield of The Pursuit in Boise sets a high standard of excellence and yet is meek to listen to God and to others. Paul was recently selected to receive our 2012 Leader of the Year award.

In our work in the academic world, we have encountered many excellent leaders as well. The most prominent of these leaders include John Anderson, Alan Cramb, Betsy Hughes (also a winner of the 2012 Leader of the Year award), Hossein Sadid, Susan Faraone, Carolyn Pelzel, Kurt Haenicke, Beth Campbell, and Carolyn Gregory.

Other clients also offer a number of examples of excellent leadership we have learned from including Bob Moss, Scott Moss, Mike Mazza (another winner of the 2012 Leader of the Year award), Brett Atkinson, Nancy Atwood, Bill Doherty, Guido DeBakker, Ella Studer, and Linda Simmons.

Of course, a book such as this has many hands involved. Thank you Coreena Tyler for your excellent research when needed and ideas in our brainstorming sessions. We extend our appreciation to the talented Sandra Cavanaugh for her ideas and energy. Sandra also participated in our brainstorming sessions. These fun sessions yielded valuable ideas from Brian Burkhardt, Katrina Burkhardt, Luke Fauver, Mike Heinz, Teri Heinz, Aubrey Monroe, Matt Monroe, Scott Swallow, and Regan Tyler.

Donna Bankhead is an incredible editor and contributed many valuable insights into how to make this effort even better. Thank you Donna for your meticulous efforts and seeing so much that we didn't. Many others encouraged us and gave us inspiration to continue and saw the value we would bring to others through leadership development. To them, we thank you and appreciate your input – Sean McDonald, Marc Herndon, Heather Hooper, Jim Hutchinson, Pastor Scott Kujath, Carol Aubitz, Jaimie and Erika Macartney, Kalvin and Liz Evans, Kevin Bell, and Dale and Bonnie Bell.

CONTENTS

Contents

PREFACE

"There isn't good or bad leadership…you are leading or you are not."
- Major Chris Whipp

Now more than ever our world needs excellent leaders. We frequently see leadership failing all around us – government, business, education, church, and families. As younger generations enter organizations, they are typically lacking in leadership skills and many may not understand the significance that strong, competent, and ethical leadership means to our society. Many experienced leaders are so busy they do not develop their leadership skills and then struggle to simply get from crisis to crisis. There are even some leaders who feel that growing as a leader is not really that important. After all, if you are in charge and getting reasonable results, that is sufficient.

Why Some Leaders Fail

- They don't understand their weaknesses and develop their leadership skills accordingly
- They don't develop their teams and direct reports
- They focus only on financial results
- They don't listen to their customers
- They are arrogant
- They lack personal integrity

Great leadership is felt throughout an organization. It sets the tone for what needs to be done, how it is to be done, and the path to achieve the desired goals. It has a major effect on the culture of an organization. When good leadership is present, people want to join the organization and those who are in it do not want to leave. In fact, studies have shown that many people desire good leadership more than a raise or promotion.

Likewise, poor leadership can be felt throughout an entire organization – and not in a good way. The real culture of the organization is the opposite of what the leaders may say it is, and many people leave the organization in frustration. Not only is the culture affected, but also the quality of the products and services is diminished, having a major effect on how well the organization performs in the marketplace.

We wrote this book because we feel strongly that leadership excellence is important in every area of our life and culture. Of course, it is easy to understand how great leadership helps a company or organization succeed and grow. In examining the leadership resources that are in the marketplace, we saw a need for a top-level approach to leadership that engaged people in self examination and self development. There are many books on leadership, many that we refer to or recommend. But they are simply books that describe principles that the reader may or may not remember or make the effort to apply to their situation. In *The Leadership Compass*, you will work – from identifying your strengths and weaknesses to reflecting on them, and onward to developing in the areas needed. You should not simply read this book, you will benefit most if you **do** this book.

Our goal is to develop better leaders in government, corporations, non-profits, universities, schools, churches, and families. It's that simple. Our experience as leaders, executive coaches, and consultants to both corporations and universities has given us insight into how to do this. We have helped leaders at all levels in these organizations through coaching, assessments, consulting and training. We hope to provide the important elements of effective leadership for current and aspiring leaders in a way they can immediately begin to assess, reflect, develop and change to be more effective and to effect change in their spheres of influence.

Not all organizations have budgets for formal leadership training and ongoing development. Therefore, this book provides the content, tools, and direction to grow current and future leaders regardless of organizational budgets. We feel it is also important to recognize that leadership goes beyond the work environment and as such, every person that desires to increase their success and effectiveness can benefit from this book, regardless of their position.

This Book Will Enable You To:

- Assess your performance in 30 leadership competencies.
- Reflect on what each competency means to your current or aspired position.
- Create a Personal Development Plan specific to your needs and goals.
- Access ideas and resources to include in your Personal Development Plan.
- Focus your attention on improving your leadership skills and behaviors.
- Create positive leadership change.
- Provide growth in your current position.
- Expand your potential to move into higher leadership positions.

The Renew Leadership Movement

There are many leadership resources in the marketplace, but despite these great resources we continue to see a breakdown at all levels of leadership. Consequently, we have started the Renew Leadership Movement, with the goal of helping people become great leaders and consequently have an impact at all levels of society.

The Leadership Compass is one part of our program; and it will help guide you to improving your leadership skills and behaviors, regardless of your job or where you are in your personal life. The Renew Leadership Movement website (**http://www.renewleadership.com**) has many other tools, blogs, resources, and forums to discuss leadership topics. Through the Renew Leadership Bookstore, you can easily access Amazon and view books we highly recommend for current and aspiring leaders. We urge you to subscribe to this site to get leadership news, access leadership resources, and participate in the blogs and forums.

Helping you become a better leader is only the first step in the Renew Leadership Movement. We hope to spread the movement to every part of society and see the benefits of excellent leadership given to our children and grandchildren. We are not happy with the status quo of leadership today and will stand tall in changing it. We hope you will also participate in the Renew Leadership Movement to continue your leadership growth and help others do the same.

INTRODUCTION

"Nothing so conclusively proves a man's ability to lead others as what he does from day to day to lead himself."

- Thomas J. Watson

Are You a Leader?

Yes! You are a leader, probably on multiple levels, and most of the content in this book is relevant to you. First, you are a leader of yourself. You make decisions about your life including day-to-day "operations" and your future plans. Most of the competencies we present in this book are very applicable to the skills and behaviors you display in your everyday life. How well you do in each competency has a major impact on your personal life.

You may also be a leader in your family and within your circle of friends. Again, the decisions you make as a leader in this environment can have a major impact on your life and the life of others. Much of what we present in *The Leadership Compass* is relevant to your role as a leader in your family and within your circle of friends.

We commonly think of leaders at the next level – local community, churches, schools and businesses. You may be a leader in one or more of these roles. Each competency we describe in this book is relevant to these leadership roles.

There are also leaders at the national level. You may aspire to be a leader at this level. It is very important that leaders at this level excel in as many competencies as possible because of the far-reaching impact they have in their performance.

Finally, today's world is smaller and smaller because of advances in technology and transportation. There are leaders in the global community who have an impact on us. You may fill this role as a global leader for a corporation, non-profit, or government agency. Consider the impact that global leaders have in their leadership role.

What level of leader are you? Most likely you lead at different levels in your personal and professional worlds. Regardless, your leadership skills and behaviors have an impact on you and those around you.

What is Leadership and Why is it Important?

There are many definitions of leadership, and what we have found is that most are either too general (the art of getting people to follow) or too specific (the practice of effectively communicating to others what needs to be done and getting their cooperation to do it).

We prefer to define leadership by its characteristics, using our competency model that encompasses what we believe are the key attributes of successful leadership. Our model (*4Ps Leadership Compass*™) consists of 30 competencies built around our 4Ps – Persuasive Vision, Positive Results, Personal Character, and People Skills. Many would consider 30 competencies far too many, but we feel that to be successful, the leader must focus on developing all of these competencies. Notice we said developing, not being perfect in all competencies. No one is excellent in all the competencies. But, if you know which are your strengths and which need improvement, you can be moving in the right direction.

Competencies are made up of various skills and behaviors that describe the leader's characteristics in detail. Much of the work you will do to improve is focused on changing your skills and behaviors that make up a competency.

Consider the following graphic which is explained in more detail in Chapter 2:

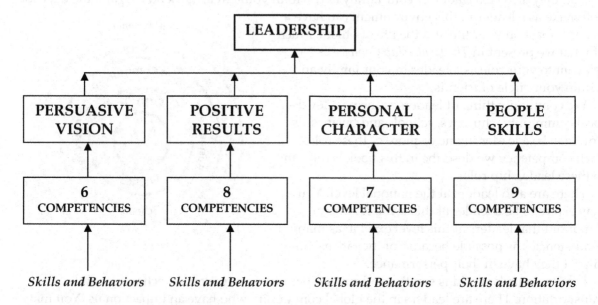

Leaders have many responsibilities, but good leaders establish the vision, set the example, guide others, and make difficult decisions with solid character and courage. Leaders are also responsible for their results and for the results of those they lead. All great leaders inspire others to achieve beyond what is expected. After all, just doing what is expected is not great, it is just average, and only average results are produced.

It is every leader's responsibility to put forward their best effort, regardless of the number of people they lead. It is also important to remember that a leader's success or failure has a direct

2

impact on others. It is vital if you are a current or aspiring leader that you take every step possible to be your best and understand your strengths and weaknesses and how to continually develop your skills. It is also important to remember that no leader has "arrived" or is perfect. It benefits every leader to honestly assess their skill level, identify specific improvements or growth areas, and then take actions to develop while leading others to do the same. Think about this last sentence a moment. If *every* leader did this, how much better would our organizations function and how much improvement in results would be experienced?

Another side benefit to this approach is that it promotes positive changes in the culture of the organization, as the norm becomes individual excellence rather than an outlook that excellence is optional. If the whole organization has this mindset, the results can be phenomenal!

The Leadership Compass

We have written *The Leadership Compass* to aid those who want to improve their leadership skills and behaviors. We have seen such an incredible demand for strong leadership in government, universities, businesses, churches, and families that we would be remiss in not providing a useful tool to enable current and prospective leaders to improve. We believe that most leaders want to take steps to excel; they just don't know how to systematically do it, even though there is an abundance of books on leadership. This book is different because it provides the system, models, and activities for leaders to move in the right direction.

Some large corporations and government agencies have leadership training, and a few might even have coaching or mentoring programs. But the vast majority of organizations do not implement comprehensive leadership development practices that increase the kind of sustainable leadership effectiveness that leads to organizational success.

Many organizations use standardized 360-degree performance assessments as part of their formal review process. While laudable on the surface, we have seen many organizations and leaders use these assessments punitively. These assessments should be used as a development tool, not as an accessory to punishment. The best organizations use them to create a positive culture of leadership *development*.

Further, leadership effectiveness and success are often measured when pre-determined and tangible results are produced, such as revenue objectives, customer satisfaction ratings, etc. While these are critically important, more often than not many organizations stop there in quantifying leadership or organizational success.

We believe there are many factors that determine a leader's or an organization's success, more than just achieving a stated goal or number. For example, reputation of the person or organization, customer satisfaction, workplace safety, and employee loyalty are just a few other factors to consider when defining success.

As leadership coaches and consultants over the last couple of decades, we have worked with leaders in large and small organizations, profit and non-profit, and have had the privilege to observe and facilitate the contributing factors that go into achieving and sustaining leadership and organizational effectiveness. Over time, we developed several leadership and development models and have used them to help leaders achieve personal, professional, and organizational success. These experiences culminated in this book for potential and current leaders so they can grow their talents and behaviors to excel as leaders in their organization.

The real opportunity lies in how individual leaders embrace a mindset of excellence and personal responsibility and then doggedly promote that excellence and responsibility within the organization they lead. This begins at the individual level, and can and should take place at all levels of the organization from the front line employee to the CEO. However, it takes an exceptional leader to accomplish this sometimes massive organizational task.

If you expect your company or organization to provide leadership development, you may have a long wait. However, even if you are participating in your organization's development opportunities, the concepts, principles, and activities in *The Leadership Compass* will serve to augment your learning and multiply your growth specific to your needs. In these stressful economic times, it is paramount that every individual commits to their professional development. To us, that means starting first with developing your leadership skills because this has a major effect on your success. Your personal success then influences your organization's success, which further benefits you and others within the organization.

> ### *Why We Need Strong Leaders*
>
> - The world is becoming more competitive in a straining economy
> - We need examples of strong and ethical leadership for our upcoming generations
> - Businesses and other organizations need strong leaders to achieve and maintain success

It is important that leaders be the best they can be in their job and other aspects of their life. Without competent leaders grounded in character, there are consequences to people, organizations, and even countries. People depend on leaders, and the success of any organization hinges on the qualities of the leaders. We believe every leader should have an understanding of their current state and a plan to improve.

Using the 4Ps Leadership Compass™ Competency Model and the corresponding tools presented in this book, any person, in any position, can control and manage their ongoing leadership growth. This book revolutionizes leadership development in that it:

- Applies to all leaders – successful, struggling, and aspiring.
- Provides a map and corresponding leadership tools for self-initiated development.
- Enhances other leadership development programs that may be part of the reader's ongoing activities.
- Provides direction to the reader's specific leadership needs, which creates focus.
- Provides real-life examples of excellence in each leadership competency.
- Gives recommendations and resources to improve in each competency, which saves valuable time.

We use compass and direction metaphors throughout the book. You are on a journey to assess your leadership skills and behaviors, reflect on the results, develop in a specific direction based on your needs, and create long-term change in your leadership skills and behaviors. *The Leadership Compass* should be your first step in creating a life-long path for leadership development.

Cultural Considerations

As you embark on this leadership development journey using *The Leadership Compass* as your guide, you will notice that most references to leadership skills and behaviors are those predominately considered best practices in western thought on leadership. It is important to keep in mind that other cultures may have variations to these behaviors that mirror their customs and practices. Therefore, if you live or work in a country that has some of these variations to leadership behaviors, take note of these differences especially as you identify actions to take when building your Personal Development Plan.

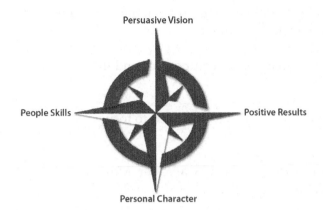

Persuasive Vision

People Skills — Positive Results

Personal Character

CHAPTER 1

How to Navigate This

Book

"We must become the change we want to see."
- Mahatma Gandhi

In *The Leadership Compass*, we have put together resources and tools that, if objectively and faithfully used, will help you grow your leadership effectiveness and bring value to those you lead and to your organization.

In **Chapter 2, The Leadership Compass**, you will be guided through our 4Ps Leadership Compass™ Competency Model. Here the skills and behaviors that are needed for greatest leadership success are described. From experience, it is our belief that if a leader exemplifies each of these competencies, then their effectiveness will be greater than that of a leader skillful in only a few of these important behaviors. This comprehensive approach produces the best leaders.

Chapter 2 also includes a description of the development model you will use throughout the book to identify your strengths and weaknesses when creating a Personal Development Plan (PDP). This model consists of four steps: Assess, Reflect, Develop, and Change.

Chapter 3, Mapping Your Direction, will walk you through the steps to create your Personal Development Plan. It includes a sample plan so you can see an example of the final stage of our process before you begin the exercises for each competency. A blank PDP is included in Appendix C.

Chapter 4, The Leadership Compass Competencies provides a brief introduction on how to proceed through each of the competency chapters. Follow the instructions here to get the most out of each competency and its associated tools.

Chapters 5 through 34 describe and focus on each of the 30 leadership competencies. This description is not an exhaustive exploration of each competency; that is what the resources are designed to provide if you need further development (based on the results of your self assessment). Within each chapter are a series of tools to help you understand the competency and assess your current location (skill and behavior level) in that competency. Each chapter also contains tools to help you create a Personal Development Plan to improve in the competency. The following is a description of the format of each competency chapter.

Competency Description: We provide a summary of the competency and the importance it has for the effective leader.

Red Flag Behaviors: A short list of behaviors that indicate you need to focus your improvement in this competency.

Case in Point: An example of how the competency is used by a leader. Most of these examples show positive behaviors in the competency.

Notes for the Aspiring Leader: Brief tips for those who desire to be stronger self leaders and those who are considering a leadership role in the future.

ASSESS Your Current Location: This is the self assessment portion of the competency chapter. Follow the instructions to take the self assessment and record your score here and on the Master Score Sheet in Appendix A.

REFLECT: This section consists of worksheets to record your highest and lowest items from the self assessment. It also includes a list of questions to stimulate your thinking about this competency.

DEVELOP: This series of tools helps you create the foundation of a Personal Development Plan for the competency. Included in the section are:

- *Develop and Renew* - A lengthy list of recommendations we have used in working as coaches with successful leaders.

- *Resources* – Books, articles, websites and other resources to consider as part of your Personal Development Plan for this competency.

CHANGE: This section includes worksheets for you to identify specific steps to improve your weaknesses or enhance your strengths in this competency. You can easily transfer this information to your Personal Development Plan (Appendix C) if you choose to focus on this competency.

It will take some time for you to go through the material and worksheets for all competencies. We recommend that you schedule approximately one hour each day until you complete all competencies. You will then be able to create your Personal Development Plan, focusing on those competencies most important to your leadership role.

The final chapter (35), **Creating Long-Term Change**, is the final step in your personal leadership development. In this chapter, we describe how you can use your Personal

Development Plan to make changes in your professional life to become a better leader. This chapter will guide you in the creation of your Personal Development Plan and give you tips on how to implement your development steps to achieve your leadership development goals.

Appendix A is a Master Score Sheet you can use to record your scores for each competency's self assessment.

Appendix B contains worksheets to help you collect and analyze the data from the self assessments to prepare your Personal Development Plan.

Appendix C contains a blank Personal Development Plan for your use.

Finally, for the greatest success in using this book for your continued leadership development, you will need a mindset that you are responsible for your growth and success. We provide many resources along with a roadmap to follow, but you will need to motivate yourself to do the work necessary to increase your effectiveness. The decision to commit to your development and success will lead to positive results over time. If you are having trouble deciding if you wish to pursue a path to improve your leadership skills, remember what Winston Churchill once said: *"We are still masters of our fate. We are still captains of our souls."* So make the commitment and take the time to be the master and captain of your fate. As a leader, you have much to gain and give in furthering your success!

The following are two brief examples of leaders who have used The 4Ps Leadership Compass™ Competency Model and tools to improve their leadership skills and behaviors:

Example 1

Carol was an entrepreneur who grew her business from a one-person flower arrangement shop to a 12-person florist business. After she hired her first two employees, she realized that she needed to provide leadership for the company. She had no strategic plan and she operated day to day, problem to problem. She sometimes got upset at her staff and didn't react well because of the stress she was under. She knew she needed to do something.

Her first step was to take her leadership assessment. This indicated to her that she was strong in decision making, oral communications, and integrity. This made her feel good, but she also saw that she was weak in talent management, conflict management, strategic thinking and financial management. She realized that if she was to grow her business, she needed to improve in these important areas.

Using the resources provided with the self assessment, she created a Personal Development Plan. She spent a little time each day focusing on the development recommendations and put her effort into learning about each of her weakest competencies.

As a result, Carol developed a well-thought-out strategic plan, spent more time coaching and mentoring her employees, and increased her understanding of critical financial issues. Soon her employees were happier and she looked forward to each day. She continued to refer to her Personal Development Plan and used it to continue her company's growth.

After a year, she needed to hire four more people and she promoted Jaimie, one of her florists, to be a manager. Her first step with Jaimie was to guide her through a self assessment and help Jaimie create her Personal Development Plan.

Example 2

Roger was excited about his new position as Director of Procurement for his company. He had studied hard and recently completed his degree program in business administration with an emphasis on procurement. He was glad the company saw the value in his education.

It wasn't long, however, until Roger was dismayed. His team did not respond well to his directions and they were resistant to change. He was working long hours and it was taking a toll on his family. Even when he came home late, he worked in his home office for another two hours each evening. He was beginning to think the promotion was not worth it and yearned for the days when he was just "one of the guys" and could leave every day at 5:00.

Janet, Roger's boss called him into her office late on a Friday. She explained that she knew things were not going well. Some people had complained to her about Roger's way of doing things, and she observed two times when Roger lost his temper with someone.

Rather than berate Roger, Janet suggested that he take a self assessment of his leadership strengths and weaknesses and put the effort into learning how to improve. She stressed that Roger needed to be as objective as possible in completing the assessment. She told Roger that she would support him in any way possible to improve his leadership skills and behaviors. She recommended that they meet weekly to assess his progress.

Roger was skeptical in the beginning, feeling that it would take time away from doing his job. Janet had recommended he do the assessment and then set aside an hour each day to work on his Personal Development Plan. Roger agreed and completed the self assessment that evening. He was surprised at the comprehensiveness of the assessment and even more startled at the results. He never thought he was weak in interpersonal skills. He always thought his communication skills were excellent. On the other hand, he did realize that he had a problem with stress management.

He used the resources supplied with the self assessment and created his Personal Development Plan. Since Roger is a morning person, he arrived at the office early each day and devoted the time from 7:00 to 8:00 to work on his development plan. Each week he met with Janet and they reviewed his accomplishments. Janet shared her ideas and he incorporated them into his plan. In a matter of weeks, he could tell he was improving in these areas. In fact, two of his team members asked him, "What happened? We were getting discouraged with you and it is like you have turned over a new leaf!"

The Leadership Compass: Mapping Your Leadership Direction is designed to methodically lead you through the steps to becoming a better leader. With objective and diligent effort you will create a Personal Development Plan customized to meet your leadership growth needs and with focused attention to your development, you will experience greater leadership success.

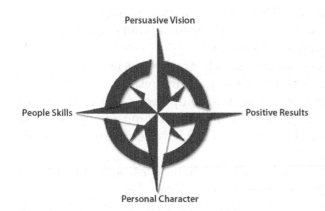

Persuasive Vision

People Skills — Positive Results

Personal Character

CHAPTER 2

The Leadership

Compass

"Know thyself."

- Plato

Every leader has strengths and weaknesses. We regard Abraham Lincoln as an excellent leader who guided America through some of its most difficult years. He demonstrated impeccable integrity, motivation, and courage. But Lincoln was also often depressed and communicated poorly. He had difficulty making decisions and hesitated to make personnel changes in his General Staff, leading to many setbacks. In his case, his strengths were so very strong that he succeeded in spite of his weaknesses.

If you think about public leaders, even those you admire, it is not difficult to identify their weakest competencies. The closer you get to understanding someone's position, the easier it is to evaluate an individual's strengths and weaknesses. For example, you probably know your boss' weaknesses better than your boss does!

It is easy to say, "A leader must be inspirational and be a good strategist." Or, "A leader must communicate clearly and manage people well." What do these statements mean? Although they may be true, how are they measured and what does success look like?

The Leadership Compass Competency Model

Over many years of research and administering leadership assessments to university and corporate leaders, we have collected data on the skills and behaviors that constitute leadership excellence and success. Through this research and the anecdotal evidence from coaching many of these leaders, we have determined that a broad-based approach in measuring leadership effectiveness helps cast the best vision for leadership excellence and provides the best framework in which to effectively grow leaders. From this research, we identified specific skills and behaviors that contribute to a leader's overall effectiveness and success. The measurement of these skills and behaviors is then used to identify what areas of focus should encompass the leader's development strategy for their ongoing improvement.

The outcome from this approach is our model of 30 leadership competencies that describe and measure a leader's strengths and weaknesses. This has led to some interesting findings. For example, in almost all businesses and universities, the weakest competency measured is Talent Management. Simply put, most leaders are poor at selecting talent, coaching, giving feedback, and developing their team members. As you can imagine, this can have serious negative effects on an organization's success.

On the other side of the spectrum, almost all leaders score well in their Commitment to Diversity. Perhaps this is because of the emphasis on diversity of hiring over the past few decades. Anecdotal comments have expanded on this by identifying that excellent leaders take advantage of a diversity of thought and opinion.

There are, of course, a myriad of other leadership competency models. They range from models that categorize leadership on four or five macro-competencies to extensive models that break leadership into a multitude of components. We have given extensive study to these models and have found, for the purposes of self development, a middle-of-the road approach is best for individual professional development.

Because we focus on the systemic development of the leader, we believe it is important to dissect leadership skills and behaviors into as many individual competencies as reasonable. This enables development activities to be as precise as needed to create positive and faster growth and results – more on this later. If leadership is described in just four competencies, the range of skills and behaviors is so large it would be difficult to manage and translate into actionable steps within a development plan. For instance, if you assessed yourself as weak in people skills, what does that mean – communication? negotiation? teamwork? – or any number of additional discrete competencies.

By the same token, it is important to group related competencies. This enables you to have a big picture of your leadership traits. Even though you may score high in some competencies and low in others, if they are related you can see trends in your performance.

We group our 30 competencies into 4 "Ps":

- Persuasive Vision
- Positive Results
- Personal Character
- People Skills

The outcome is our 4Ps Leadership Compass™ Competency Model. We believe that each of the four points on the Leadership Compass are vital to every leader in their professional effectiveness and to their ability to contribute significantly to the success of the organization they participate leading in.

Let's look at each of these leadership compass points in more detail.

4Ps Leadership Compass™ Competency Model

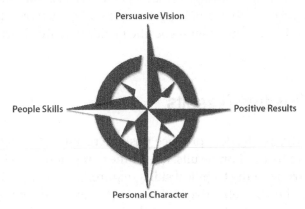

Persuasive Vision

Leaders must create a persuasive vision for their team or organization. Without a vision, planning cannot take place. Without a vision, it is difficult for a leader to be inspiring. Without a vision, the team will be unclear as to what direction to go.

But simply having a vision is not enough. The vision must be creative and serve to motivate and inspire others. It must be the result of strategic thinking by the leader and others who have input into the vision.

By persuasive, we mean that the vision itself will influence others to follow. But the leader must also use influencing tactics to maintain momentum and to "sell" the path to achieve the vision. A persuasive vision must also make sense. It must be tangible and understood by others, and the benefits to the organization and people must be apparent.

> ### *Persuasive Vision Competencies*
> - Creativity
> - Influencing
> - Inspiration
> - Motivation
> - Planning
> - Strategic Thinking

Political leaders excel at creating a vision when they are running for office. While they may be successful at communicating the vision and influencing others, they may very well have difficulty when reality strikes and they win the election.

Thus, having a persuasive vision (and excelling at the competencies that make it up) is not enough. The vision needs to be attainable and more importantly, the leader needs to know the path to achieve it and lead those in the organization through the specific actions to reach the vision. For example, in his 2008 campaign for the presidency, Barack Obama set a vision of

> ### *Notable Leaders Strong in Persuasive Vision*
> - Fred Smith (FedEx)
> - Martin Luther King Jr.
> - Ronald Reagan
> - Winston Churchill
> - Dwight Eisenhower

"Hope and Change." While many would say they liked the vision and it inspired and motivated them, others would say that the vision was too vague and did not provide enough clarity on its meaning and what specific actions were needed to get there.

The key message is that a persuasive vision can be incredibly powerful and rally others. However, that is only part of a leader's responsibility. An organization's vision has to have clarity and be followed with specific tactics that are clearly communicated, understood, and achievable.

Positive Results

Effective leaders produce positive results. They achieve their goals and objectives. Strong leaders are focused on results, one of the competencies which support this category. In addition, they are strong in the technical skills required for their position and are well-respected as being an expert.

Leaders effective in this category are also committed to quality in all they do and produce. They are not hesitant to make informed decisions, and they manage their time well. If tasked to find new business for their organization, they do it well and are customer focused.

A prime example of an effective leader who produced positive results is the late Steve Jobs with Apple. Jobs coupled his extreme skills as a visionary with the competencies to create positive results – customer focus, technical skills, business development, decision making, and financial management. He led his team to produce his visionary products by staffing his leadership team with people very similar to himself.

> **Positive Results Competencies**
>
> - Business Development
> - Commitment to Quality
> - Customer Focus
> - Decision Making
> - Financial Management
> - Focus on Results
> - Technical Skills
> - Time Management

> **Notable Leaders Strong in Positive Results**
>
> - Steve Jobs (Apple)
> - Bill Gates (Microsoft)
> - Vince Lombardi
> - Meg Whitman (eBay)

On the other hand, one of the most challenging leadership positions is as the manager of a sports team. If a team is expected to do well, but in reality performs weaker than expected, the manager (not the players) takes the responsibility and often loses their job.

Personal Character

The most effective leaders excel in this category. We can think of many leaders who have been strong in the other three categories, but a failure in character brought about their demise, such as Richard Nixon and Ken Lay (Enron). Most character failures bring about the resignation or reassignment of the leader, such as in the examples above. Some, however, take a long road of rehabilitation to regain their reputation to leave a positive legacy (Bill Clinton, Michael Milkin). Leaders must do what is right to gain the trust of others and establish their credibility.

Credibility is based on honesty and ability to do the job. It is the foundation that every leader builds their organization on, day in and day out. Customers, peers, and team members must trust an effective leader. Without trust, there will not be followers for long.

Leaders are also followers, and must show their humbleness to be good followers. Everyone has a boss – even a CEO must report to a Board of Directors or Trustees; politicians are accountable to their constituents; and entrepreneurs must meet the needs of their customers. While some leaders may not always be in the role of a follower, they set the example in their organization by listening to the input of others, acknowledging mistakes and taking responsibility for outcomes of their team. They do not shift the blame to others.

Personal Character Competencies

- Courage
- Credibility
- Followership
- Initiative
- Integrity
- Stress Management
- Trust

Leaders must sometimes be courageous and make a hard decision or solve a difficult problem. Often, doing the right thing versus taking the easiest or most profitable approach takes a good deal of courage, especially if there is opposition. The most effective leaders do not hesitate to be courageous and demonstrate their best talents in difficult situations. They also know how to manage their stress level so it does not become infectious and create anxiety in others. They excel in managing their work-life balance and have interests outside of the workplace.

Notable Leaders Strong in Personal Character

- Abraham Lincoln
- Mother Theresa
- Florence Nightingale
- Martin Luther
- Billy Graham

Probably the most important competency for a leader is integrity. The most effective leaders do what is right and are anchored with a strong set of ethics. They hold the bar high for others they lead or even come in contact with. An effective leader never compromises on their integrity – never.

As a final note on personal character, it is often minimized as an important factor to leadership success. However, a leader's character is often mirrored within the organization. So for example, if you have a bully type leader who allows dishonest practices, others within the organization are likely to follow these behaviors. Not only will the workplace become difficult to work in, the organization itself will suffer greatly. Outstanding personal character in a leader really does matter and this is why it is part of the Leadership Compass and is supported by relevant competencies.

People Skills

Leaders need people who willfully and aggressively follow their lead to achieve success. People skills are essential, but unfortunately, the lack of skills in this area leads to the demise of many leaders. The competencies in this category cover a wide range of skills and behaviors. Many leaders do well in some competencies, but are weak in others.

Effective leaders have good interpersonal skills, meaning they are liked and people enjoy working with them and for them. They are considerate of people's needs. They manage people well, care about their individual goals, and accept the responsibility to develop the talents of others. They also provide positive feedback when a job is done well and constructive feedback when a person needs to change a behavior.

Teamwork is an essential competency that requires people skills. Team members can be vastly different and have competing interests. Consequently, teams can be complex to lead. Effective leaders know how to build a team and focus their energy on achieving the team's goals. When conflict arises, the effective leader challenges it and works toward the best outcomes, whether they are involved in the conflict or it is among team members.

Effective leaders embrace change and realize that it is their responsibility to craft the outcome for people. They proactively communicate the change and manage its outcomes. They lead through the change using effective communication, patience, and understanding of the difficulties that people transitioning through change experience.

The most effective leaders are adept at negotiation. Whether with a customer or resolving an issue within their organization, the leader strives to achieve the best outcome of any negotiation using ethical negotiation tactics.

People Skills Competencies
• Change Leadership
• Commitment to Diversity
• Communications
• Conflict Management
• Interpersonal Skills
• Negotiation
• Problem Solving
• Talent Management
• Teamwork

Effective communication skills are required for any leader to be successful. Leaders know what to communicate (and when) and are skilled in influencing how others receive the communication. It is critical that the leader effectively listen and display the body language that confirms to the receiver that listening is taking place.

Notable Leaders Strong in People Skills
• Colin Powell
• Ronald Reagan
• Margaret Thatcher
• Bill Clinton
• Dale Carnegie

Finally, leaders look at individuals as people who bring talents to their team regardless of their background, ethnicity, religion, or other orientation. They are considerate of others and seek out diversity, including differences of opinion and ideas.

Leadership Competency

As you can see from this overview of the Leadership Compass and the 4Ps, leadership competency is vital to a leader's success and to the overall health of the organization in which they lead. You may have also noticed that some competencies could perhaps fall into more than one P or directional on the Compass. When making the final assessment of how each competency interrelates to other competencies to increase a leader's effectiveness, we chose the Compass directional which promotes the greatest success in that P for a leader (See Figure on next page).

For example, Influencing falls under Persuasive Vision, but also has many correlations to People Skills because, after all, you are influencing people. However, effective influencing is needed to promote and implement the vision of the organization, which is what drives the plans, tasks, and behaviors of the people within the organization.

As you continue through this book, you will notice how each of the competencies build upon each other to complete each of the 4Ps, with the overall model forming the general characteristics of effective and successful leaders.

Every leader has multiple weaknesses, especially when viewed through the lens of an in-depth competency model such as this. It is important to note that while this model depicts ideal leadership skills and behaviors, it also provides leaders with the vision and direction needed to increase their propensity to greater effectiveness and success. Remember, success for a leader and for the organization they represent takes a lot of thought, effort, commitment, and frequent change. This takes us to the next layer of the 4Ps Leadership Compass™ Competency Model – leadership development.

Before we move on, we feel it is important to reiterate that discrete behaviors, skills, and attitudes all form the competencies within the 4Ps Leadership Compass™

4Ps Leadership Compass™ Competency Model

Persuasive Vision

Creativity
Influencing
Inspiration
Motivation
Planning
Strategic Thinking

People Skills

Change Leadership
Commitment to Diversity
Communications
Conflict Management
Interpersonal Skills
Negotiation
Problem Solving
Talent Management
Teamwork

Positive Results

Business Development
Commitment to Quality
Customer Focus
Decision Making
Financial Management
Focus on Results
Technical Skills
Time Management

Personal Character

Courage
Credibility
Followership
Initiative
Integrity
Stress Management
Trust

Competency Model. If a leader exhibits competency in these areas, they are more likely to succeed and to help their people and organization succeed. There are however outside factors that can affect behavior and sometimes impede performance. Therefore, we recommend that leaders seek out professional resources in addition to our leadership development model, if they are having difficulty in any of the following areas:

- Mood difficulties (depression, mental illness, etc.)
- Situational difficulties (relational, extreme conflict, etc.)
- Physical health difficulties (seek and follow professional care)

While these factors will not always affect a leader's performance, in most cases they do, so it is important to be aware not only for yourself, but for those you lead.

Leadership Development

No leader will attain perfection in all the competencies we have identified. We are all works in progress. Successful leaders understand this and therefore analyze their performance, results, and plans while making the necessary adjustments and changes that provide forward progress toward greater success. In other words, it is a continuous process of assessing, reflecting, developing, and changing that advances a leader's effectiveness.

Those leaders who do not embark on this continuous process typically stall in their growth and results, lose interest in their work, succumb to mediocrity, or in extreme cases, are susceptible to unethical practices because they do not have a compass or foundation to guide their actions and decisions.

There are a variety of reasons leaders may choose not to continuously develop, grow, and improve; some may include:

Examples of Why Leaders May Not Develop, Grow, and Improve

Common Reasons	Examples	Possible Attitude	Our Thoughts
Excuses	"I'm too busy; it is not that important."	Growth, development and change are not viewed as important.	As people, we focus our energy on our priorities. Is being your best a priority?
Self-Perception	"I'm already doing great and don't need to improve."	Fear of inward reflection, possible results, and the needed effort to change.	It takes courage to honestly face our shortcomings, and it does take time and effort. Are you worth it? Is your career worth it?
Deflecting	"It is not my fault; that is my organization's responsibility."	Lack of personal responsibility and accountability.	People, especially in positions of authority, must take personal responsibility.
Motive	Hiding a failure.	Dishonesty and self-deception.	The easiest action to take is not always the right action. Weigh your decisions with what is right to avoid this dangerous slippery slope.

If you are honest with yourself, one or two of these thoughts have crossed your mind in the past. Remember, if you are a leader it does not mean that you are perfect; it means that you are responsible for doing the right thing! That responsibility begins with you, because the opposite of responsibility is reckless leadership, and the consequences affect not only you, but also others. Your actions, or lack of actions, to grow and improve set the example for your organization. If you are taking responsibility for your continuous development, others are likely to follow.

Taking responsibility for your personal leadership development has tangible rewards and will likely:

- Improve your overall results.
- Inspire others to do the same, therefore improving their performance.
- Bring greater success to your organization.
- Open up new professional opportunities.
- Discourage poor behavior patterns because your example and behavior set the norm for your team or organization.

Let's further analyze leadership development within the constructs of the 4Ps Leadership Compass™ Competency Model. We highlight these steps because without a plan to increase effectiveness, it is much more difficult to experience improvement. On the other hand, by following this method, your path to leadership success is greatly enhanced. In later chapters, we will guide you through the specific instructions for building your Personal Development Plan.

Four discrete steps to successful leadership development lead to improvement and greater effectiveness:

1. **Assess** – First, you need to understand your current state as a leader, primarily your strengths and weaknesses. This step provides you with a snapshot of your current performance using the self assessment in each competency chapter. It is vital that this step be done objectively, honestly, and as accurately as possible, as the results determine the quality of improvements you will achieve.

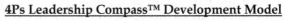

4Ps Leadership Compass™ Development Model

2. **Reflect** – Next, it is important to reflect on your results. Because the self assessment is quite detailed, you may discover skills or behaviors that you hadn't thought of before, especially as you link them to your specific position along with your current behavior. This step will help you form the most beneficial development actions in the next step.

3. **Develop** – This step is where the hard work begins as you identify the specific actions you will take to improve in your weakest areas and how you can leverage your strengths to increase your overall effectiveness. For best results, be specific in your actions related to your position, use the development recommendations we provide in each competency chapter, and set specific dates that you will accomplish these actions.

4. **Change** – Finally, you will experience the process of positive change — changed behaviors and improved skills, as well as a few awkward moments while you are learning or re-learning a particular skill. Change takes time and consistent effort so you will need to be committed and may wish to reach out to a peer for accountability and feedback if it is a particularly difficult area. Additional tips on how to successfully implement change are provided in Chapter 35.

The 4Ps Leadership Compass™ Competency and Development Models provide the structure for development and the foundation for successful leadership behaviors and skills needed for effective leadership. Now the choice to move forward is up to you.

Important And Often Overlooked Leadership Traits

Before beginning your journey through *The Leadership Compass*, we ask that you pause and think about the kind of leader you want to be. Perhaps you have experienced good and bad leaders and can make a judgment based on your experience. However, we would like you to consider several common traits that great leaders possess in order to maintain a following and create success for themselves, others, and their organization. Many of these characteristics are embedded within the Leadership Competency Model competencies. However, we want to emphasize and expand on their importance to long-term, successful leadership because they are often not talked about, overlooked, or in many cases, misunderstood and undervalued. We recommend that, after reviewing these leadership traits, if you decide you need further understanding and development in them, be sure to incorporate appropriate actions into your Personal Development Plan.

Leading with Compassion

The most effective leaders are compassionate – they truly care about people, especially their followers. Your leadership stint is only temporary; you will eventually retire and even pass on. Compassion is the one characteristic of a leader that can make or break a leader's legacy. Wouldn't you want your followers to be talking about you and your leadership compassion years after you are no longer a leader? On the other hand, would it be more important to you to achieve as many goals as possible by whatever means possible at the expense of others? Effective leaders can be effective without treating others harshly. In fact, we believe compassion adds to not detracts from success.

As you go through each competency, think about what it means to your style as a leader to be compassionate. In a blog, Marie-Claire Ross lists seven ways to bring more compassion to your leadership style:

- Listen, listen, and listen again. Great leaders actually listen more than they talk. When talking to staff members, they ask more questions and listen.

- Assume the best of others. People usually try to do the right thing and sometimes they make mistakes. Find out why they did what they did and help them get back on the right track.

- Keep your emotions in check.

- Be interested in others. Great leaders are interested in those who work with them at all levels.

- Accept responsibility. You are 100% responsible for your life. Blaming others and creating excuses diminishes the respect others have for you.

- Be open to feedback. Don't argue. Listen and respond by changing where needed.

- Support others in their career. It has been said that the number one responsibility of a leader is to develop other leaders.

In addition to assessing your strengths and weaknesses in the self assessment for each competency, strive to be a compassionate leader.

Leading with Humility

Unfortunately, humility has gained a bad reputation in many cultures as a negative characteristic for leaders. It is often thought to mean that a humble person has a low opinion of themselves, that they are spineless and weak, or that humbleness is not compatible with a vibrant intellect and personality.

Sometimes describing the opposite of something helps to enhance the understanding of the true meaning of the word. The following traits or behaviors are the opposite of humility:

- Narcissism. People who are narcissistic think it is all about them. They make very poor leaders. They may get a lot done but quickly alienate any followers.
- Conceit. The conceited person thinks they are the best, when in fact, the opposite may be true.
- Arrogance. No one likes to follow an arrogant leader. And the arrogant leader will blame the followers who fall by the wayside.
- Pride. The prideful leader carries conceit to new levels. They believe in themselves to a fault.

We have probably all been in positions at some point during our career where we have served under leaders who have one or more of these characteristics. It is not only quite painful to follow their lead, but more important, it sets a terrible example of leadership. The behaviors can be infectious and affect the entire organization's culture. They stifle growth, seriously damage motivation, cause creativity and quality to suffer, and decrease productivity.

Now, look at some of the characteristics of humility that you will find in an excellent leader:

- Has an accurate — not exaggerated — opinion of their own importance.
- Respects and embraces the perspective of a diversity of people and ideas.
- Views self as equal to others, regardless of their position.
- Receptive and appreciative of other's ideas.
- Gives credit to others when success is achieved.
- Does not blame others or deflect problems.

Those who lead with humility understand that not all good, virtue, and knowledge originates with them. They understand that others around them, regardless of their position, experience, age, gender, and so forth, have something to offer, and they can learn and benefit from them. Strong, humble leaders should set this example to others within an organization and with their teams to keep the culture growing, positive, and vibrant. If you find yourself acting without genuine humility, take positive steps to grow in this area. You may need a change of thinking, but positive results will follow.

Leading to Serve

It is a common perception that leaders are to be served by their followers. This practice has been in existence for thousand of years, across many nations, and we still see it played out in countries that have kings, queens, and dictators as their rulers. Even in modern day business organizations, we may see this practice, although with a more subtle approach.

Many great leaders have taken a different approach and view themselves as servants of others – team members, customers, and community. When we take a close look at leaders as servants versus leaders who expect to be served, the contrast is sharp as shown in the chart on the following page:

Leaders as Servants	Leaders Who Expect to be Served
Listen to others.	Consider themselves above listening.
Ensure that their team has what it needs to be successful.	Expect their team to make do with what they have and take a hands-off approach to problems.
Create an environment that is transparent and fosters open communication.	Uses knowledge and information as power and leverage.
Show empathy toward others with actions that demonstrate caring.	May voice empathy but the words are without substance.
Earn respect through actions.	Demand respect based on their position.

When you serve others that you lead, your actions show that you care and that you are open and transparent. You are there to help your team be successful. You look after and protect those you lead. As you have the opportunity, look to serve those you lead. If you do so, loyalty, respect, and quality results will follow.

Self-Initiated Development

Over the years, we have worked with a variety of leaders, especially in the executive coaching environment, and we continually stress the importance of initiative when it comes to improving behavior and performance. It really is a choice and unfortunately, some do not make this choice, typically because of the effort involved.

Earlier we briefly mentioned the consequences of not pursuing ongoing professional development. However, we want to leave you with a few thoughts on self-initiated development, as it is a basic and foundational principle to success.

- No one can do this for you.
- You are ultimately responsible for your successes or failures.
- Others depend on your competence.
- You may be held accountable for your lack of competence.
- You are important (not solely because of your position) and deserve the positive outcomes that result from continued development.
- You are in control; therefore can determine your route and destiny.
- You can make a difference in your own life and the lives of others by taking a self-initiated development direction.

As you embark on this journey seek others who can encourage you, support your efforts, hold you accountable, and mentor or coach you. Development and change take time and commitment, but with honest and diligent effort, you will experience many of the rewards that we spoke of earlier. The positives to your career with this approach cannot be overstated. So here we go!

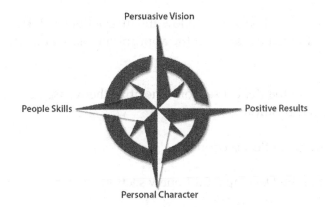

Persuasive Vision

People Skills

Positive Results

Personal Character

CHAPTER 3

Mapping Your

Direction

"A goal without a plan is just a wish."
- Antoine de Saint-Exupery

To be an effective leader, you need a plan to continually develop your skills and behaviors. Leaders cannot be satisfied with the status quo. Business (and life) moves fast, and leaders must continually improve to not only be better leaders, but to keep pace with other leaders and ever changing environments.

In this chapter, you will learn how to create your Personal Development Plan (PDP). It is created by you and is *your* map forward to becoming a better leader. Using the information in this book and the results of your self assessment, you will create a PDP that is customized for you. It will not fit anyone else. It focuses on the competencies in which you need improvement. It identifies actions to take that fit your needs and schedule.

Your PDP will list a lot of things you must do. Fulfilling the goals you set will not be easy. Learning anything takes focus and work, and improving your leadership skills and behaviors is no exception. Later in this chapter we will give you some tips to make it easier for you to accomplish your goals using the PDP. First, however, we will give an overview of the steps to prepare your PDP and discuss how to identify the actions you will take as part of your plan. Finally, at the end of this chapter, we will show you a sample PDP for one competency to give you an idea of what an effective PDP looks like. Keep in mind, yours will be different in many ways because it is customized to your needs and your position.

Steps to Prepare Your Personal Development Plan

1. Read the front matter to each competency chapter – Description, Notes to an Aspiring Leader, Case in Point, and Red Flag Behaviors.

2. Take the Self Assessment (Assess Your Current Location). Follow the instructions to take the assessment and calculate your score. Record the score in the appropriate place and on the Master Score Sheet in Appendix A.

3. List your highest and lowest scored items in the Reflect section. Prioritize them based on their importance to your current or aspired position.

4. Think about and answer the questions in the Reflect section.

5. Review the recommendations provided in the Develop And Renew section.

6. In the Change section, list the specific actions you will take to enhance a strength or improve a weakness in this competency. Refer to the Reflect, Develop and Renew, and Resources sections to give you ideas on actions to take.

7. If this competency is one that you choose to focus on developing, transfer the information in the Change section to your Personal Development Plan in Appendix C.

8. To develop your overall PDP, follow the instructions in Appendix C.

Tips to Prepare Your Personal Development Plan

Your PDP is serious business. It is your path forward to becoming a more effective leader. Therefore, we offer the following tips to help you create a plan that works for you.

1. **Prioritize Development.** After completing the self assessment for all the competencies in our model, choose which you will focus on developing first. You should select those that are most critical for your current or aspired position. However, if you scored well in a competency, we would advise not including it in your PDP immediately.

   Use the Master Score Sheet in Appendix A to determine competencies in which you need immediate improvement and are part of your current or aspired role. You can always come back later to further develop your skills and behaviors in the competencies in which you scored well (strengths).

2. **Use Action Verbs.** When you create your actions in the CHANGE section for each competency, use action verbs. This makes the action a true action. For example, if you think reading a book about the competency will help you, use the term "Read…" to list the action item. Another example would be, "Talk to Jason Herk about his experiences in developing his credibility."

3. **Create a Realistic Schedule.** Ensure that the schedule you create as part of the PDP is realistic. Nothing is more demoralizing in this effort than not being able to accomplish all the actions by the scheduled date. Give thought to your scheduling, and factor in the time you need to do your job and other parts of your life. However, your schedule should be aggressive so you can accomplish your goals in a timeframe in which you can quickly see results. It is better to focus on fewer competencies and be aggressive in your actions and schedule than to tackle too many competencies at once with many action steps to improve.

4. **Change Your Thinking.** Lasting change comes from changing our thinking. If you desire to change in a certain area, give time to change your thinking about it. Our tendency is to repeat certain behaviors over and over, even if we are trying to change. But a change in our thinking supports the creation of new behaviors. For example, you may find influencing difficult or be stuck in a particular pattern of influencing others. As you learn more about influencing, you may be uncomfortable using different influencing tactics, so make sure you understand the different techniques and the value of each. In many cases, we need to retrain our thinking when using new approaches. This takes time, repetition, and often awkwardness in the beginning.

5. **Stay Motivated.** When discouraged, which will happen sometimes during this process, reflect on your behaviors and the impact they have on your organization, the people around you, and your future career goals. Motivate yourself by thinking about how your improvement will benefit your career and those who you come in contact with – your team, peers, and family. You may even want to reward yourself when you complete major steps on your Personal Development Plan to help stay motivated.

Another method that works well to keep on task with your development is to team with a peer who is also using *The Leadership Compass*. You can then hold each other accountable for assignments and help keep each other motivated.

Sample Personal Development Plan

Creating a Personal Development Plan is NOT the purpose of this book. Nor are the efforts you take as you progress through the competencies. The purpose is to create change in you, change that is meaningful to you as a leader. A PDP that sits on a shelf does not change you or your behaviors. Put it center on your desk. Refer to it daily and celebrate your successes.

The following shows a sample Personal Development Plan for one competency (Time Management). Yours may look similar, but it also may look very different from this sample, depending on the action steps you identify to develop in each competency. Use this sample as a guide in creating your PDP in Appendix C.

SAMPLE PERSONAL DEVELOPMENT PLAN (PDP)

Competency: Time Management

Score: 62%
(from Appendix A)

General Steps for this Competency:

Actions (See Change Section)	Resources Needed	Date Compl.
Read *Time Management: The SID Way.*	Purchase through website or Amazon.	5/20
Talk with Jason Elias about his time management techniques.	Schedule time with Jason.	5/4
Talk with my spouse about my work-life balance needs.	Set aside time to talk about this issue.	5/4
Talk with team members about my meeting management skills. What are their impressions and feedback?	Set meeting time to meet with each team member.	5/4

Item-Related Steps:

Item (See Reflect Section)	Score	Actions (See Change Section)	Resources Needed	Date Compl.
I know how much time I am spending on various jobs.	2.0	Track my time on each job for 1 week.	Develop a log to use or find a sample online.	4/22
I delegate time-consuming tasks when appropriate.	2.0	Talk with my team about what tasks they are comfortable with me delegating. Assess skills level of each team member for specific tasks.	Set up one-on-one meetings.	5/2
I manage meeting agendas appropriately.	1.0	Begin creating meeting agendas for those I am responsible for.	Research some sample agendas; ask T. Bossum.	4/22
I leave contingency time in my schedule to deal with the unexpected.	1.0	When developing my daily schedule, allow an hour free time in both morning and afternoon to use as contingency time.	Daily schedule	4/22
I am organized and it is easy for me to find what I need.	1.0	Get assistance from Heather to organize my office.	Suitable time for her to devote to the task.	5/6

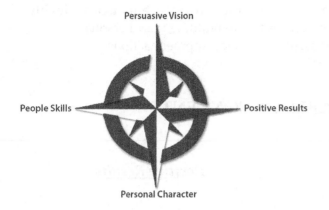

Persuasive Vision

People Skills — Positive Results

Personal Character

CHAPTER 4

The Leadership Compass Competencies

"It is necessary … for a man to go away by himself … to sit on a rock … and ask, "Who am I, where have I been, and where am I going?"
- Carl Sandburg

On the following pages, you will study about and take the Leadership Compass Self Assessment for each competency, along with analyzing your score and creating your personal development actions for each competency. The sections of each chapter have been described in Chapter 1.

The self assessment consists of an assessment for each of the 30 competencies, grouped by P, described in Chapter 2. At the beginning of each competency self assessment are instructions on how to complete it. Follow the instructions for scoring and recording your score on the Master Score Sheet in Appendix A. Based on the results of this self assessment, you will then develop your Personal Development Plan as described in Chapters 3 and 35.

It is important that you be as objective and honest as possible. In fact, step out of yourself and try to view your skills and behaviors from the perspective of others that you interact with on a regular basis. One way to do this is to think of two or three people you work closely with, perhaps a direct report, a peer, and your boss. As you take each self assessment, think of them by name (and visualize them) and consider how you think they would score each item. The more honest and objective you are in completing each self assessment, the more useful the results will be for you.

Identify the competencies that are most appropriate to your current or aspired position. It is not necessary that you complete the self assessments in the order provided, although we highly recommend that you complete all relevant competencies before building your Personal Development Plan. This process will help you prioritize your development actions.

COMPETENCY TABLE OF CONTENTS

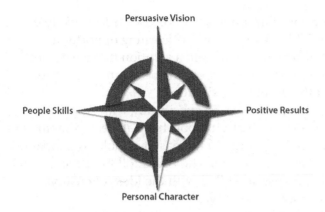

Persuasive Vision

People Skills

Positive Results

Personal Character

CHAPTER 5

Creativity

(Persuasive Vision)

"Creativity is inventing, experimenting, growing, taking risks, breaking rules, making mistakes, and having fun."
– Mary Lou Cook

Because we are executive coaches, people often ask us, "What do you do?" One response we think is apropos is that as coaches we work with a person to trigger creative thinking to solve problems or deal with situations. People being coached are looking for innovative solutions.

Creativity, a quality more traditionally associated with artistic endeavors, has been slow to find its place in the business world outside of marketing or advertising. In truth, it is at the core foundation of every entrepreneurial enterprise. Many believe that creativity is associated with a particular personality or gene inherent to a certain type of person. This skill involves qualities such as the propensity to take risks or to turn a problem on its head to gain a new perspective. This type of creativity is a skill that can be learned and is valuable to every leader.

Most of us are more creative than we demonstrate. We are taught to be conservative in our thinking and fear being penalized for suggesting new or unique ideas. You and your team should generate ideas without initially judging them – that comes later as you determine the risks and cost of adopting them.

Creativity is also a motivator. It is challenging and personally rewarding to the members of your team to find unique solutions to problems or issues that arise. This endeavor can be deeply satisfying to many people and keep the organization vibrantly moving in a positive direction.

Creativity has many applications in the day-to-day world of the manager and leader. In problem solving, the creative person can choose from a greater number of alternative solutions. In conflict management, the leader often must come up with a creative solution to bring people and ideas together. Even in everyday management situations, creativity can help us come up with more innovative ways of doing things – and often ways of doing them faster, cheaper, and better. These creative ideas often come from putting together a diverse team to look at a situation. A diverse team brings together a variety of experiences and perceptions of a situation, usually leading to a creative result.

To increase your creativity, look for new patterns of information. Look for the least likely or odd ideas or solutions and ask, "What's missing?." Look on failures as learning opportunities. Take the time to be creative. Sometimes we are in such a rush to gain a solution that we do not fully consider all alternatives. Sleep on a problem or situation. Often, the best or most unique solution comes when we are not thinking about the problem or situation.

Think of the creativity that has occurred over the past 20 years, specifically with Apple products – music, video, books, communication, and productivity tools have all been combined in devices that are smaller than a calculator was in recent history. In the past, technology companies did not seek out and hire creative people; they wanted engineers who could follow specifications in creating a product. Today, high technology companies are filled with the ideas of creative people who engineer new products that make us more productive.

Creativity relies on freedom first, structure later. After you come up with your ideas, subject them to all the tests and criticism that any other potential solution is given. Creativity lies in the way solutions are generated, not in how they are tested.

Red Flag Behaviors

- You do not encourage team members to brainstorm ideas or solutions to problems.
- When faced with a problem, you choose a path or solution immediately, without considering alternatives.
- You ignore innovative ideas or solutions from your team members.
- You have linear thinking and approach every situation looking for the logic behind it.
- You select team members for projects strictly based on the requirements and their skills related to the project.
- You think creative people do not belong in your organization – you want doers, not thinkers.

Case in Point

Lara was facing a dilemma. Her department's largest customer was filled with poor communicators. No one in the customer's organization would return calls promptly, and it often caused delays in production as her team waited for a response. Finally, she realized that she needed to solve the problem, but she had no ideas on how to do so.

She decided to put together a team to brainstorm solutions. Rather than just use her team, she also selected some creative people from other departments. She even included a few people who did not normally work with the customer. She thought that a diversity of ideas, including those from people who did not know the customer, may help solve the problem.

During the brainstorming session, Lara was surprised at the number of creative ideas that were presented. No idea was dismissed until all ideas were captured. The team then assessed the possible outcomes of each idea and the risks involved.

The team decided to invite the customer's team to an offsite meeting so they could discuss solutions. All core team members and Lara's boss, Carolyn, would attend to demonstrate the corporate commitment to improving communications.

The team planned to keep the meeting low-key and discuss other topics as well as communications to show commitment to this customer. Because it was the holiday season, the team would provide refreshments to keep the meeting less formal. Instead of attacking the customer about their poor communication and the effects it had on Lara's team, they decided that Carolyn should approach the issue from the customer's perspective. Carolyn would clearly show that the communication problem has an effect on the customer's desired schedule.

Notes for the Aspiring Leader

Creativity in leadership is becoming more important, particularly in high-technology companies. As an aspiring leader, learn to think out of the box. Push yourself to consider all alternatives in problem solving. Seek out creative people to observe and learn from. Take the time to come up with new and unique ideas, and do not be afraid to bring them to the attention of your leadership.

Assess Your Current Location – Creativity

(Persuasive Vision)

Instructions: Read each of the skills and behaviors below. As objectively as possible, score yourself for each according to the following scale: 1 = strongly disagree; 2 = disagree; 3 = agree; 4 = strongly agree. If a behavior is not appropriate for your current or aspired position, check the N/A column.

SKILL OR BEHAVIOR	1	2	3	4	N/A
I provide a safe environment for team members to brainstorm ideas.					
I am open to new ideas when solving problems or assessing situations.					
When team members are trying new approaches, I handle failures with understanding and create a learning moment.					
I cultivate a culture that rewards innovative ideas.					
I assemble teams with an eye toward diversity of culture, thought, background, and education when possible.					
When coaching subordinates, I encourage them to come up with alternatives to solve a problem or situation.					
I reward initiative.					
I encourage experimentation.					
I strive to make work exciting and interesting for teams.					
I build teams with diverse points of view to solve problems or generate ideas.					
I look for and consider the least likely solutions to a problem or situation.					

Continue on next page.

34

Assess Your Current Location – Creativity

(Persuasive Vision)

SKILL OR BEHAVIOR	1	2	3	4	N/A
I push people to get out of their comfort zone.					
I tend to think out of the box when analyzing problems or issues.					
SCORES FOR CREATIVITY (Total check marks in each column and multiply by the heading for the column. Record your scores here.)					

TOTAL SCORE FOR CREATIVITY: _____

(Add scores from Columns 1, 2, 3, and 4. Record the total above and on the Master Score Sheet in Appendix A. Also, count the number of N/As and record on the Master Score Sheet.)

Reflect – Creativity

Scoring Analysis

List Your Four Highest Scored Items (Strengths)

Note: If you have multiple items with the same high score, choose the four items that are most related to your current or aspired position.

Item	Score

List Your Four Lowest Scored Items (Weaknesses)

Note: If you have multiple items with the same low score, choose the four items that are most related to your current or aspired position.

Item	Score

Reflect – Creativity Questions

Think through the following questions about creativity:

- When have you had to come up with a creative solution to a problem?

- What kinds of obstacles do some organizations have in place that limit leaders and staff from being creative?

- Think of the most creative person you know. Describe the value they bring to a work situation using their creativity.

- Is it possible to be too creative? What are the consequences of working with someone who is too creative?

- What can you do in your organization to stimulate creativity or use it to solve problems or issues?

- Steve Jobs was a leader who valued and practiced creativity. What were the results for him and Apple?

Develop – Creativity

Develop and Renew

Consider the following development tactics to help improve your skills and behaviors in creativity. Identify which tactics would be valuable to include in your Personal Development Plan (PDP) if you choose to improve in this competency.

- Assemble teams that offer a diversity of background, culture, experience, and education. Diversity brings a different perspective on solving problems and providing ideas. We often get set in our own ways due to our background, culture, and experience and do not see alternative solutions because they are not part of our experience.

- Encourage experimentation by allowing low-impact failures. Reward success but do not react negatively to failures. Encourage team members to understand why an approach failed. This can be done by leading team members in a review of the attempted solution to determine why it failed. Perhaps the idea was good but an obstacle in the implementation caused the failure. Always consider what could have been done differently when an initiative fails.

- Remove the restraints. What is preventing you from being more creative? Are you a perfectionist? Being creative means you will not always get everything right and things may get a little messy at first. Are you worried about what other people may think? Don't be, for you will stimulate the best solutions and ideas by being creative.

- Think out loud. Often the best ideas come when we talk it out with someone else as a sounding board.

- Learn to sleep on a problem or issue. Moving away from the situation often enables you to think more clearly and with openness when you return.

- Turn a problem upside down. How does this change the perspective? Does it help to see the root cause of a problem or situation?

- Set an example by being willing to approach problems and situations in new ways. Ask questions when someone poses a solution or idea. You set an excellent example when you ask questions to stimulate thinking about a problem or new idea. Even if you know the solution will work, continue to ask questions so that you model creative thinking to your team members.

- Use brainstorming techniques. Have group members think of all possible ideas or solutions with the understanding that none are considered ridiculous. Get them to think out of the box. Often, brainstorming works more effectively if the leader is not present. Give the team a set amount of time to brainstorm and then listen to their solutions or ideas. Do not pass judgment, but be sure to explore each idea with questions to stimulate their thinking. Unless the idea is not practical, support their collaboration and choice of the right solution or idea. If it is not practical, take the time to explain the obstacle preventing implementation of their solution or idea.

- Review a situation that occurred in the past that resulted in a failure or less-than-positive result. Have team members come up with different ways that things could have been done. This post-mortem exercise stimulates their thinking and will create a better environment for creativity in the future.

- Always ask, "What if?" Get yourself and team members to always think of consequences of each approach. If you have a conference room or location where you always brainstorm ideas or solutions to problems, make a sign that says "What if?" and post it in the room.

- Accept that some people are more creative than others. Group people together that are opposites in this area, and you will find that the result is much better. The creative team members will push the boundaries and come up with innovative ideas and solutions. Those who are less creative will keep the ideas and solutions within the allowable bounds of implementation.

- Create the right environment by rewarding creative ideas and solutions. Creativity is contagious. If people know that creativity is expected, they will not be afraid to come up with innovative solutions.

- Expect creativity. When leaders shoulder the burden of responsibility for innovation, team members will shirk it. It is easy to follow a leader who is creative and provides all the answers. Challenge your team members to think for themselves and be sure they know it is safe for them to push the boundaries to come up with great ideas.

- Develop a system to reward creativity. When people know that the organization rewards new ideas, they will try more often to generate them. By the same token, if someone comes up with a creative solution or new way of doing things and it fails, do not punish them. Rather, as a team, review what went wrong and learn from the mistake.

- Get people involved and immersed in problems. Leaders should not solve problems in isolation. The more creative minds that are applied to a problem, the greater the range of potential solutions.

- Periodically regroup organizational teams. Some teams grow stale with age. Teams that work together for long periods of time tend to do things the same way over and over, and they do not stimulate their thinking to come up with new ideas on how to do things.

Resources

Books

Beaudan, Eric. *Creative Execution: What Great Leaders Do to Unleash Bold Thinking and Innovation*. San Francisco: Jossey-Bass, 2012.

Ceserani, Jonne. *Big Ideas: Putting the Zest into Creativity and Innovation at Work*. London: Kogan Page, 2011.

DeBono, Edward. *Creativity Workout: 62 Exercises to Unlock Your Most Creative Ideas*. Berkeley, CA: Ulysses Press, 2008.

DeGraff, Jeff. *Creativity at Work*. San Francisco: Jossey-Bass, 2002.

Drucker, Peter F. *Innovation and Entrepreneurship*. New York: Harper, 2006.

Foster, Jack. *Ideaship: How to Get Ideas Flowing In Your Workplace*. San Francisco: Berrett-Koehler, 2001.

Harvard Business Essentials (compiler). *Managing Creativity and Innovation*. Cambridge: Harvard Business Press, 2003.

Hesselbein, Frances. and Rob Johnston. *On Creativity, Innovation, and Renewal: A Leader to Leader Guide*. San Francisco: Jossey-Bass, 2002.

Hiam, Alexander. *The Manager's Pocket Guide to Creativity*. Amherst, MA: HRD Press, 1999.

Linkner, Josh. *Disciplined Dreaming: A Proven System to Drive Breakthrough Creativity*. San Francisco: Jossey-Bass, 2011.

Mattimore, Bryan W. *Idea Stormers: How to Lead and Inspire Creative Breakthroughs*. San Francisco: Jossey-Bass, 2012.

Rich, Jason. *Brain Storm: Tap Into Your Creativity to Generate Awesome Ideas and Remarkable Results*. Franklin Lakes, NJ: Career Press, 2003.

Websites

David Parrish is a creativity consultant and offers good information at: http://www.davidparrish.com/page.asp?pgid=108&pgsid=30.

An excellent blog article can be found at: http://www.sprocketwebsites.com/Blog/tabid/190/EntryId/79/Creativity-and-Business.aspx.

The Art of Work website offers creative ideas at: http://creativebusinessstrategies.blogspot.com/.

Change – Creativity

Instructions

Using the table below and on the next page, refer to the items you listed in the Reflect – Creativity worksheet and identify specific actions you will take to improve your weaknesses or enhance your strengths in each area. Refer to the Develop and Renew section on the previous pages for action ideas, keeping in mind the needs of your current or aspired position.

You can have multiple actions for each item you intend to focus on. In the first section, list the actions that are specific to the items you listed in the Reflect – Creativity section. On the following page, list any actions you will take that are general to this competency and are related to more than one scored item. Finally, prioritize your actions based on the need for your current or aspired position. These actions will become part of your Personal Development Plan (PDP) for this competency in Appendix C.

Actions to Improve Weakness or Enhance Strength	Priority

Continue on next page.

Change – Creativity

Actions to Improve Weakness or Enhance Strength	Priority

Other Actions You Will Take Related to Creativity (not related to the identified strongest or weakest items)	Priority

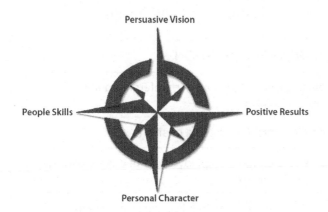

Persuasive Vision

People Skills — Positive Results

Personal Character

CHAPTER 6

Influencing

(Persuasive Vision)

"It takes time to persuade men to do even what is for their own good."
– Thomas Jefferson

How well someone influences others determines, to a large degree, their leadership success. It also determines how well the leader gets things done and gains the support of others. Everyone is constantly influencing others, whether it is to get someone to do something, gaining someone's support for an initiative, or convincing others to think a certain way. The greatest leaders (and sometimes the most damaging) are those who can influence the best.

However, some leaders are not successful in their influencing tactics. We tend to use the tactic or approach that we are most comfortable with, not the tactic or approach that would work best with a particular individual, group or situation. Leaders must consider who they are trying to influence and use the tactic that the recipient prefers, not necessarily the one with which they are most comfortable.

Leaders must influence with integrity. They should not use negative tactics such as threats, manipulation, or intimidation. Leaders who use these negative tactics quickly lose credibility. But these tactics are used more frequently than we might admit. Many leaders use these tactics because of their personality or when they sense that using these tactics is the best way to get things done. When driven by short-term pressures to produce, it is easy for a leader to fall back on these methods.

The ability to effectively influence others is also dependent upon your organizational and personal power. For example, a vice president of an organization has more organizational power than a project manager or administrative assistant. Each of us derives some power from the organization we work for, and this power can be used to effectively influence others. We also may have personal power, such as authority in a specific situation, having a doctorate degree, or extensive experience.

Terry Bacon (1994) describes 14 influencing tactics, 10 positive and four negative:

TACTIC	BRIEF DESCRIPTION
Legitimizing	Using authority or credentials to explain and influence; referring to the organization's processes and procedures.
Logical Persuasion	Using facts, logic, or evidence to explain or justify a position.
Appealing to Friendship	Asking based on friendship; relying on friendship, loyalty, or a past relationship to get what you want; asking for personal favors.
Socializing	Behaving in a warm and friendly manner so as to influence strangers to cooperate.
Consulting	Asking the influencee to help you arrive at an acceptable solution; appealing to the influencee's expertise.
Stating	Simply saying what you want or what you think.
Appealing to Values	Inspiring cooperation by appealing to the influencee's values, emotions or feelings.
Modeling	Inspiring the influencee to behave in a certain way by setting an example; leading by example.
Exchanging	Giving something of value to the influencee in exchange for what you want; negotiating or bargaining something.
Alliance Building	Getting a number of people together to influence another; more powerful as a group.
Avoiding (neg.)	Failing to act or respond; behaving passive-aggressively.
Threatening (neg.)	Describing punishment or other negative consequences.
Intimidating (neg.)	Using a size or power differential to get your way.
Manipulating (neg.)	Withholding information; lying, deceiving, misleading, or disguising your feelings or intent.

We can't conclude an introduction to influencing without a brief discussion of influencing upward. This can include your boss, your boss' boss, peers with substantial power, and even customers. The ability to influence upward depends on one very important characteristic – the ability to build a relationship with those you need to influence. You need to know your boss and others in this category. Building a relationship with those you need to influence helps in many ways, but most importantly in determining the best influencing tactics to use in a situation.

Red Flag Behaviors

- You influence others by being demanding or using intimidation.
- You have difficulty influencing upward.
- You dislike ideas that others bring to you.
- You try to influence all your direct reports the same way.
- You overuse your organizational power to influence others.
- You dislike trying to convince others of your plans or ideas.

Case in Point

(Please see the Case in Point on page 32 that sets the stage for this scenario.)

After her brainstorming meeting with the team, Carolyn accepted their recommendation and set up the meeting with the customer to solve the communication problem. Now she had to determine how she would present her case to the customer to solve the problem.

She had worked with this customer for two years but did not have a strong relationship with George, their vice president who would be leading the customer's team. She knew he was an engineer and had been with the company for almost 20 years. However, her colleague, Phyllis, had worked for George for many years. Carolyn reached out to Phyllis to learn more about George. She learned that because he was an engineer, he assessed situations and made decisions based on logic. Phyllis also felt that George had a very strong loyalty to his company and always did what was right for his organization.

Phyllis' insight helped Carolyn develop a strategy that would likely influence George to solve the problem. First, she would express her commitment to solving the problem because she believed in the success of George's company. She would also use logic to show that the communication problem had an impact on the project's schedule. She would show the negative impact that delays would have for George's company. To close, she would recommend some solutions to the problem, showing the benefits of each to George's company. She would strive to remain positive throughout the conversation, stressing the importance of solving the problem to the success of both companies.

Notes for the Aspiring Leader

Learning how to effectively influence will help you grow in an organization.
Always use positive influencing tactics and do not tolerate negative tactics.
Use your organizational power wisely.

Assess Your Current Location – Influencing

(Persuasive Vision)

Instructions: Read each of the skills and behaviors below. As objectively as possible, score yourself for each according to the following scale: 1 = strongly disagree; 2 = disagree; 3 = agree; 4 = strongly agree. If a behavior is not appropriate for your current or aspired position, check the N/A column.

SKILL OR BEHAVIOR	1	2	3	4	N/A
I effectively influence up, down, and across the organization.					
I take the time to think about how others should be effectively influenced.					
I methodically plan how to influence others to take a position or do a task.					
I understand the different influencing tactics.					
I gain acceptance of new ideas among difficult audiences.					
I consider who needs to be influenced for each situation.					
I have a reputation for being an effective influencer.					
I do not tolerate the use of negative influencing tactics, such as manipulation or threats.					
I effectively influence upward.					
I use appropriate influencing tactics with direct reports.					
I know my personal influencing preference.					
I do not intimidate or threaten people to influence them.					
I use my organizational power appropriately.					
I learn the background of those I need to influence so that I know what tactics work with each.					

Continue on next page.

Assess Your Current Location – Influencing

(Persuasive Vision)

	1	2	3	4	N/A
SCORES FOR INFLUENCING (Total check marks in each column and multiply by the heading for the column. Record your scores here.)					

TOTAL SCORE FOR INFLUENCING: _____

(Add scores from Columns 1, 2, 3, and 4. Record the total above and on the Master Score Sheet in Appendix A. Also, count the number of N/As and record on the Master Score Sheet.)

Reflect – Influencing

Scoring Analysis

List Your Four Highest Scored Items (Strengths)

Note: If you have multiple items with the same high score, choose the four items that are most related to your current or aspired position.

Item	Score

List Your Four Lowest Scored Items (Weaknesses)

Note: If you have multiple items with the same low score, choose the four items that are most related to your current or aspired position.

Item	Score

Reflect – Influencing Questions

Think about the following questions about influencing:

- Think about how you are influenced. What influencing tactics work on you?

- How do you respond to negative influencing tactics, such as threats, manipulation, or intimidation?

- Think of three individuals who are close to you, either personally or professionally. How do you influence each of them?

- Why do you think it is important to be a good influencer as you become a leader in an organization?

- Have you had the experience of working for someone who used the power of their position to influence others? How was that experience for you?

- Can loyalty to an organization be effectively used as an influencing tactic?

Develop – Influencing

Develop and Renew

Consider the following development tactics to help improve your skills and behaviors in influencing. Identify which tactics would be valuable to include in your Personal Development Plan (PDP) if you choose to improve in this competency.

- Consider the influencing techniques you use to convince others of a decision or to do a task. How could you do things differently to be more successful? Identify different influencing techniques you can use for the individuals you need to influence. Build a chart that shows each positive influencing tactic described earlier. List your team members next to their preferred influencing tactic. If you are unclear, ask them the tactic they prefer.

- When faced with your next decision or initiative, consider what would be a winning solution for each stakeholder (including you). Keep in mind that you cannot always create a winning situation or result for everyone, but at this point simply identify what would be a winning solution for each. How can you use this information to influence others?

- When you are preparing to present a new idea in hopes of garnering support, identify all the stakeholders and those impacted by the idea. After identifying them, think of the benefits of the proposed idea to each stakeholder. When you present the idea, emphasize the benefits to each.

- Building the trust of others to gain their support takes time. People want to see what happens when others trust you first. Can you be relied upon? Will you maintain confidences? If you are consistent, you will gain the trust and confidence of others. What role does trust play in the ability to influence others?

- List your peer leaders and team members. Identify what motivates each. How can you use this understanding when you need to influence them?

- Be cautious not to use negative influencing techniques such as avoidance, manipulation, threats, or intimidation.

- Character and credibility are also important for successful influencing. If you consistently demonstrate excellent character and have demonstrated that you deserve credibility, you will be more successful in influencing others. If you are not respected for your character, or have demonstrated that you are not credible, it will take much more convincing to influence others.

Resources

Books

Bacon, Terry. *Leadership Through Influence*. Durango, CO: Lore International Institute, 1994.

_____. *Elements of Influence*. New York: AMACOM, 2011.

Bhargava, Rohit. *Likeonomics: The Unexpected Truth Behind Earning Trust, Influencing Behavior, and Inspiring Action*. New York: Wiley, 2012.

Carnegie, Dale. *How to Win Friends & Influence People*. New York: Simon and Shuster, 2009.

Cohen, Allan. *Influencing Up*. New York: Wiley, 2012.

Daly, John. *Advocacy: Championing Ideas and Influencing Others*. New Haven, CT: Yale University Press, 2012.

Goldstein, Steve and Robert B. Cialdini. *Yes!: 50 Scientifically Proven Ways to Be Persuasive*. New York: Free Press, 2009.

Kendrick, Tom. *Results Without Authority: Controlling a Project When the Team Doesn't Report to You*. New York: AMACOM, 2006.

Larson, Elizabeth and Richard Larson. *The Influencing Formula*. Watermark Business Publications, 2012.

McIntosh, Perry and Richard A. Luecke. *Increase Your Influence at Work*. New York: AMACOM, 2011.

O'Conner, Joseph and John Seymour. *Introducing NLP: Psychological Skills for Understanding and Influencing People*. Thorsons, 1993.

Patterson, Kerry et al. *Influencer: The Power to Change Anything*. New York: McGraw-Hill, 2007.

Schlimm, Dirk. *Influencing Powerful People: Engage and Command the Attention of the Decision Makers to Get What You Need to Succeed*. New York: McGraw-Hill, 2011.

Widener, Chris. *The Art of Influence: Persuading Others Begins With You*. New York: Crown Business, 2008.

Websites

The Influence at Work website offers a blog and other resources at: http://www.influenceatwork.com/.

A blog regarding how to influence visitors to your website can be found at: http://www.businessmarketingblog.org/how-to-win-business-and-influence-visitors/.

Change – Influencing

Instructions

Using the table below and on the next page, refer to the items you listed in the Reflect – Influencing worksheet and identify specific actions you will take to improve your weaknesses or enhance your strengths in each area. Refer to the Develop and Renew section on the previous pages for action ideas, keeping in mind the needs of your current or aspired position.

You can have multiple actions for each item you intend to focus on. In the first section, list the actions that are specific to the items you listed in the Reflect – Influencing section. On the following page, list any actions you will take that are general to this competency and are related to more than one scored item. Finally, prioritize your actions based on the need for your current or aspired position. These actions will become part of your Personal Development Plan (PDP) for this competency in Appendix C.

Actions to Improve Weakness or Enhance Strength	Priority

Continue on next page.

Change – Influencing

Actions to Improve Weakness or Enhance Strength	Priority

Other Actions You Will Take Related to Influencing (not related to the identified strongest or weakest items)	Priority

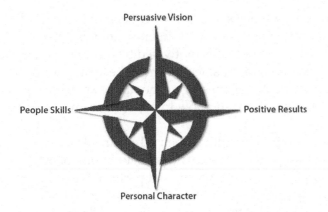

Persuasive Vision

People Skills — Positive Results

Personal Character

CHAPTER 7

Inspiration

(Persuasive Vision)

"If your actions inspire others to dream more, learn more,
do more and become more, you are a leader."
– John Quincy Adam

When leaders provide inspiration, they motivate others to perform to their fullest potential. Passion, purpose, and meaning help make a leader inspirational. The ability to communicate that passion, purpose, and meaning to others helps establish the inspirational culture of an organization.

In a recent survey of over 1500 managers, 55% of respondents stated that inspiration was what they most liked to see in leaders. People want to be inspired and perform at their best. Typically when asked what makes a great leader, people say it is someone who inspires others to do something. To do this, leaders need to provide passion, purpose, and meaning to those around them.

We often think of inspirational leaders as being charismatic and extroverted. This is not always the case; many are quiet and even introverted (Steve Jobs, Bill Gates). However, their passion is clear to others, and they easily and confidently communicate purpose. Inspirational leaders clearly express a vision that is directly connected to the needs and values of both the organization and individuals. The vision is obvious to those in the organization and can even be used as a marketing tool to those outside the organization.

Inspirational leaders also provide strong strategic focus. They are good at ensuring that the business only does those things that add real value. They are adept at communicating the strategic focus, and this focus is at the heart of the decisions they make. In addition, to experience inspiration people need to feel included. For real inclusion, people need to feel intimately connected to the actions and processes leading to the accomplishment of both the organization's and their individual goals.

The big picture view is also a characteristic of inspirational leaders. They see beyond the immediate need and put the current situation into perspective. They can communicate a vision beyond the day-to-day work and communicate the vision with passion that is contagious.

Inspiration is closely connected with two other competencies in our 4Ps Leadership Compass™ Competency Model: motivation and integrity. Taking a closer look at each, motivation is a key component of inspiring others to take action. But, each individual is motivated by different values and circumstances (money, time off, recognition, etc.) Inspirational leaders must be aware of what motivates others and include those factors in their inspirational message. One can be an inspiring leader, yet fail to achieve the goals because they do not understand how to motivate team members.

To be most effective, inspirational leaders must also be principled. Their ethics are above reproach and they are deeply committed to doing things right. Their values are built on honesty, character, openness, and respect for people. Inspirational leaders who do not perform with integrity may have short-term results, but in the long term they will lose their followers. Think of how many leaders you may have admired and been inspired by, only to see them fall by making a mistake in ethics or integrity. Just today, a leader I admired and was inspired by was arrested for driving while intoxicated. Yes, I may admire some things he does, but I can't say that he inspires me anymore. Just as trust can be damaged or lost in the blink of an eye, an inspiring leader can lose it all with just one mistake. Fortunately, most leaders will make the right decisions and stay in a position whereby they can inspire others to do their best and be their best.

Red Flag Behaviors

- You do not know or do not communicate your organization's vision.
- You express your dislike of the organization's vision.
- You do not encourage others and overreact when they make mistakes.
- You view your work as just a job and you let others know your view.
- When something goes right, you do not hesitate to take credit.
- You do not feel it is your responsibility to inspire or motivate others.

Case in Point

Contrary to popular belief, the winter of 1777/1778 was not abnormally cold or snowy for a Pennsylvania winter. Nonetheless, it was cold, wet, icy, and demoralizing to George Washington's Continental Army. The army had just been driven south from New York City and New Jersey. They had little food and their clothes were in tatters, and many were without shoes.

But the actions of George Washington up to that encampment and during the long winter inspired many of the army to do their best. Baron Friedrich von Stueben, a Prussian mercenary, led the soldiers in drills throughout the winter at Washington's direction. This kept the soldiers occupied and better trained for the spring offensive to come.

General Washington moved throughout the encampment every day, encouraging the soldiers and tending to their problems. His very presence in the cold, wet weather every day inspired his soldiers to make it to the next day. Yes, some gave up and went home. But many chose to stay and suffer for the greater good, the preservation of their country. Many of their letters that have been preserved speak of General Washington's inspiring words and presence during the difficult time.

Notes for the Aspiring Leader

Thank about what inspires you. Do you see the big picture? Are you able to communicate benefits to your team and peers to stimulate inspiration? Focus on establishing yourself as a leader of high integrity, because without integrity, inspiration will be short-lived.

Assess Your Current Location – Inspiration

(Persuasive Vision)

Instructions: Read each of the skills and behaviors below. As objectively as possible, score yourself for each according to the following scale: 1 = strongly disagree; 2 = disagree; 3 = agree; 4 = strongly agree. If a behavior is not appropriate for your current or aspired position, check the N/A column.

SKILL OR BEHAVIOR	1	2	3	4	N/A
I inspire others to perform at their highest potential.					
I work to establish an inspirational culture in the organization.					
I provide strong strategic vision.					
I demonstrate passion for my organization's strategic vision.					
I work to connect people intimately with actions and processes leading to accomplishment of goals.					
I demonstrate humbleness, particularly around areas of success.					
I demonstrate a great desire to learn and improve.					
I share credit and praise where appropriate.					
I accept responsibility for mistakes.					
I clearly express a vision that is directly connected to the needs and values of the organization.					
I encourage others.					
I frame my messages to be positive.					
I use analogies or tell stories to inspire others.					
I always act with integrity to ensure that my inspirational message is not damaged by my actions.					
I consider how people are motivated and relate these motivators to how I inspire them as much as possible.					

Continue on next page.

Assess Your Current Location – Inspiration

(Persuasive Vision)

	1	2	3	4	N/A
SCORES FOR INSPIRATION (Total check marks in each column and multiply by the heading for the column. Record your scores here.)					

TOTAL SCORE FOR INSPIRATION: _____

(Add scores from Columns 1, 2, 3, and 4. Record the total above and on the Master Score Sheet in Appendix A. Also, count the number of N/As and record on the Master Score Sheet.)

Reflect – Inspiration

Scoring Analysis

List Your Four Highest Scored Items (Strengths)

Note: If you have multiple items with the same high score, choose the four items that are most related to your current or aspired position.

Item	Sore

List Your Four Lowest Scored Items (Weaknesses)

Note: If you have multiple items with the same low score, choose the four items that are most related to your current or aspired position.

Item	Score

Reflect – Inspiration Questions

Think about the following questions about Inspiration:

- What leaders have inspired you? What did they do that gave you inspiration?

- Have you ever been in a situation where you were not inspired? How did it affect your performance?

- Can inspirational leaders fail? Can you think of an example of a leader who was initially inspirational but did not carry through in their performance?

- Do you believe that an inspirational leader can drive a team to do extraordinary things, far beyond what is expected?

- What limits inspiration?

Develop – Inspiration

Develop and Renew

Consider the following development tactics to help improve your skills and behaviors in inspiration. Identify which tactics would be valuable to include in your Personal Development Plan (PDP) if you choose to improve in this competency.

- Think of an inspirational leader in your organization. What attributes make them inspirational? Why do they appeal to you and others? Observe what they do and consider what they say and how they say it. What inspires them? If you don't know, ask them. Ask them if they can mentor you to be more inspiring.

- Consider how you could become more inspirational. Do you have a vision? Do you have passion for the vision? Can you give meaning to others around the vision? How well do you communicate the vision to others?

- Think about your vision. How does it relate to others, or is it too personal and applicable only to you? Your vision is important, but it may be different from others' vision. If you focus your leadership strictly around what inspires you, it may be difficult to inspire others. Consider how you can reframe your vision to lead to the success of the organization.

- What does it mean to have your vision clearly connected to the needs of the organization and to individuals? If the vision is connected to the needs of the organization but not to individuals, what might be the result? Your vision is important to the success of the organization, and people can appreciate that. However, their individual vision may be different from yours, but still be related to the success of the organization. Always consider others' vision and how it is connected to their success and that of the organization.

- Integrity is critical to the inspirational leader. Think of some leaders who may have been inspirational but lacked integrity. Throughout history, there have been inspirational leaders who lacked integrity and bad things happened as a result. Inspirational leaders ground their behaviors and actions in integrity.

- Think about the needs of others. An inspirational leader gives people what they want and need within their capabilities. Do you think about the needs of others? Do you provide adequate rewards based on the person's needs? Do you provide what people need to get the job done? A leader can give an inspirational talk about a vision or project, but if they fail to provide the needed resources their credibility suffers.

- Strive to include all people in your organization. Try to get them intimately connected to your vision by showing the importance they play in achieving the vision. Seek out those who do not seem to be inspired by your vision. Talk with them one-on-one to encourage them to support you and the organization. Ask them what their barriers are to contributing to the success of the organization.

- Inspirational leaders must be aware that their behaviors are being constantly scrutinized. Focus on acting with integrity and above reproach.

- When communicating your vision, do not hesitate to draw on experience outside your sector. Give the vision life beyond simply being a goal to achieve. Many leaders are good storytellers and can illustrate a concept in an inspiring way using experiences from other industries, their own history, or from other people.

- Inspirational leaders are also risk takers; they even tend to bend the rules a bit. They tolerate and encourage this in their followers. But, inspirational leaders are also smart risk takers and do not put the organization at risk to achieve a lofty vision.

- People respond to inspirational leaders because these leaders listen to others. Inspirational leaders ask for and respect what their people tell them about how to do things better. They also provide the resources to ensure that the solutions are delivered.

Resources

Books

Adair, John. *The Inspirational Leader: How to Motivate, Encourage, and Achieve Success*. London: Kogan Page, 2009.

Bates, Suzanne. *Motivate Like a CEO: Communicate Your Strategic Vision and Inspire People to Act*. New York: McGraw-Hill, 2008.

Bench, Marcia. *Becoming an Inspirational Thought Leader: Turn Your Setbacks Into Opportunities and Change the World With Your Gifts*. High Flight Press, 2012.

Biviji, Yusuf. *Inspirational Leadership: A Few Select Thoughts and Quotes For All of Us to Learn and Use*. Charleston: CreateSpace, 2012.

Evans, Jeff. *Inspirational Presence: The Art of Transformational Leadership*. Morgan James Publishing, 2009.

Greenleaf, Robert. *Servant Leadership: A Journey into the Nature of Legitimate Power & Greatness*. Mahwah, NJ: Paulist Press, 2002.

Hayes, Merwyn and Michel Coner. *Start With Humility: Lessons From America's Quiet CEOs on How to Build Trust and Inspire Followers.* The Greenleaf Center for Servant Leadership, 2010.

Hiam, Alexander. *Motivational Management: Inspiring Your People for Maximum Performance.* New York: AMACOM, 2006.

Luce, Donald and Brian McDermott. *Time Out for Leaders: Daily Inspiration for Maximum Impact.* Nova Vista Publishing, 2006.

Maxwell, John. *The 21 Indispensible Qualities of a Leader.* Nashville, TN: Thomas Nelson, 2007.

_____. *Go for the Gold: Inspiration to Increase Your Leadership Impact.* Nashville, TN: Thomas Nelson, 2008.

Michellie, Joseph. *The Zappos Experience: 5 Principles to Inspire, Engage, and WOW.* New York: McGraw-Hill, 2011.

Myers, Betsy. *Take the Lead: Motivate, Inspire, and Bring Out the Best in Yourself and Everyone Around You.* Atria Books, 2011.

Secretan, Lance. *Inspirational Leadership: Destiny, Calling and Cause.* 2003.

_____. *Inspire: What Great Leaders Do.* New York: Wiley, 2004.

Sinek, Simon. *Start with Why: How Great Leaders Inspire Everyone to Take Action.* New York: Portfolio, 2009.

Zenger, John et al. *The Inspiring Leader: Unlocking the Secrets of How Extraordinary Leaders Motivate.* New York: McGraw-Hill, 2009.

Change – Inspiration

Instructions

Using the table below and on the next page, refer to the items you listed in the Reflect – Inspiration worksheet and identify specific actions you will take to improve your weaknesses or enhance your strengths in each area. Refer to the Develop and Renew section on the previous pages for action ideas, keeping in mind the needs of your current or aspired position.

You can have multiple actions for each item you intend to focus on. In the first section, list the actions that are specific to the items you listed in the Reflect – Inspiration section. On the following page, list any actions you will take that are general to this competency and are related to more than one scored item. Finally, prioritize your actions based on the need for your current or aspired position. These actions will become part of your Personal Development Plan (PDP) for this competency in Appendix C.

Actions to Improve Weakness or Enhance Strength	Priority

Continue on next page.

Change – Inspiration

Actions to Improve Weakness or Enhance Strength	Priority

Other Actions You Will Take Related to Inspiration (not related to the identified strongest or weakest items)	Priority

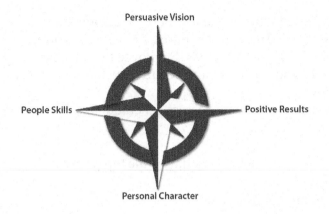

CHAPTER 8

Motivation

(Persuasive Vision)

"People often say that motivation doesn't last. Well, neither does bathing - that's why we recommend it daily."

– Zig Ziglar

In the previous chapter, we described how leaders get people to follow them because they are inspirational. Although this is true, and people want to be inspired, there are other factors that cause them to do a good job or be committed to the goals of the organization.

Motivation comes from within each person; the leader ultimately cannot motivate people. However, the leader establishes the conditions where people motivate themselves. Each person has a different set of motivators. What motivates one person may not work with another. Leaders must recognize people for who they are and help them find their own way forward by making the best use of their own strengths and abilities.

Motivation can be a challenge for some leaders. They may say, "The person has a job. I expect them to do it well and in return they get a paycheck." However, researchers have learned that workers are more motivated by emotional rather than economic factors. Thus, getting people involved, recognizing achievements, and giving attention are often more important in developing motivation and sustaining it than a pay raise or bonus. This does not mean that money does not motivate; it surely does. However, the emotional factors have a greater impact and sustain motivation better.

One of the best ways to motivate a team is to have a strong and well-communicated vision. People need to know where the organization is going, how it intends to get there, and what it means to them. It is leadership's responsibility to set the vision and communicate it in a way that it motivates others.

A major issue in motivation is the generational differences that often are present between a leader and followers. Young workers do not necessarily follow the traditional styles and patterns of workplace behavior. Senior leaders often assume that the younger generation will define and measure success the way they themselves do.

It was only 20 to 30 years ago when workers started with a company or organization and expected to stay with the organization until retirement. This is rarely the case in today's world; workers readily move to another company if it better suits their needs. Employee turnover is a leading problem for human resource professionals, and much of it can be attributed to companies not understanding how to motivate their workforce.

Cam Marston (2007) focuses his work on effective management across generational differences in the workplace. He describes young workers as:

- Having a work ethic that no longer mandates a 10-hour work day as the top priority.
- Being easily competent in new technologies.
- Having tenuous, if non-existent, loyalty to an organization.

In today's world, it is important that leaders understand their workforce and learn what motivates them to achieve their personal goals. Only then can the leader hope to make the linkage from their personal goals to the organization's goals.

Leaders must be aware of the practical things that motivate people – money, time off, recognition, inclusiveness, etc. Remember – some people live to work, while others work to live. For some people, their job or position is only a means to an end, with the end being the activities or things that the person enjoys or values most.

Leaders are also responsible for motivating themselves. Followers do not follow a lazy leader. People like to work for a leader who has goals and strives to achieve them. Think about what motivates you and how you can build a life to meet those needs.

Red Flag Behaviors

- You cannot identify what motivates each member of your team.
- You feel that getting paid should be enough motivation for others to do a good job.
- You tell others to improve in their weak areas, but do not guide them in how to do it.
- You do not encourage others; rather, you look for their mistakes and berate them for poor performance.
- You have difficulty managing people who are different from you – generational, gender, race, etc.

Case in Point

Kate's team had been working on the project for six months, and it would be another long six months before it was finished. Most weeks, the team put in overtime. Three times they needed to work over a weekend to meet a crucial deadline. They were tired, and Kate could see that the project was taking a toll on them.

Kate explained to Ed, her director, that she needed to do something to boost morale. Ed recommended that she be creative and consider what motivated each of the five team members. He told her to do what it would take to stay on track and produce a quality product. Together they set a budget and Kate gave a lot of thought to what motivates each of her team members.

After agreeing on a budget with Ed, Kate planned a celebration party to note the halfway point of the project. She set the date for a Thursday afternoon and announced that after the party, everyone would be given a long weekend. Near the conclusion of the party she recognized verbally and in a personal letter a significant contribution each team member had made over the past six months. Finally, she presented each team member with a gift certificate to take their spouse or significant other to a nice dinner, recognizing the sacrifice that they made as well. To close the party, Kate introduced Ken, the CEO. He thanked the team members, spoke about the importance of their project, and spent a few minutes talking with each team member and encouraging them individually.

When the team returned to work the following Monday, each person thanked Kate. They all stated that the party, time off, and gift certificates reenergized them for the coming six months until the project is completed.

Notes for the Aspiring Leader

Think about what motivates each member of your team. If you are not sure, have a discussion with each and learn more about them. Be careful not to judge others' motivators. What works for you may not be important to others. In fact, you may learn from others what is really important and what motivates you.

Assess Your Current Location – Motivation

(Persuasive Vision)

Instructions: Read each of the skills and behaviors below. As objectively as possible, score yourself for each according to the following scale: 1 = strongly disagree; 2 = disagree; 3 = agree; 4 = strongly agree. If a behavior is not appropriate for your current or aspired position, check the N/A column.

SKILL OR BEHAVIOR	1	2	3	4	N/A
I am aware of what motivates me.					
I develop a vision for team efforts.					
I communicate my organization's vision in a way that is clear and directly relates to organizational goals.					
I work to understand motivators for each team member.					
I work to ensure that every team member is motivated to achieve.					
I work to help team members demonstrate respect for others and their needs.					
I am aware of organizational incentive and recognition programs.					
I am considerate of each team member's special needs.					
I am aware of when I need to encourage others.					
I capitalize on people's strengths and help them develop in their weak areas.					

Continue on next page.

Assess Your Current Location – Motivation
(Persuasive Vision)

	1	2	3	4	N/A
SCORES FOR MOTIVATION (Total check marks in each column and multiply by the heading for the column. Record your scores here.)					

TOTAL SCORE FOR MOTIVATION: _____

(Add scores from Columns 1, 2, 3, and 4. Record the total above and on the Master Score Sheet in Appendix A. Also, count the number of N/As and record on the Master Score Sheet.)

Reflect – Motivation

Scoring Analysis

List Your Four Highest Scored Items (Strengths)

Note: If you have multiple items with the same high score, choose the four items that are most related to your current or aspired position.

Item	Score

List Your Four Lowest Scored Items (Weaknesses)

Note: If you have multiple items with the same low score, choose the four items that are most related to your current or aspired position.

Item	Score

Reflect – Motivation Questions

Think about the following questions about motivation:

- What motivates you to do a good job?

- What de-motivates you? Think of a time when you were de-motivated. What did it feel like? How did it affect your productivity?

- What are some motivators for people on your team? Your peers?

- Shouldn't people simply be motivated by having a job (and pay check)?

- What motivates you outside the work environment?

- Have you seen a team that is highly motivated? What is the impact on productivity and results?

Develop – Motivation

Develop and Renew

Consider the following development tactics to help improve your motivation skills and behaviors. Identify which tactics would be valuable to include in your Personal Development Plan (PDP) if you choose to improve in this competency.

- The best way to motivate a team is to focus on leading the team and enabling them to achieve their full potential through their own efforts. Don't micro-manage. Rather, describe to the team what their goal is and what your expectations are. Then step back and monitor progress. Step in if your expectations are not being met or if the team does not appear to be going in the right direction.

- The leader's greatest role in motivating is to recognize people for who they are and to help them find their own way forward by making best use of their own strengths and abilities. In this way, achievement, development, and recognition will come naturally to the person. Do you know the strengths and abilities of each of your team members?

- Think about your team members. What motivates each? Money? Recognition? Time off? Other factors? Talk to each and develop a relationship with them. This will help you understand what is important to them.

- Be aware of generational differences on your team and how that affects what motivates the team members. How do you feel about the younger members of your team who may be motivated differently from you? Do you judge them and question their loyalty to the project or organization?

- Be sure your organization has a clear vision of the future. Communicate the vision to the team and keep it as a driving force in daily operations and decision making. Everyone should know the vision of the organization. It is your job, as a leader, to communicate the vision clearly and show team members the relationship between what they are doing and the achievement of the vision. People need to know that their work is important.

- Treat people fairly. Nothing de-motivates someone more than the feeling that they are being treated unfairly. Sometimes, in our quest to honor or reward people who do a good job, we overlook someone who also contributed to the effort. We are right to reward people for doing a good job, but it is risky if you do not consider everyone who may have contributed. It is also de-motivating to others if someone is rewarded who did not fully participate in a project's success.

- Help people find the value in what they are doing and work toward ensuring that people are doing what they like to do. Work to build people's confidence and recognize their uniqueness. Help them develop their creativity and seek meaning in what they do.

Resources

Books

Blanchard, Ken and Don Shula. *The Little Book of Coaching: Motivating People to be Winners.* New York: Harper Business, 2001.

Chandler, Steve and Scott Richardson. *100 Ways to Motivate Others: How Great Leaders Can Produce Insane Results Without Driving People Crazy.* Pompton Plains, NJ: Career Press, 2012.

Conley, Chip. *Peak: How Great Companies Get Their Mojo from Maslow.* San Francisco: Jossey-Bass, 2007.

Deems, Richard and Terri Deems. *Leading in Tough Times: The Manager's Guide to Responsibility, Trust, and Motivation.* Amherst, MA: HRD Press, 2003.

Glanz, Bargara. *Handle With Care: Motivating and Retaining Employees.* New York: McGraw-Hill, 2002.

Green, Thad. *Motivation Management: Fueling Performance by Discovering What People Believe About Themselves and Their Organizations.* Palo Alto, CA: Davies-Black Publishing, 2000.

_____. *The Belief System: The Secret to Motivation and Improved Performance.* Hays Group, 2003.

Grey, Mattison and Jonathan Manske. *The Motivation Myth: The Simple Yet Powerful Key to Unlock Human Potential and Create Inspired Performance and Achievement.* Charleston, SC: CreateSpace, 2012.

Hiam, Alexander. *Motivational Management: Inspiring Your People for Maximum Performance.* New York: AMACOM, 2006.

Kruse, Kevin. *Employee Engagement 2.0. How to Motivate Your Team for High Performance.* Charleston, SC: CreateSpace, 2012.

Latham, Gary P. *Work Motivation: History, Theory, Research, and Practice,* Thousand Oaks, CA: Sage, 2011.

Marston, Cam. *Motivating the "What's In It For Me" Workforce: Manage Across the Generational Divide and Increase Profits.* New York: Wiley, 2007.

Maslow, Abraham. *Motivation and Personality.* New York: Harper Collins, 1997.

_____, Abraham. *Toward a Psychology of Being.* San Francisco: Wiley, 1998.

_____, Abraham. *Maslow on Management*. San Francisco: Wiley, 1998.

Myers, Betsy. *Take the Lead: Motivate, Inspire, and Bring Out the Best in Yourself and Everyone Around You*. Atria Books, 2012.

Stratheford, Michael. *Motivating Employees: How to Keep Employees Happy While Maximizing Productivity*. Amazon Digital Services, 2012.

Thomas, Kenneth W. *Intrinsic Motivation at Work: What Really Drives Employee Engagement*. San Francisco: Berrett-Koehler, 2009.

Scott, Wayne et al. *Motivating Others: Bringing Out the Best in People*. Bloomington, IN: 1st Books Library, 2001.

Segovia, W. Oliver and Bill George. *Passion and Purpose: Stories from the Best and Brightest Young Business Leaders*. Cambridge: Harvard Business Review, 2011.

Websites

Wikipedia offers extensive discussion of motivation theories at: http://en.wikipedia.org/wiki/Motivation http://www.businessrulesgroup.org/bmm.shtml.

The Incentive Performance Center offers an excellent article on motivation in the workplace: http://www.incentivecentral.org/business_motivation/why_motivation.1856.html.

Other Resources

The following video is an excellent talk on the science of motivation by Dan Pink: http://www.ted.com/talks/dan_pink_on_motivation.html.

Change – Motivation

Instructions

Using the table below and on the next page, refer to the items you listed in the Reflect – Motivation worksheet and identify specific actions you will take to improve your weaknesses or enhance your strengths in each area. Refer to the Develop and Renew section on the previous pages for action ideas, keeping in mind the needs of your current or aspired position.

You can have multiple actions for each item you intend to focus on. In the first section, list the actions that are specific to the items you listed in the Reflect – Motivation section. On the following page, list any actions you will take that are general to this competency and are related to more than one scored item. Finally, prioritize your actions based on the need for your current or aspired position. These actions will become part of your Personal Development Plan (PDP) for this competency in Appendix C.

Actions to Improve Weakness or Enhance Strength	Priority

Continue on next page.

77

Change – Motivation

Actions to Improve Weakness or Enhance Strength	Priority

Other Actions You Will Take Related to Motivation (not related to the identified strongest or weakest items)	Priority

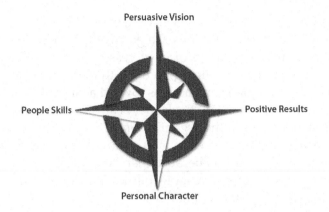

CHAPTER 9

Planning

(Persuasive Vision)

"Good fortune is what happens when opportunity meets with planning."

– Thomas Alva Edison

Planning involves many activities at a number of levels. At the highest level, leaders must have strategic plans to guide their activities over a period of time. At the micro level, leaders must think about their activities each day – what to accomplish, and how to accomplish it with the available resources. In between, there is a lot of planning that must be done involving projects, teams, proposals, and meetings.

Let's begin at the lowest level. All leaders have a to do list, whether on paper, on their computer, or in their head. The to do list itemizes all the short- and long-term work that must be done – tasks, phone calls, e-mails, meetings, etc.

The next level of planning consists of thinking about the upcoming day and creating a plan to get through the day in the best way possible. Most of us plan in this way; as we travel to work or after we arrive, we mentally focus on the tasks to be done, meetings to attend, and problems to solve.

Instead of planning on the fly, however, effective leaders give considerable time and thought to what they will do and how they will do it. Their to do list is much more than a reminder tool; it is the framework for their success.

We strongly recommend you set aside 20 to 30 minutes at least twice a week as sacred time. During this time you should be uninterrupted and focus only on what you need to do. No computer, no phone calls, no text messaging. Spend the full amount of time you set aside focusing on your to do list and how to accomplish the tasks on it.

After reviewing your to do list, the time can seem to stretch forever. But we recommend going to the next level during this time and asking some key questions about your list; What tasks could be delegated to someone else? What do you not really need to do? What tasks do you do to avoid doing tasks that are more difficult? Finally, ask if you can take a different approach in doing each task that would lead to more efficiency or a better result. Sacred time, if used regularly, will lower your stress level and improve your confidence in getting the right things done through planning.

The next level of planning is for the successful completion of projects or initiatives. Without detailed planning on how a project is to be managed, a myriad of things can go wrong. Project managers plan schedules, budgets, quality, and resources to insure project success.

Strategic planning is the highest level of planning. Strategic planning involves thinking about your organization's goals and objectives and gearing your plans and actions toward achieving them. In addition to helping create the organization's strategic plan, the leader is also responsible for communicating the plan and gaining the buy-in of others in the organization.

The most important role of the leader in strategic planning, however, is to ensure that the steps are taken that will lead to success. Leaders struggle with execution because there are always obstacles that impact it. For example, the demands of your normal responsibilities may leave you with minimal time to focus on the execution of the strategic plan's initiatives.

McChesney (2012) describes three disciplines of execution to help:

- Focus on the wildly important.
- Act on the lead measures. Measure the most high impact areas your team must do to reach their goals.
- Keep a compelling scorecard. Know where you are on the path to success.

Successful leaders have a handle on both macro planning (such as project planning or personal development planning) and micro planning (such as day-to-day tasks). They are organized and know what they are doing to execute larger plans. They use tools to know the priority of each task and what should be done next. They constantly measure their results and adjust their plans when necessary.

Red Flag Behaviors

- You do not plan what you are going to work on each day; you simply focus on the task in front of you, regardless of its priority.
- You do not set objectives for a project.
- You do not communicate strategic or project plans to your team.
- You refuse to change plans when faced with new information or a change.
- You do not have an agenda for meetings.
- Your work area is totally disorganized, and you have difficulty finding what you or someone else may need in the mess.

Case in Point

Chris is an excellent planner. He needs to be. As a Project Manager for Interior Construction for the building of one of the nation's largest airport terminals, he is constantly busy with hundreds of tasks running through his mind at all times.

What makes Chris an excellent planner? First, he sets aside 20 minutes each morning for quiet time to think about what needs to be accomplished that day. All his tasks are directly related to the vision he set forth for the completed project. If the task doesn't align with the vision, it isn't on his list. He is not afraid to say no to any task not related to completing the project within budget, on schedule, and with the best quality.

Chris always has his to do list and calendar with him. Before he became tech savvy he kept his list and schedule on paper. But now he is using his iPad. Throughout the day, he completes a task and marks it off. When a new task comes up or he gets a meeting request, he reviews his task list and schedule to determine when it can be completed or if the meeting conflicts with another event. Because he is constantly connected via e-mail and his planning tools, he can communicate responses quickly and solve problems on the run.

Others have noticed that Chris always knows what needs to be done, and so they have adopted some of his planning tools themselves. The CEO was so impressed with Chris' planning tools, he provided iPads for all the other managers. Chris now teaches a one-hour class to the managers to show them how to effectively plan using the tools, including the most important tool – his sacred time to plan his work for the day.

Notes for the Aspiring Leader

Learn how to plan by observing others. Learn what planning tools work for those who seem to have it all together. Evaluate those tools and determine if they will work for you. Participate in strategic planning, and learn how to communicate to get buy-in on the organization's path to success. Be sure to have a plan for your professional development.

Assess Your Current Location – Planning

(Persuasive Vision)

Instructions: Read each of the skills and behaviors below. As objectively as possible, score yourself for each according to the following scale: 1 = strongly disagree; 2 = disagree; 3 = agree; 4 = strongly agree. If a behavior is not appropriate for your current or aspired position, check the N/A column.

SKILL OR BEHAVIOR	1	2	3	4	N/A
I acquire appropriate resources to achieve outcomes.					
I adapt work plans in response to new information or change.					
I continually balance competing or ill-defined demands of scope, time, cost, quality, needs, and expectations.					
I delegate tasks to others when appropriate.					
My plans are directly linked to the organization's strategic plans.					
I establish performance objectives to keep projects on schedule.					
I always have an agenda for meetings.					
My work area is organized, and I can easily find what I need.					
I identify tasks and establish priorities.					
I integrate strategic plans into project, program, and policy plans.					
I provide tools and processes to work teams to accomplish work plans.					
I use organizational tools to accomplish plans.					

Continue on next page.

Assess Your Current Location – Planning

(Persuasive Vision)

SKILL OR BEHAVIOR	1	2	3	4	N/A
I use quiet (sacred) time to think about tasks and plans.					
I understand my organization's strategic plans.					
I communicate the details of plans to those involved and stakeholders.					
I use goals, milestones, and control mechanisms to measure and manage.					
SCORES FOR PLANNING (Total check marks in each column and multiply by the heading for the column. Record your scores here.)					

TOTAL SCORE FOR PLANNING: _____

(Add scores from Columns 1, 2, 3, and 4. Record the total above and on the Master Score Sheet in Appendix A. Also, count the number of N/As and record on the Master Score Sheet.)

Reflect – Planning

Scoring Analysis

List Your Highest Four Scored Items (Strengths)

Note: If you have multiple items with the same high score, choose the four items that are most related to your current or aspired position.

Item	Score

List Your Four Lowest Scored Items (Weaknesses)

Note: If you have multiple items with the same low score, choose the four items that are most related to your current or aspired position.

Item	Score

Reflect – Planning Questions

Think about the following questions about planning:

- Think of a big project you've worked on that was successful. How much planning took place before and during the project? Do you feel planning added to the success of the project?

- When planning a project or initiative, what components of a plan need to be considered?

- What are the differences between short-term planning and strategic planning?

- Have you worked on a project that was not well planned? What were the results? What could have been done differently?

- How does planning relate to other leadership competencies, such as Focus on Results, Time Management, Creativity, Problem Solving, and Talent Management?

Develop – Planning

Develop and Renew

Consider the following development tactics to help improve your skills and behaviors in planning. Identify which tactics would be valuable to include in your Personal Development Plan (PDP) if you choose to improve in this competency.

- List your current projects and tasks. Identify the goals, milestones, and control mechanisms for each. For any that do not have these three elements, develop them.

- List your team's projects. Identify how you are measuring progress on each. If you do not have measures in place, work with your team to identify how progress can be measured and how the process can be integrated with each project.

- Build time into your schedule for sacred time. Devote at least 20 minutes every other day to think strategically about how you are doing things. This should be quiet, uninterrupted time devoted to creative thinking about what needs to be done, what is working, and what is not working.

- Evaluate how well your peer leaders and team members evaluate tasks and establish priorities. Identify who may need additional development or mentoring in this area. Talk with them about programs that can help or mentoring you can provide.

- Are there any resources you need that are consistently difficult to obtain? Identify these resources and develop a strategy to smooth the relationships or process toward getting them.

- We suggest that you and your peer leaders periodically evaluate how your administrative support staff is being utilized. Is your administrative team being overworked? Are there situations where some teams or leaders misuse their administrative support? Could your support teams be reorganized to provide support that is more effective? Consider these and similar questions when evaluating how well your organization uses administrative support.

- Use technology tools to manage your time and your task list. A number of tools are available, and we recommend experimenting with them to determine which work for you.

- Build a responsibility matrix that lists your responsibilities, those of your peer leaders, and those of your individual team members. Are there any overlapping responsibilities? Are there any important areas that are not under anyone's responsibility? Review your matrix with the appropriate people to clarify any unclear responsibilities.

- To improve your delegation skills, it is first important that you identify where you are falling short. Think about instances when you have delegated tasks. Have you delegated the tasks to the appropriate person with sufficient guidance and support? Consider talking with your team members about this issue and get feedback about their perceptions. Develop a list of questions about delegation before meeting with them, and be open to their feedback and responses.

- At the beginning of a project, it is important that you work with your team to identify the tools, resources, expectations, and processes that they will need to be successful. Take the time to listen to their concerns and requests. If you commit to provide something to them, be sure you fulfill the commitment. Also, develop a habit of continually checking with your team to ensure that they have what they need.

Resources

Books

Baca, Claudia M. *Project Manager's Spotlight on Change Management*. San Francisco: Jossey-Bass, 2005.

Bossidy, Larry et al. *Execution: The Discipline of Getting Things Done*. New York: Crown, 2002.

Bradbary, Dan and David Garrett. *Herding Chickens: Innovative Techniques for Project Management*. San Francisco: Jossey-Bass, 2005.

Brassard, Michael. *The Memory Jogger 2: Tools for Continuous Improvement and Effective Planning*. Goal/QPC, 2010.

Harvard Business School Press. *Managing Projects: Pocket Mentor Series*. Cambridge: Harvard Business School Press, 2006.

Frame, J. *Managing Projects in Organizations: How to Make the Best Use of Time, Techniques, and People*. San Francisco: Wiley, 2009.

Gevurtz, Franklin A. *Gevurtz's Business Planning*. New York: Foundation Press, 2008.

Hartman, Amir. *Ruthless Execution: What Business Leaders Do When Their Companies Hit the Wall*. London: FT Press, 2003.

Kendrick, Tom. *The Project Management Tool Kit: 100 Tips and Techniques for Getting the Job Done Right*. New York: AMACOM, 2004.

Manas, Jerry. *Napoleon on Project Management: Timeless Lessons in Planning, Execution and Leadership*. Nashville, TN: Thomas Nelson, 2008.

McChesney, Chris et al. *The 4 Disciplines of Execution: Achieving Your Wildly Important Goals.* New York: Free Press, 2012.

Ognek, Mike. *Maneuver Management: Planning and Communication for Business Success.* Charleston, SC: CreateSpace, 2012.

Pascal Dennis and Jim Womack. *Getting the Right Things done: A Leader's Guide to Planning and Execution.* Lean Enterprise Institute, 2007.

Tomczyk, Catherine A. *Project Manager's Spotlight on Planning.* San Francisco: Jossey-Bass, 2005.

Websites

Wikipedia offers an excellent overview of project management: http://en.wikipedia.org/wiki/Project_management.

Mindtools presents tools for various parts of project management and planning: http://www.mindtools.com/pages/main/newMN_PPM.htm.

Other Resources

The Project Management Institute is the focal point of project management learning and certification. See them at http://www.pmi.org

Change – Planning

Instructions

Using the table below and on the next page, refer to the items you listed in the Reflect – Planning worksheet and identify specific actions you will take to improve your weaknesses or enhance your strengths in each area. Refer to the Develop and Renew section on the previous pages for action ideas, keeping in mind the needs of your current or aspired position.

You can have multiple actions for each item you intend to focus on. In the first section, list the actions that are specific to the items you listed in the Reflect – Planning section. On the following page, list any actions you will take that are general to this competency and are related to more than one scored item. Finally, prioritize your actions based on the need for your current or aspired position. These actions will become part of your Personal Development Plan (PDP) for this competency in Appendix C.

Actions to Improve Weakness or Enhance Strength	Priority

Continue on next page.

89

Change – Planning

Actions to Improve Weakness or Enhance Strength	Priority

Other Actions You Will Take Related to Planning (not related to the identified strongest or weakest items)	Priority

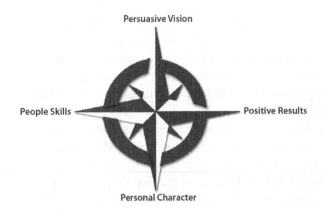

Persuasive Vision

People Skills

Positive Results

Personal Character

CHAPTER 10

Strategic Thinking

(Persuasive Vision)

"Traditional thinking is all about "what is."
Future thinking will also need to be about "what can be."
- Edward de Bono

Strategic thinking is about analyzing opportunities and problems from a broad perspective and understanding the potential impact your actions might have on others. Strategic thinkers visualize what might or could be and take a holistic approach to day-to-day issues and challenges. And they make this an ongoing process rather than a one-time event (Harvard Business School Press, 2010).

Strategic thinkers ask questions and challenge assumptions about how things work in their organization. They gather complex and sometimes ambiguous data and interpret it. The strategic thinker uses insights gained to make smart choices and select appropriate courses of action.

Why is strategic thinking important to a leader? Harvard (2010) describes five reasons:

- You can chart a course for your group that is aligned with the organization's overall strategy.
- You make smart long-term decisions that complement and align with the decisions that others in your organization are making.
- You gain your employees' commitment to supporting your decisions.
- You boost your group's performance and maximize business results.
- You foster a culture that supports fresh thinking and embraces strategic initiatives.

Strategic thinkers have future focus. They constantly consider how the conditions in which their group and company operate may change in the coming months and years. They keep an eye out for opportunities that may prove valuable in the future, as well as threats that may loom.

Another attribute of strategic thinkers is that they have a positive outlook. They view challenges as opportunities, and believe that success is possible. This positive outlook is infectious throughout the organization. But strategic thinkers must also be flexible and be able to adapt approaches and shift ideas when new information suggests the need to do so.

Strategic thinkers are open to new ideas from supervisors, peers, and outside stakeholders. They take criticism well and do not get defensive about it. They want to do what is best, and if they are going in the wrong direction, they invite feedback. They continually work to broaden their knowledge and experience so they can see connections and patterns across seemingly unrelated fields of knowledge. This understanding of the cause and effect linkages is one of the elements that helps the strategic thinker make wise decisions.

Finally, strategic thinkers are curious. They are genuinely interested in what is going on in their group, company, industry, and wider business environment. They are engaged at all levels.

We must make a distinction between strategic thinking and strategic planning. This competency focuses on strategic *thinking*, as described in the above paragraphs. To gain some clarity on the differences, one could say that you can do strategic thinking without a complete strategic planning process, but you cannot do successful strategic planning without strategic thinking. The goal of strategic thinking is to develop the mindset to view things strategically, with an eye to the future and awareness of the intended results. (Note: We recommend that you also review the previous competency, Planning, because of its relationship with Strategic Thinking.)

Thus, we can think strategically all the time, but focus on strategic planning often much less. Strategic thinking is not limited to those in planning. It is beneficial to everyone to participate in strategic thinking.

Strategic thinking is a great asset to problem solving and helps the leader understand multiple perspectives and a diversity of ideas. Often, strategic thinkers can generate a wide range of options, visualize new possibilities, and formulate fresh approaches to their work. Strategic thinkers can objectively analyze a situation and evaluate the pros, cons, and implications of any course of action.

Every leader must engage in strategic thinking to be successful. Not doing so can be disastrous. For example, assume you need to drive from Seattle to Miami. Also assume that you need to do it in four days, can only spend $400 on fuel, and cannot use any interstate highways. Under these conditions you would not immediately jump in your car in Seattle, point it southeast, and begin driving. You would engage in strategic thinking about the problem.

First, you would consult a map and determine the best route. You would calculate how many miles you needed to drive each day. You would consider where you could stop to rest, and so on. Strategic thinking helps you get to where you need to be in the best way possible. Strategic thinking helps you know what to plan in your strategic plan. In our example, knowing how to use a map, locate hotels, and detour around congested cities are examples of strategic thinking. The strategic plan is the result.

The hallmark of strategic thinking is considering and defining the medium to long-term business objectives and expectations for the future, and then working backward to the present situation as an analysis and decision making tool for the leader. This provides the much needed big picture and creates a feeling of direction and growth (strategic planning), along with a sense of progress. If any organization makes decisions without adopting a comprehensive strategic thinking procedure, it risks being hasty and uninformed in its decisions and deprives itself of the creativity and insight that strategic thinking can provide.

Red Flag Behaviors

- You do not view your organization's strategic plans as being important.
- You do not focus on the future, even the next day; you focus on what you are currently working on, regardless of its priority.
- You make decisions without thinking through the consequences.
- You do not think about better ways of doing things.
- You discourage others from making changes to better things.
- You cannot describe or communicate the purpose of your group and how it interrelates with the organization's plans.
- You dislike making long-term decisions.
- You do not seek out multiple perspectives on important issues.

Case in Point

Brian was known as the big picture guy. As the team grew, it was difficult at times for everyone to know what the end result of the project was to be and how it related to the company. Brian was always the one to be able to put each task into perspective. He was driven by the vision of the end result and how all the pieces fit together. It helped that he was able to communicate the vision to his team, but more importantly, communicate how each task benefited the project and the company's strategic vision.

When faced with problems, Brian always thought about how the potential solutions affected the whole project and company. He was also the one who asked others who were making decisions to consider what the unintended consequences may be. More than once, his queries caused another manager to rethink a decision because they had not thought about long-term implications of the decision.

Brian's team appreciated his strategic thinking and knew that if they ever were unclear about why they were doing something, Brian would have an answer for them. His communication of the vision and the path to achieve it was a strong motivator for his team.

Notes for the Aspiring Leader

Develop your strategic thinking skills by observing a successful strategic thinker who makes decisions, considers a wide set of alternatives, and seeks the big picture view of things. Don't always be satisfied with your first thoughts - push your thinking to the next right answer. Consider challenges as opportunities to improve the future for you and your organization.

Assess Your Current Location – Strategic Thinking

(Persuasive Vision)

Instructions: Read each of the skills and behaviors below. As objectively as possible, score yourself for each according to the following scale: 1 = strongly disagree; 2 = disagree; 3 = agree; 4 = strongly agree. If a behavior is not appropriate for your current or aspired position, check the N/A column.

SKILL OR BEHAVIOR	1	2	3	4	N/A
I am able to understand multiple perspectives on important issues.					
I anticipate emerging trends and lead the organization to address them.					
I appropriately communicate priorities to others with enthusiasm.					
I build commitment to my organization's strategy and vision.					
I determine strategic objectives and set priorities.					
I develop effective plans for my organization consistent with the organization's mission and vision.					
I effectively translate the vision of my organization into tactics and initiatives.					
I examine issues with a long-term perspective.					
I operate with a clear sense of direction.					
I am able to shift my thinking when presented with new or additional information.					
I use a diversity of ideas, opinions, approaches, and people to develop strategy.					

Continue on next page.

Assess Your Current Location – Strategic Thinking

(Persuasive Vision)

SKILL OR BEHAVIOR	1	2	3	4	N/A
I am genuinely interested in what is happening in my organization and my industry.					
I set aside time each week to think about the future.					
I strive to broaden my knowledge and experience.					
I welcome new ideas and can readily connect them to my plans for the future.					
I visualize new possibilities and bring fresh approaches to what I do.					
I objectively evaluate situations and assess the pros, cons, and implications.					
I ask questions and challenge assumptions about how things are working in the organization.					
I have a positive outlook and view challenges as opportunities.					
I am a catalyst for organizational change consistent with my organization's strategy.					
SCORES FOR STRATEGIC THINKING (Total check marks in each column and multiply by the heading for the column. Record your scores here.)					

TOTAL SCORE FOR STRATEGIC THINKING: _____

(Add scores from Columns 1, 2, 3, and 4. Record the total above and on the Master Score Sheet in Appendix A. Also, count the number of N/As and record on the Master Score Sheet.)

Reflect – Strategic Thinking

Scoring Analysis

List Your Four Highest Scored Items (Strengths)

Note: If you have multiple items with the same high score, choose the four items that are most related to your current or aspired position.

Item	Score

List Your Four Lowest Scored Items (Weaknesses)

Note: If you have multiple items with the same low score, choose the four items that are most related to your current or aspired position.

Item	Score

Reflect – Strategic Thinking Questions

Think about the following questions about strategic thinking:

- Does your organization put an emphasis on thinking strategically? If so, how do they do this?

- How can you help define, support and/or lead your organization's strategic goals and vision?

- How does strategic thinking help an organization achieve its goals?

- Do you think strategically about your future (both in your professional and personal life)?

- How does strategic thinking help you in other leadership competencies, such as Focus on Results, Customer Focus, Decision Making, and Problem Solving?

Develop – Strategic Thinking

Develop and Renew

Consider the following development tactics to help improve in your strategic thinking skills and behaviors. Identify which tactics would be valuable to include in your Personal Development Plan (PDP) if you choose to improve in this competency.

- Do you feel that your team and your peer leaders understand your organization's strategies? If not, consider how you can communicate your support for the strategies and the impact that they have on the organization's success. Challenge those strategies that you do not see as beneficial.

- Think about a situation you are faced with or a decision you need to make. What are the pros, cons, and implications of each alternative? Consider all the options and determine how you can develop a plan consistent with the strategic plans of your organization.

- Help your team members see the cause and effect of situations and decisions.

- List the issues that you have dealt with lately. Which could have long-term impacts that you may have overlooked? How could you have better examined each with an eye toward the long-term perspective?

- Consider meeting with your team to review the organization's strategies and the impact of success or failure. Does your team have a clear understanding of the organization's strategies and vision? Do team members understand their role in helping the strategies be successful? Meet with your team on a regular basis to discuss organizational strategies and their impact.

- Take some time and think about additional improvements that you would like to see in your organization and your team. Prioritize them and begin to champion the most impacting changes. Discuss with other leaders and your team.

- Consider meeting with your peer leaders and team on a regular basis to brainstorm improvements and assign actions to initiate steps to accomplish them. The outcome of each meeting should be a list of prioritized improvements and action items for accomplishing the highest-priority items.

- List future opportunities for your organization and team. How clear are you about each opportunity? Are the opportunities realistic? How can you visualize and communicate these opportunities to your team?

- Draw a chart that links your team's tactics and initiatives with the strategic vision of the organization. If you have difficulty, consider brainstorming with other leaders. When completed, ensure that your team understands the linkages between what they do and the organization's vision.

- Consider surveying team members to assess how well they understand the linkages between what they do and the organization's vision. This survey can tell you and your peer leaders whether better communication of the vision needs to take place. There may also be a disconnect between the tactics and initiatives of team members and the vision that needs to be addressed.

Resources

Books

Ackermann, Fran and Ian Brown. *The Practice of Making Strategy: A Step-by-Step Guide.* Thousand Oaks, CA: Sage Publications, 2005.

Bandrowski, James. *Corporate Imagination Plus: Five Steps to Translating Innovative Strategies Into Action.* New York: Free Press, 2000.

Birnbaum, Bill. *Strategic Thinking: A Four Piece Puzzle.* Douglas Mountain Publishing, 2004.

Cusumano, Michael and Constaninos Markides. *Strategic Thinking for the Next Economy.* New York: Wiley, 2001.

Darden, Katie. *Strategic Goal Planning – Determining Your Core Values – A Creative Approach to Taking Charge of Your Business and Life.* Career Life Press, 2012.

Dixit, Avinash and Barry Nalebuff. *Thinking Strategically: The Competitive Edge in Business, Politics, and Everyday Life.* New York: Norton, 1993.

Freedman, Mike and Benjamin Tregoe. *The Art and Discipline of Strategic Leadership.* New York: McGraw-Hill, 2003.

Harvard Business Review. *Harvard Business Review on Advances in Strategy.* Cambridge: Harvard Business School Press, 2002.

Harvard Business School Press. *Thinking Strategically.* (Pocket Mentor). Cambridge: Harvard Business Review Press, 2010.

Horwath, Rich. *Deep Dive: The Proven Method for Building Strategy, Focusing Resoruces, and Taking Smart Action.* Greenleaf Book Group Press, 2009.

Hultman, Ken. *Values-Driven Change: Strategies and Tools for Long-Term Success.* iUniverse, 2006.

Krogerus, Mikael; Tschappeler, Roban; Earnhart, Philip and Piening, Jenny. *The Decision Book: 50 Models for Strategic Thinking.* New York: Norton, 2012.

Wilson, Ian. *Subtle Art of Strategy: Organizational Planning in Uncertain Times.* New York: Praeger, 2003.

Wootton, Simon and Terry Horne. *Strategic Thinking: A Nine Step Approach to Strategy and Leadership for Managers and Marketers.* London: Kogan Page, 2010.

Websites

Wikipedia offers an excellent description of strategic planning at http://en.wikipedia.org/wiki/Strategic_planning.

From The Free Management Library: http://managementhelp.org/strategicplanning/index.htm.

Center for Simplified Strategic Planning, Inc. http://www.cssp.com/ Many strategic planning tools, articles, and other resources.

Ten keys to strategic planning for non-profits and foundations: http://www.tccgrp.com/pdfs/per_brief_tenkeys.pdf.

Change – Strategic Thinking

Instructions

Using the table below and on the next page, refer to the items you listed in the Reflect – Strategic Thinking worksheet and identify specific actions you will take to improve your weaknesses or enhance your strengths in each area. Refer to the Develop and Renew section on the previous pages for action ideas, keeping in mind the needs of your current or aspired position.

You can have multiple actions for each item you intend to focus on. In the first section, list the actions that are specific to the items you listed in the Reflect – Strategic Thinking section. On the following page, list any actions you will take that are general to this competency and are related to more than one scored item. Finally, prioritize your actions based on the need for your current or aspired position. These actions will become part of your Personal Development Plan (PDP) for this competency in Appendix C.

Actions to Improve Weakness or Enhance Strength	Priority

Continue on next page.

Change – Strategic Thinking

Actions to Improve Weakness or Enhance Strength	Priority

Other Actions You Will Take Related to Strategic Thinking (not related to the identified strongest or weakest items)	Priority

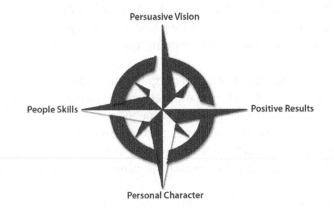

Persuasive Vision

People Skills — Positive Results

Personal Character

CHAPTER 11

Business

Development

(Positive Results)

"Make a customer, not a sale."
– Katherine Barchetti

Business Development consists of all marketing and sales activities needed to grow an organization. It is essential for the viability and growth of any business. Leaders are typically involved in business development in some role, whether as a sales leader, or as an executive with customer responsibilities. Both roles are involved in setting strategy or presenting the company's services or products to potential customers.

Business development activities include:

- Marketing
- Branding
- Identifying opportunities
- Account planning and management
- Developing differentiation
- Relationship building
- Proposal development
- Presentations

Often we think of business development as being totally in the purview of the marketing and sales teams. This is not the case, however. Operational leaders are often involved in most, if not all, of these activities. Think about how often operational leaders and project mangers are involved in writing proposals, developing technical solutions, or participating in meetings with a customer.

Bacon and Pugh (2004) describe business development as analogous to the game of chess. In chess, the game is segmented into three phases, opening game, middle game, and end game. Each game has a different strategy and role in winning, with middle game being the most important part of the game.

In business development, opening game is focused on getting your organization known in the marketplace through strategy development, communication to the market, and branding. You are conditioning the buyers in your market to think of you when they have a need.

Middle game consists of establishing a relationship with a customer and learning about their needs. You also communicate your differentiators to the customer in middle game and show them why it is in their best interest to choose you. In effect, you are conditioning the customer to want to work with you.

Creating a proposal and presentation to the customer are the primary end-game activities. Building on the knowledge you gained in middle game, you can create a clearly differentiated proposal that communicates to the customer, in a formal way, what you have been emphasizing in middle game – why they should choose you. In end game, you are conditioning the deal so that it is favorable to you but gives the customer what they need to solve their problems.

A key part of business development is the creation of positive differentiators and communicating them to the marketplace and your customers. What makes you different? Differentiation takes place on many levels, but often the key to winning is the creation of positive *behavioral* differentiators. These behaviors help a customer make the decision to work with you because they *want* to work with you.

Another key part of business development is understanding the difference between features and benefits. Features describe what your organization offers. Benefits are what the features do for your customer. Customers buy benefits, not features. You should always describe what your organization offers in terms of benefits to the customer.

It is important that every leader in an organization have an understanding of business development. Without an emphasis on business development, an organization will whither and die. Leaders must mentor their direct reports in their business development responsibilities, even if they are limited to simply having customer contact. Today's business world is extremely competitive, and the organization that perfects its business development activities will grow in the marketplace.

Red Flag Behaviors

- You do not enjoy being around customers.
- You do not enjoy delivering presentations to customers.
- You do not see that business development is an important activity for everyone in the organization.
- You are uncooperative with the marketing and sales people in your organization.
- You do not look for opportunities to contribute to the growth of your organization.

Case in Point

Jay was an engineer and loved doing the technical work it involved but he accepted a promotion to be Director of Technical Services. He quickly realized that he would have much more customer contact in the new position and would be responsible for major parts of his company's proposals and customer presentations.

His first step was to meet with the Director of Business Development to learn what was expected of him in these areas. After learning that creating proposals and customer presentations was much different than anything he had previously done, he signed up for a course in proposal development. To improve his skills in customer presentations, he attended a two-day workshop that gave him confidence in presenting his company's position on a bid to a customer.

After creating his first proposal, he sought feedback from other key people in the organization. He learned that he needed to improve his skill level and agreed to be mentored by the Director of Business Development. Soon, Jay was able to manage the creation of excellent proposals and with his new confidence in presentation skills, he was comfortable presenting solutions to potential customers.

Although he was still an engineer, he now had a better understanding of his leadership role in business development. His next steps were to train his key team members so they could assist him in creating proposals and be groomed for leadership positions themselves. In every team meeting he stressed that everyone in the company was in sales and should learn as much as possible about business development and how to interact with customers.

Notes for the Aspiring Leader

Learn business development, regardless of your position. Get comfortable representing your company to customers. Focus on learning how to communicate what your organization offers in terms of benefits to the customer.

Assess Your Current Location – Business Development

(Positive Results)

Instructions: Read each of the skills and behaviors below. As objectively as possible, score yourself for each according to the following scale: 1 = strongly disagree; 2 = disagree; 3 = agree; 4 = strongly agree. If a behavior is not appropriate for your current or aspired position, check the N/A column.

SKILL OR BEHAVIOR	1	2	3	4	N/A
I understand my role in my organization's business development process.					
I ensure that my direct reports understand the importance of their role in growing the organization's business.					
I develop and maintain strong relationships with potential and existing customers.					
I know and follow my organization's business development processes.					
I work to develop positive differentiation with potential and existing customers.					
I know and follow through on the perception that our organization wants to have in the marketplace.					
I share information about a customer or opportunity with the appropriate people in my organization as we prepare an offer.					
I develop customer-focused proposals. (Customer-focused proposals clearly show an understanding of the customer's needs and express what you will do in terms of benefits to the customer.)					

Continue on next page.

Assess Your Current Location – Business Development

(Positive Results)

SKILL OR BEHAVIOR	1	2	3	4	N/A
I develop and deliver customer-focused presentations. (Customer-focused presentations clearly show an understanding of the customer's needs and express what you will do in terms of benefits to the customer.)					
I deliver dynamic and exciting presentations that capture the attention of the audience.					
I create and use detailed key account plans to drive account activities.					
I proactively communicate with potential and existing customers.					
I work closely with potential and existing customers to understand their needs and provide solutions.					
I identify opportunities with either potential or existing customers.					
I communicate potential opportunities to the appropriate business development person in my organization.					
I review our business development processes after each opportunity to learn how they can be improved.					

Continue on next page.

Assess Your Current Location – Business Development

(Positive Results)

	1	2	3	4	N/A
SCORES FOR BUSINESS DEVELOPMENT (Total check marks in each column and multiply by the heading for the column. Record your scores here.)					

TOTAL SCORE FOR BUSINESS DEVELOPMENT: _____

(Add scores from Columns 1, 2, 3, and 4. Record the total above and on the Master Score Sheet in Appendix A. Also, count the number of N/As and record on the Master Score Sheet.)

Reflect – Business Development Questions

Scoring Analysis

List Your Four Highest Scored Items (Strengths)

Note: If you have multiple items with the same high score, choose the four items that are most related to your current or aspired position.

Item	Score

List Your Four Lowest Scored Items (Weaknesses)

Note: If you have multiple items with the same low score, choose the four items that are most related to your current or aspired position.

Item	Score

Reflect – Business Development Questions

Think about the following questions about business development:

- Do you feel you can contribute to the business development activities of your organization but are not considered for that role? If so, what can you do to become more involved?

- Is business development as important as production, service delivery, or operational excellence?

- What is the difference between sales and business development?

- Consider someone who is excellent in business development. What makes them effective?

- What is the relationship between business development and other leadership competencies such as Integrity, Communications, Strategic Thinking, Focus on Results, and Commitment to Quality?

Develop – Business Development

Develop and Renew

Consider the following development tactics to help improve your business development skills and behaviors. Identify which tactics would be valuable to include in your Personal Development Plan (PDP) if you choose to improve in this competency.

- Everyone in the organization has a role in business development. As a leader, emphasize this to everyone and look for teaching moments in your interactions. If you see someone behave in a way that damages business development or is not customer focused, correct this behavior. Consider providing training to everyone in the organization that focuses on his or her role in business development.

- Leaders are responsible for implementing a business-development culture in an organization. A business-development culture stresses excellent relationships with customers and focuses on what an organization can do to achieve their business goals. Leaders should constantly stress how people in their organization can demonstrate behaviors that contribute to building better relationships with customers.

- Technical leaders should take steps to learn as much as possible about business development. If business development is a weakness for you, identify the areas you need to improve by reviewing your score for each of the items. If possible, find a business-development mentor who will help you learn and experience business-development activities.

- Know your organization's business-development processes and your specific role in them. Every organization is different. How do you interact with others in your organization to build business? What groups depend on you for input into the business-development process? Does your team have a good understanding of how your organization pursues and acquires new business? If not, make it a point to mentor them in the processes to excel at business development.

- What are your organization's strengths and weaknesses in this area? If your organization is strong in an area, capitalize on this strength. For example, if your products are the best quality in the marketplace, this fact should be emphasized in every contact that your people have with customers. Conversely, if building relationships is a weakness, provide training and experience in relationship building techniques.

- Business success is contingent on the success of both sales and operations. It is easy to understand how sales plays into business development, but operations has an equally important role. If projects are not completed to the customer's delight, they will not come back to you with more business. Operations also plays a key role in creating business-development strategies and responses to customers. Often, customers look at an organization to determine how well operations and sales work together as an indicator of the kind of support they will receive when doing business with you.

- Understand that you and your people create positive and negative differentiators from the competition. You should strive to ensure that you always create positive differentiators. There are four types of differentiation you need to consider – operational, reputation, pricing, and behavioral. You need to assess how well you do in each area. For example, what is your reputation in the marketplace? How do you stack up (in the eyes of potential customers) against the competition? What perceptions do you need to reinforce? What perceptions do you need to change?

- Model behaviors that you see others excel in, especially in developing customer relationships. Find someone you can model who is excellent in business development. What characteristics help them excel in this competency? How do they create positive behavioral differentiation?

- Evaluate your organization's proposal processes. Do you win most of the contracts for which you submit proposals? If not, why not? Review your proposal processes and determine how they can be changed to be more successful. Are your proposals customer focused? Do they communicate in terms of benefits to the customer? Is every proposal effort a crisis? If so, how can you do things more methodically and get better results.

- Do you have key account plans for your most critical customers? Having a key account manager responsible for the growth of business with a key customer is essential. Key account managers must have detailed plans and strategies to ensure that they can service the account well to maintain and build business with the key account.

- Leaders should emphasize the development of zippered relationships with customers. This means that you establish and nurture relationships at multiple levels between the organizations. This strengthens the relationship between the organizations and minimizes the impact if changes occur in either organization.

- If you, as a leader, see how the business-development process could be improved, take action to implement the improvement. If you are new to an organization, you have the opportunity to look at the processes more objectively and provide valuable input into how things could be done better. Ask questions about why things are done the way they are done. If you know a better way of doing things, bring it up and see the reaction. Perhaps the company does things the way they do because that is the way it has been done for many years. You have the opportunity to help change things and improve the business-development processes.

Resources

Books

Bacon, Terry and David Pugh. *The Behavioral Advantage*. New York: AMACOM, 2004.

Griffin, Jill. *Customer Loyalty: How to Earn It, How to Keep It*. San Francisco: Jossey-Bass, 2002.

Hall, Stacey and Jan Brogniez. *Attracting Perfect Customers: The Power of Strategic Synchronicity*. San Francisco: Berrett-Koehler, 2001.

MacPherson, Duncan. *Breakthrough Business Development: A 90-Day Plan to Build Your Client Base and Take Your Business to the Next Level*. New York: Wiley, 2007.

Morgen, Sharon. *Selling With Integrity: Reinventing Sales Through Collaboration, Respect, and Serving*. San Francisco: Berrett-Koehler, 1999.

Rainey, David L. *Sustainable Business Development: Inventing the Future Through Strategy, Innovation, and Leadership*. Cambridge: Cambridge University Press, 2010.

Sant, Tom. *Persuasive Business Proposals: Writing to Win More Customer, Clients, and Contacts*. New York: AMACOM, 2003.

Scheessele, William B., et al. *60 Insights for Mastering Business Development*. Charleston, SC: CreateSpace, 2012.

Sorensen, Hans Eibe. *Business Development: A Market-Oriented Perspective*. New York: Wiley, 2012.

Websites

The Association of Proposal Management Professionals can be found at: http://www.apmp.org.

Excellent articles on business strategy development can be found at http://businessdevelopmentstrategy.net/.

Although a commercial site, OST offers an excellent number of business development articles and blogs, especially in the area of proposal development. See them at http://www.ostglobalsolutions.com/blog/.

Change – Business Development

Instructions

Using the table below and on the next page, refer to the items you listed in the Reflect – Business Development worksheet and identify specific actions you will take to improve your weaknesses or enhance your strengths in each area. Refer to the Develop and Renew section on the previous pages for action ideas, keeping in mind the needs of your current or aspired position.

You can have multiple actions for each item you intend to focus on. In the first section, list the actions that are specific to the items you listed in the Reflect – Business Development section. On the following page, list any actions you will take that are general to this competency and are related to more than one scored item. Finally, prioritize your actions based on the need for your current or aspired position. These actions will become part of your Personal Development Plan (PDP) for this competency in Appendix C.

Actions to Improve Weakness or Enhance Strength	Priority

Continue on next page.

Change – Business Development

Actions to Improve Weakness or Enhance Strength	Priority

Other Actions You Will Take Related to Business Development (not related to the identified strongest or weakest items)	Priority

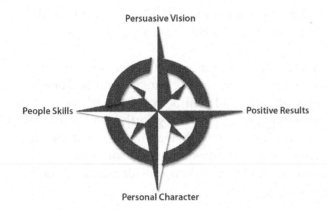

Persuasive Vision

People Skills — Positive Results

Personal Character

CHAPTER 12

Commitment to

Quality

(Positive Results)

"Mere allocation of huge sums of money for quality will not bring quality."

– W. Edwards Deming

Think of companies that offer high-quality products or services. They offer high-quality products or services because their leaders have created a culture that emphasizes quality from top to bottom in the organization. High-quality products and services do not just happen; they are created by organizations that plan quality and have a culture of excellence.

Leaders must set high expectations for quality in their organization. They must notice opportunities to improve quality and take action to do so. They must seek honest feedback from their customers and listen to them. Without quality, a company sacrifices customers, revenue, and ultimately its own existence.

The first step in demonstrating a commitment to quality is to ensure that processes are in place that support quality. These processes may be formalized and follow industry methodologies such as Six Sigma. George (2003) describes the Four Keys of Lean Six Sigma as:

- Delight your customers with speed and quality.
- Improve your processes.
- Work together for maximum gain.
- Base decisions on data and facts.

The second step is to ensure that standards for quality are set and communicated. The quality standards must be developed by, or at minimum supported by, the leadership team and infused into the culture of the organization.

Finally, monitor quality to insure you are achieving your standards. Quality checks and measurement should be an ongoing effort that leads to continuous improvement of your products or services.

To create a culture that emphasizes high quality, the leader must not only enforce quality standards but also provide incentives to others to identify ways that things could be done better. For example, each week all managers in all departments of all facilities of Ritz Carlton meet via conference call. During this highly-structured meeting, managers bring forth ideas to help make the Ritz Carlton experience better for all customers. The ideas are listed and assigned for further analysis. Not all ideas are adopted - some require too much investment and some may have negative effects that the suggester was not aware of; but all are given consideration. Michelli (2005) describes the points of the Ritz Carlton Gold Standard:

- Define and Refine – Set the foundation, communicate the core identity and culture; be relevant.
- Empower Through Trust – Select, don't hire; it's a matter of trust.
- It's Not About You – Build a business focused on others, support front-line empathy.
- Deliver WOW! – The ultimate guest experience, turn WOW! Into action.
- Leave a Lasting Footprint – aspire, achieve, teach – sustainability and stewardship.

How often do you listen to your customers about quality? Although some organizations seek feedback from customers using a survey or online questionnaire, are the results analyzed and actions taken? Consider better ways you could receive feedback from your customers. Would a scheduled meeting be possible? If so, it demonstrates to the customer that you care about them and the quality of the products they are buying.

Companies in service industries, such as restaurants and hotels, must be even more aware of their customers' opinions in today's world of social media. Many customers routinely post online reviews on services such as Yelp or Tripadvisor, and bad reviews can cause a business serious damage.

Red Flag Behaviors

- You feel it is more important to get something done with imperfections than to get it done right.
- You do not view quality from the perspective of a customer.
- You think quality is overrated and production volume or making a sale are more important.
- You overlook imperfections by others in either products or services.
- You reward team members who produce more but with quality problems, and not those who focus on quality.
- You do not figure out how to measure quality; rather, you say you will know it when you see it.

Case in Point

Rand owned a small business that manufactured model train sets. Over the past year, he noticed that the percentage of trains that were returned for defects had nearly doubled from the previous year. This had a major impact on his bottom line, as well as his professional reputation. He knew he needed to do something, so he searched for a quality expert and selected the best applicant, Julie Benson.

During Julie's first month, she reviewed the entire design and production process. After her analysis of the returns and the processes, she implemented a quality control system that insured every train set met specific standards at each step of the production process. She also trained the line workers to look for specific parts that were causing many of the defects. After hearing the results from the line workers, she knew that part of the problem was the motor set. It was not sufficiently insulated to withstand the heat beyond about one hour of track time. This resulted in wires shorting in the set, causing the locomotive to burn out.

Julie recommended one of two solutions to Rand. Her preferred solution was to add a new part to the motor to absorb the heat. The other was to investigate the possibility of buying the motors from a more reliable source. Rand chose the second solution because it was easier than adding a new step to the production process.

Julie's next step was to monitor the quality of the new motors to ensure that they did not repeat the problem or introduce any new problems. Her analysis showed that the new motors worked fine, and returns dropped to even lower levels than the original rate.

Notes for the Aspiring Leader

The quality of products or services that your organization provides is reflective of you personally. Strive to build a strong reputation for quality over your career. Be a champion and spread the quality culture throughout your organization.

Assess Your Current Location – Commitment to Quality

(Positive Results)

Instructions: Read each of the skills and behaviors below. As objectively as possible, score yourself for each according to the following scale: 1 = strongly disagree; 2 = disagree; 3 = agree; 4 = strongly agree. If a behavior is not appropriate for your current or aspired position, check the N/A column.

SKILL OR BEHAVIOR	1	2	3	4	N/A
I actively seek methods to improve the quality of products or services.					
I continually strive to add value to products, services, and other areas of involvement.					
I create high expectations for an organization-wide quality culture.					
I notice opportunities to improve quality and take actions to do so.					
I seek feedback in areas of perceived team or organizational weakness.					
I seek feedback from internal and/or external customers regarding quality.					
I recognize team members who demonstrate a focus on quality.					
I establish processes to check quality throughout product development or service delivery.					
I strive to differentiate myself and my organization through high-quality products or services.					
I develop and enforce quality standards for my organization.					

Continue on next page.

Assess Your Current Location – Commitment to Quality

(Positive Results)

SKILL OR BEHAVIOR	1	2	3	4	N/A
I resist efforts from others to produce inferior quality products or deliver poor quality service.					
I know what to measure to insure quality and when to measure it.					
I simplify complex processes without negatively impacting quality.					
I am dedicated to providing organization-wide common systems for insuring quality.					
I am skilled at figuring out the processes needed to get things done.					
I am committed to continuous improvement through empowerment and management by data.					
I leverage technology to positively impact quality.					
I am aware of customer reviews on social media and quickly address valid negative reviews.					
SCORES FOR COMMITMENT TO QUALITY (Total check marks in each column and multiply by the heading for the column. Record your scores here.)					

TOTAL SCORE FOR COMMITMENT TO QUALITY: _____

(Add scores from Columns 1, 2, 3, and 4. Record the total above and on the Master Score Sheet in Appendix A. Also, count the number of N/As and record on the Master Score Sheet.)

Reflect – Commitment to Quality

Scoring Analysis

List Your Four Highest Scored Items (Strengths)

Note: If you have multiple items with the same high score, choose the four items that are most related to your current or aspired position.

Item	Score

List Your Four Lowest Scored Items (Weaknesses)

Note: If you have multiple items with the same low score, choose the four items that are most related to your current or aspired position.

Item	Score

Reflect – Commitment to Quality Questions

Think about the following questions about commitment to quality:

- Does your organization put an emphasis on commitment to quality? If so, how do they do this?

- How do you feel when you buy a product or encounter service that reflects poor quality? Do you ever say, "I will never buy from that company again.?" Do you tell others about your poor experience?

- Name some companies or organizations that have a reputation for excellent quality products or services. Why do you think they have this reputation?

- What are some ways that you can instill a commitment to quality in your team or direct reports?

- How can the leadership of an organization help it gain a reputation for quality products or services?

Develop – Commitment to Quality

Develop and Renew

Consider the following development tactics to help improve your commitment to quality. Identify which tactics would be valuable to include in your Personal Development Plan (PDP) if you choose to improve in this competency.

- As a leader, take steps to initiate a review of how your products or services can be improved. Discuss with all appropriate stakeholders, and identify achievable improvements. Prioritize improvements and create an improvement plan.

- Consider steps you could take to create a culture within your organization that seeks opportunities to improve quality and to be proactive in doing so.

- When we hear about a concern with a product or service, we typically place it on our priority list. These actions can easily become overcome by events or other tasks needing completion. When you hear a concern, make a note of it and speak to stakeholders about it as soon as possible. Concerns with products or services should rank very high on your priority list. To be proactive in this area, it is important that you develop a relationship with customers so they are comfortable bringing their concerns to you.

- Identify how you can demonstrate that you are concerned with the accuracy and completeness of projects and tasks. What obstacles do you face in becoming more concerned with accuracy and completeness? How can you overcome these obstacles?

- Is adding value part of your organization's culture? We recommend that as a leader you define what added value means to your organization and take steps to create a culture which encourages value to be added at all levels.

- Be aware of what is being said on social media sites about your organization. This is especially important for restaurants and places of lodging. Share both positive and negative reviews with your team.

Resources

Books

ASQ Quality Management Division, et al. *The Quality Improvement Handbook*. ASQ Quality, 2006.

Bhote, Keki. *The Ultimate Six Sigma: Beyond Quality Excellence to Total Business Excellence*. New York: AMACOM, 2002.

Cochran, Craig. *The Continual Improvement Process: From Strategy to the Bottom Line*. Chico, CA: Paton, 2003.

Deming, W. Edwards. *The Essential Deming: Leadership Principles From the Father of Quality*. New York: McGraw-Hill, 2012.

George, Michael. *The Lean Six Sigma Pocket Toolbook: A Quick Reference Guide to 100 Tools for Improving Quality and Speed*. New York: McGraw-Hill, 2004.

George, Michael et al. *What is Lean Six Sigma?* New York: McGraw-Hill, 2003.

Mitra, Amitava. *Fundamentals of Quality Control and Improvement*. New York: Wiley, 2008.

Pande, Pete and Larry Holpp. *What is Six Sigma?* New York: McGraw-Hill, 2002.

Roberson, Russell. *Quality: Tenets on Leadership*. Charleston, SC: CreateSpace, 2011.

Rose, Kenneth. *Project Quality Management: Why, What, and How*. Plantation, FL: J. Ross Publishing. 2005.

Smith, Dick et al. *Strategic Six Sigma: Best Practices from the Executive Suite*. New York: Wiley, 2002.

Van Tiem; Darlene, et al. *Fundamentals of Performance Improvement: A Guide to Improving People, Process, and Performance*. San Francisco: Pfeiffer, 2012.

Walter, Mary. *The Deming Management Method*. Perigee Books, 1988.

Websites

See the American Society for Quality at www.asq.org.

See articles in Quality Digest at: www.qualitydigest.com.

Inc. Magazine provides an excellent article on quality at http://www.inc.com/guides/2010/09/5-ways-to-improve-quality.html.

Change – Commitment to Quality

Instructions

Using the table below and on the next page, refer to the items you listed in the Reflect – Commitment to Quality worksheet and identify specific actions you will take to improve your weaknesses or enhance your strengths in each area. Refer to the Develop and Renew section on the previous pages for action ideas, keeping in mind the needs of your current or aspired position.

You can have multiple actions for each item you intend to focus on. In the first section, list the actions that are specific to the items you listed in the Reflect – Commitment to Quality section. On the following page, list any actions you will take that are general to this competency and are related to more than one scored item. Finally, prioritize your actions based on the need for your current or aspired position. These actions will become part of your Personal Development Plan (PDP) for this competency in Appendix C.

Actions to Improve Weakness or Enhance Strength	Priority

Continue on next page.

Change – Commitment to Quality

Actions to Improve Weakness or Enhance Strength	Priority

Other Actions You Will Take Related to Commitment to Quality (not related to the identified strongest or weakest items)	Priority

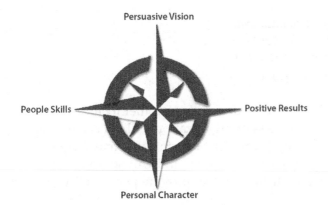

Persuasive Vision

People Skills — Positive Results

Personal Character

CHAPTER 13

Customer Focus

(Positive Results)

"There is only one boss. The customer. And he can fire everybody in the company from the chairman on down, simply by spending his money somewhere else."

- Sam Walton

Almost all organizations and leaders have customers. We usually think of customers as those who buy our products or services; however, customers can be internal or external. Sometimes those who work in administrative positions with no direct access to an organization's external customers forget that the success of the organization depends on how well they serve their internal customers. For example, a director of Human Resources may not directly interface with the company's customers, but her customers include all the company's employees, outside vendors, senior leadership, and her peers in other parts of the business. If she does not focus on serving her customers, their morale may be lower and those who actually interface with external customers may not do their best job.

Customer focus is defined as an individual and organizational orientation toward satisfying the needs of potential and existing customers. To meet these needs, you must know what they are. Too often, people assume they know what is important to a customer. Rather than make this assumption, talk with your customers and learn what their key issues are and how you can serve them to their satisfaction.

Solomon (2012) believes that the key to customer focus is to be proactive, not reactive. He stresses that it is a customer trend to expect anticipatory service in today's internet world. The edge will be created for those who anticipate customer needs and desires and are proactive in meeting (or exceeding) those needs and desires.

This is why many businesses try to learn as much as possible about their best customers. Hotels gain an edge if they know their frequent customers like a particular type of room, a certain style of pillow, or a particular snack that can be pre-positioned in the room on arrival.

It is also important to follow through on all commitments and meet them 100% of the time. Solomon went on to write a short poem that sums up the relationship between you and your customers:

"If you can anticipate,
You can differentiate.
If customers feel at home,
They're unlikely to roam."

There is a very simple answer to the question, "Why bother with customer focus?" If you don't focus on existing and potential customers, your business or organization will not achieve its potential, and in fact stands a good chance of failing. Think of restaurants you may frequent. Some you return to on a regular basis. Others you have visited once and will not return due to poor quality food or service. Eventually, those establishments that provide poor quality products or services will fail.

One approach we have found that increases customer focus is to take the attitude that you are the customer's advocate in your organization. Put yourself in the customer's place and question everything to determine if it will benefit the customer or not. Being the customer's advocate also enables your organization to more readily adopt behaviors that are above and beyond. It is these types of behaviors that differentiate your business from the competition.

Inghilleri (2010) describes four elements of customer satisfaction:

- Perfect product
- Caring delivery
- Timeliness
- Effective problem resolution process

Think of the organizations and companies you deal with, and compare their approach to Inghilleri's elements. You will return to those businesses that meet his elements of customer satisfaction and will be reluctant to return to those that do not meet your standards for customer focus.

Leaders determine whether their organization is customer focused or not. Followers emulate the behaviors of leaders, especially when dealing with potential and existing internal or external customers. Be observant of customer-focused behaviors you come in contact with in your daily life. What can you learn from others in this important area?

Red Flag Behaviors

- You do not believe that the customer is always right.
- You do not attempt to understand customers' needs.
- You pride yourself on being difficult to work with (from a customer's perspective).
- Deadlines are a nuisance and you rarely meet them.
- You talk negatively to your peers and team about customers.
- You make promises to customers but do not follow through.

Case in Point

I recently read a story about Jia Jiang who challenged himself to be rejected every day for 30 days (see http://www.entresting.com/blog/100-days-of-rejection-therapy). He was rejected on his first two days but on the third his premise fell apart. He went to a Krispy Kreme doughnut shop and requested five doughnuts put together in the shape and color of the Olympics symbol in fifteen minutes.

Jackie Braun, the shift leader at the Austin, Texas, store took his order and went into the back of the store. Within 15 minutes she reappeared with Jia's order. He was amazed. But because Jackie was not satisfied with her work, she gave Jia the doughnut creation free of charge.

Check out Jia's blog to read the stories of his other days, where he was much more successful in getting rejected.

Another Case in Point

I (Ben) was traveling on business and contracted food poisoning. I felt that if I had a few more hours of sleep I would feel better and be able to go to my next meeting that evening. I had already been up all night and was sick and exhausted. At the front desk I asked if I could stay a few hours past checkout time and I was refused. I asked if they were full and was told, "No, but it is against our policy to extend checkout time." I explained my circumstances, but the desk clerk indicated by her body language that she could not care less. In exasperation I asked for a manager, but was refused.

I left the hotel in disgust and began the drive to my next hotel on the other side of Dallas. When I arrived at my new hotel, the desk clerk remarked that I didn't look well. I explained the situation and she said to immediately go to my room to rest and that I could finish my check-in later. As I was leaving for the room she said to not go to sleep for ten minutes. I was unclear why but shortly after arriving at my room there was a knock on the door. When I answered, it was a restaurant employee with a bowl of chicken soup and ginger ale. I thanked him and asked to sign the check. He said, "No, this is compliments of the front desk."

Ever since that experience I have pointed to the Marriott Hotel in Plano, Texas, as an example of excellent customer focus and urged people to patronize this establishment. I also wrote a nice letter to the manager thanking the front desk clerk for her customer focus.

Notes for the Aspiring Leader

The core of success in any business is being focused on customers. Who are your customers and what are you doing to ensure that you are meeting or exceeding their needs and desires? What can you do to learn how to listen to customers so that you can anticipate their needs and desires?

Assess Your Current Location – Customer Focus

(Positive Results)

Instructions: Read each of the skills and behaviors below. As objectively as possible, score yourself for each according to the following scale: 1 = strongly disagree; 2 = disagree; 3 = agree; 4 = strongly agree. If a behavior is not appropriate for your current or aspired position, check the N/A column.

SKILL OR BEHAVIOR	1	2	3	4	N/A
I consistently strive to delight customers by giving more than expected.					
I admit my mistakes and take steps to fix them.					
I consistently meet deadlines for deliveries to customers.					
I advocate for customers within my organization.					
I strive to provide value to customers.					
I am proactive in identifying customers' needs and issues.					
I model positive customer-focused behaviors.					
I proactively seek feedback from customers and listen to their comments.					
I seek to understand my customers' key issues.					
I am easy to do business with.					
I follow through with what I commit to a customer.					
SCORES FOR CUSTOMER FOCUS (Total check marks in each column and multiply by the heading for the column. Record your scores here.)					

TOTAL SCORE FOR CUSTOMER FOCUS: _____

(Add scores from Columns 1, 2, 3, and 4. Record the total above and on the Master Score Sheet in Appendix A. Also, count the number of N/As and record on the Master Score Sheet.)

Reflect – Customer Focus

Scoring Analysis

List Your Four Highest Scored Items (Strengths)

Note: If you have multiple items with the same high score, choose the four items that are most related to your current or aspired position.

Item	Score

List Your Four Lowest Scored Items (Weaknesses)

Note: If you have multiple items with the same low score, choose the four items that are most related to your current or aspired position.

Item	Score

133

Reflect – Customer Focus Questions

Think about the following questions about customer focus:

- How do you react when you are treated well by someone you are doing business with in your personal life?

- How do you feel about the phrase, "The customer is always right"?

- Do you feel your leaders cultivate a culture of customer focus? If yes, how are your leaders doing this?

- How can you monitor your team members or direct reports to insure they are customer focused?

- Do you think everyone in your organization knows who their customers are?

Develop – Customer Focus

Develop and Renew

Consider the following development tactics to help improve your skills and behaviors in customer focus. Identify which tactics would be valuable to include in your Personal Development Plan (PDP) if you choose to improve in this competency.

- All contributors in successful organizations must model customer-focused behaviors. In particular, they must strive to understand a customer's needs, issues, goals and objectives. Consider whether you communicate well enough with customers to understand their needs. Also, consider your attitude toward customers in front of your team and peers. It is easy to focus our frustrations on customers and complain about them being needy or difficult to work with. If you realize that you sometimes engage in this negativity, take steps to immediately change this behavior.

- You should continue to foster a culture in your team which strives to not only meet but to exceed customer expectations. This will help insure the viability of your organization and help permeate this attitude throughout all layers of the organization. Consider taking steps to be more proactive in meeting and exceeding customer needs and building a culture in the organization that strives to always be the best for customers.

- To achieve maximum effectiveness, it is critical that you are very responsive to customer needs and requests. Rather than feel that customer needs or requests are an intrusion, you should anticipate and fulfill them as soon as possible. It is also important to know when a customer is requesting something out of scope or something that is not within your organization's capabilities. When this occurs, you must explain the situation with tact.

- Develop a list of questions for your customer that would stimulate a discussion regarding their level of satisfaction. Consider all areas that are important, such as satisfaction with your products or services, their attitude, issues that may be surfacing, and so on. After developing this list, assess how much information you already know and identify your next steps in confirming it as well as seeking out more information.

- Consider convening a meeting with selected customers to solicit their ideas on improvements to your products or services that would better meet their needs. After gathering this data, develop a plan with your peers to consider how to implement each improvement.

- When developing rapport with individuals in the customer's organization, be sure to convey a sense of sincerity. Your actions should communicate your authentic concern for the customer's success and issues they face in achieving success. Sincerity is established in many ways, but one way is to get to know each individual and provide value-added information or help in meeting their needs and achieving their goals.

Resources

Books

Brinkman, Rick and Rick Kirschner. *Love Thy Customer: Creating Delight, Preventing Dissatisfaction, and Pleasing Your Hardest-to-Please Customer*. New York: McGraw-Hill, 2005.

Buckingham, Richard. *Customer Once, Client Forever: 12 Tools for building Lifetime Business Relationships*. New York: Kiplinger Books, 2001.

Cochran, Craig. *Becoming a Customer-Focused Organization*. Chico, CA: Paton, 2006.

Cook, Sarah. *Customer Care Excellence: How to Create an Effective Customer Focus*. Philadelphia: Kogan, 2011.

Frei, Frances and Anne Morriss. *Uncommon Service: How to Win by Putting Customers at the Core of Your Business*. Cambridge: Harvard Business Review, 2012.

Galbraith, Jay. *Designing the Customer-Centric Organization: A Guide to Strategy, Structure, and Process*. San Francisco: Jossey-Bass, 2005.

Heil, Gary, et al. *One Size Fits One: Building Customer Relationships One Customer and One Employee at a Time*. New York: Wiley, 1999.

Inghilleri, Leonardo. *Exceptional Service, Exceptional Profit: The Secrets of Building a Five-Star Customer Service Organization*. New York: AMACOM, 2010.

Johnson, Michael and Anders Gustafsson. *Improving Customer Satisfaction, Loyalty and Profit*. New York: Jossey-Bass, 2000.

Manning, Harley and Kerry Bodine. *Outside In: The Power of Putting Customers at the Center of Your Business*. New Harvest, 2012.

McDonald, Ben and Sidney McDonald. *Customer Focus for Leaders and Managers*. Boise, ID: Benchmark Learning International, 2011.

Michelli, Joseph. *The New Gold Standard: 5 Leadership Principles for Creating a Legendary Customer Experience Courtesy of the Ritz-Carlton Hotel Company*. New York: McGraw-Hill, 2008.

Miller, Ray. *That's Customer Focus!: The Overworked and Underappreciated Manager's Guide to Creating a Customer-Focused Organization*. Charleston, SC: BookSurge Publishing, 2008.

Solomon, Micah. *High-Tech, High-Touch Customer Service: Inspire Timeless Loyalty in the Demanding New World of Social Commerce*. New York: AMACOM, 2012.

Szwarc, Paul. *Researching Customer Satisfaction and Loyalty: How to Find Out What People Really Think*. Philadelphia: Kogan Page, 2005.

Treacy, Michael and Fred Wiersama. *The Discipline of Market Leaders: Choose Your Customers, Narrow Your Focus, and Dominate Your Market*. Basic Books, 1997.

Websites

HRM Business offers an excellent article on what a customer-focused organization looks like at http://www.hrmbusiness.com/2009/03/customer-focused-organization.html.

Change – Customer Focus

Instructions

Using the table below and on the next page, refer to the items you listed in the Reflect – Customer Focus worksheet and identify specific actions you will take to improve your weaknesses or enhance your strengths in each area. Refer to the Develop and Renew section on the previous pages for action ideas, keeping in mind the needs of your current or aspired position.

You can have multiple actions for each item you intend to focus on. In the first section, list the actions that are specific to the items you listed in the Reflect – Customer Focus section. On the following page, list any actions you will take that are general to this competency and are related to more than one scored item. Finally, prioritize your actions based on the need for your current or aspired position. These actions will become part of your Personal Development Plan (PDP) for this competency in Appendix C.

Actions to Improve Weakness or Enhance Strength	Priority

Continue on next page.

Change – Customer Focus

Actions to Improve Weakness or Enhance Strength	Priority

Other Actions You Will Take Related to Customer Focus (not related to the identified strongest or weakest items)	Priority

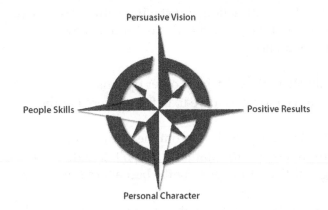

Persuasive Vision

People Skills — Positive Results

Personal Character

CHAPTER 14

Decision Making

(Positive Results)

"Choices are the hinges of destiny."

– Pythagoras

Decision making is the process of selecting from several choices and taking action. We make decisions every day. For leaders, making decisions is a large and very important part of their job. Think about the past 24 hours – how many decisions did you need to make? Many, I am sure – some small and inconsequential ones and some that may have had significant impact.

Decision making is an important leadership competency. Leaders must not only make decisions, they must make the right decisions at the right time. Effective leaders consider all alternatives, assess the risks and consequences of each, and make a decision based on what is right in the situation.

One of the major issues with decision making that we hear in coaching is that people tend to delay difficult decisions. Some people are concerned that they will make the wrong decision; therefore, they make no decision. In reality, no decision is a decision as well. Consider your decision making process. Do you search for the cause of the problem that requires a decision? Do you consider all the alternatives? Do you evaluate the risks associated with each decision?

Decisions should be made based on information. Leaders should seek as much information as possible to factor into their thinking about a decision. This may require the leader to reach out to others for information or to assign team members to get information. Ignoring information can lead to making the wrong decision. Sometimes decision makers ignore information due to their personal biases. Decision making should be bias free and based on information. The opinions of others may be important and should be considered, but be careful that your decisions are not biased based on your seeking out the opinions of others you know will agree with you.

Decisions cause a change to the status quo. When a decision is made, a change is made. Airely (2010) explains this in more detail. The more choices you are given, the more pull the status quo has and the more likely you are to not make a decision. This is further aggravated by a fact in business – sins of commission (doing something) are punished more than sins of omission (not doing anything). Thus, the status quo has a strong attraction. But staying with the status quo is a business-killer; decisions need to be made to continue growth and excellence in any organization. Airely describes what to do in this situation:

- Never think of the status quo as the only alternative. Identify other options.
- Ask yourself if you would choose the status quo alternative if, in fact, it were not the status quo.
- Avoid exaggerating the effort or cost involved in switching from the status quo.
- If you have several alternatives that are superior to the status quo, don't default to the status quo just because you are having a difficult time picking the best alternative. Force yourself to choose.
- Always remind yourself of the objectives and examine how they would be served by the status quo.

Decisions should always be made with integrity. When considering all options for a decision, leaders should always seek to do what is right. Personal gain should not play a role in a decision involving the team or organization. Even one decision that is not made with integrity can have significant ramifications. For example, if people feel you made a decision that will bring you personal gain, their trust in you will diminish and you will lose credibility.

People expect leaders to be skilled decision makers. They do not expect perfection and not every decision will be the right one. But decisions must be made and they must be made with due diligence at the appropriate time. In complex decisions, it is important to assess the ramifications of each alternative, assess the risks involved, and determine how each alternative will affect others. Decisions should not be made rashly or quickly.

Red Flag Behaviors

- You avoid making decisions.
- When faced with a decision, you make it before exploring all the alternatives and potential consequences.
- You prefer the status quo and dislike making changes.
- Many of your decisions are made from emotion and not clear, rational thought.
- You do not collect information from others when making decisions.
- Your decisions are biased toward your own personal agenda.

Case in Point

It was not an easy decision to make. Jerry ran a small business on the east side of the city. He had an offer for the land on which his business sat. He could take the offer and move, or he could ignore it and stay at this location. If he moved, there was no question he would take his business to the far west end of the city where there was a larger market for his specialty foods. But if he moved, he felt confident that most of his staff would not desire to travel the 30 miles to the new location.

Jerry thought about his decision and researched the alternatives in depth. He thought about all the unintended consequences, such as hiring and training new staff. He also considered his employees and their loyalty. Many had been with him for the six years he had been in business. He also sought out some expert advice from other small businesses that had changed location. This made him realize that he would have to invest in advertising in the new area, and he should consider how much it would cost to move his equipment to the new location.

After gathering as much information as possible, Jerry spent some time thinking about the possible move and considering the financial implications. He recalled when he opened six years ago that he assured his customers that he would be a fixture in the community and they could rely on him to meet their needs. Many of these customers still visited his shop weekly.

After much thought, Jerry made his decision and is now entering his eighth year at the same location. But you can also visit Jerry's new location on the west side of the city, managed by one of his best employees. It seems that the longer Jerry thought about his decision, the more apparent it became that he could not leave his original location, but there was nothing stopping him from opening his second location.

Notes for the Aspiring Leader

Not all your decisions will be easy, nor will they always have a good result. Leaders make decisions, even if they are difficult. Effective leaders make good decisions based on information. Learn how to gather and evaluate information, and your decisions will more likely be the right ones.

Assess Your Current Location – Decision Making

(Positive Results)

Instructions: Read each of the skills and behaviors below. As objectively as possible, score yourself for each according to the following scale: 1 = strongly disagree; 2 = disagree; 3 = agree; 4 = strongly agree. If a behavior is not appropriate for your current or aspired position, check the N/A column.

SKILL OR BEHAVIOR	1	2	3	4	N/A
I make timely decisions.					
I define the problem or issue before making a decision.					
I gain input from others about the problem or decision (as appropriate).					
I seek to learn the potential causes of a problem before making a decision.					
I use divergent thinking processes such as brainstorming to identify alternatives.					
I evaluate alternatives to determine the best decision.					
I evaluate the risks of each alternative.					
I communicate decisions to the appropriate stakeholders.					
I monitor the results of decisions.					
I evaluate what can be learned from decisions and the process in which they are made.					
SCORES FOR DECISION MAKING (Total check marks in each column and multiply by the heading for the column. Record your scores here.)					

TOTAL SCORE FOR DECISION MAKING: _____

(Add scores from Columns 1, 2, 3, and 4. Record the total above and on the Master Score Sheet in Appendix A. Also, count the number of N/As and record on the Master Score Sheet.)

Reflect – Decision Making

Scoring Analysis

List Your Four Highest Scored Items (Strengths)

Note: If you have multiple items with the same high score, choose the four items that are most related to your current or aspired position.

Item	Score

List Your Four Lowest Scored Items (Weaknesses)

Note: If you have multiple items with the same low score, choose the four items that are most related to your current or aspired position.

Item	Score

Reflect – Decision Making Questions

Think about the following questions about decision making:

- Have you ever worked with someone who makes quick decisions when needed? Did that make you feel confident?

- What obstacles are sometimes in place that cause decision making to be difficult?

- How does it feel when you work for someone who is always hesitant to make decisions?

- Do people make better decisions when they consider the decision themselves or if they bring together a team to make a decision?

- What are the consequences if you do not make decisions in a timely manner?

- What types of data or information should you consider when making decisions in your field?

Develop – Decision Making

Develop and Renew

Consider the following development tactics to help improve your decision making skills and behaviors. Identify which tactics would be valuable to include in your Personal Development Plan (PDP) if you choose to improve in this competency.

- Consider a decision you are in the process of making. List the stakeholders and those impacted by the decision that you need to collaborate with during the process. After you have completed the list, determine when the best time to collaborate with each. Then take steps to implement your plan.

- Be liberal in trying to determine who the stakeholders in a decision may be. It is better to collaborate with too many people than to ignore a key stakeholder. Also consider who will be impacted by a decision and the best timing to discuss with them - before or after the decision is made. Each decision is different and requires you to think about the process of collaboration and communication.

- List three behaviors you need to change to become more flexible in your decision making when provided with more information. When faced with a decision, think of these behaviors when new information is presented.

- When faced with your next decision, determine when the decision should be made. Does it need to be made immediately? If not, when does it impact others if the decision is not made?

- Consider keeping a running list of decisions that you need to make. Include a date when the decision needs to be made. You may also want to include the consequences if the decision is not made by the scheduled date. This will help you develop a habit of being responsive to making decisions in a timely manner.

- When faced with your next decision, build a matrix that identifies the information you need to make the decision. Include a column identifying where you can get the information or who has the information you need. After completing the matrix, use it as a guide to compile the information you need.

- What behaviors should you change to become more resolute and confident in your decision making? List them. After making a decision, think of these behaviors and use them to be more resolute in your decision making.

- Collaboration does not absolve a decision maker from taking responsibility. Have the courage and integrity to not only take responsibility for good decisions, but also for those that turn out badly. When taking responsibility for a bad decision, ensure that you can articulate what you learned from the experience.

- When faced with your next significant decision, perform a risk identification, assessment, and mitigation for each alternative. Review your risk identification, assessment, and mitigation data with other stakeholders. Use the information presented in the developmental resources for this item as a guide.

Resources

Books

Airely, Dan. *Predictably Irrational: The Hidden Forces that Shape Our Decisions*. New York: Harper, 2010.

Bazerman, Max H. and Don Moore. *Judgment in Managerial Decision Making.* New York: Wiley, 2008.

Drucker, Peter. et al. *Harvard Business Review on Decision Making*. Cambridge: Harvard Business School Press, 2001.

Drummond, Helga. *The Art of Decision Making*. New York: Wiley, 2001.

Hammond, John. et al. *Smart Choice: A Practical Guide to Making Better Decisions*. New York: Crown Business, 2002.

Harvard Business Review. *Harvard Business Review on Making Smart Decisions*. Cambridge, MA: Harvard Business Review Press, 2011.

Jones, Morgan. *The Thinker's Toolkit: Fourteen Skills for Making Smarter Decisions in Business and in Life*. New York: Random House, 1995.

Klein, Gary. *Sources of Power: How People Make Decisions*. Boston: MIT Press, 1999.

Krogerus, Mikael. et al. *The Decision Book: 50 Models for Strategic Thinking.* New York: Norton, 2012.

Lehrer, Jonah. *How We Decide*. Mariner Books, 2010.

Maruska, Don. *How Great Decisions Get Made*. New York: AMACOM, 2006.

Mooz, Hal and Jeff Henley. *Make Up Your Mind: A Decision Making Guide to Thinking Clearly and Choosing Wisely.* New York: Wiley, 2012.

Murnighan, John and John Mowen. *The Art of High-Stakes Decision Making: Tough Calls in a Speed-Driven World*. New York: Wiley, 2002.

Plous, Scott. *The Psychology of Judgment and Decision Making.* New York: McGraw-Hill, 1993.

Roth, Byron and John Mullen. *Decision Making: Its Logic and Practice.* Lanham, MD: Rowman & Littlefield, 2002.

Russo, Edward and Paul Schoemaker. *Winning Decisions: Getting it Right the First Time.* New York: Crown Business, 2001.

Welch, David. *Decisions, Decisions: The Art of Effective Decision Making.* Amherst, NY: Prometheus Books, 2001.

Yates, Frank. *Decision Management: How to Assure Better Decisions in Your Company.* San Francisco: Jossey-Bass, 2003.

Websites

A Lexicon of Decision Making. See http://faculty.fuqua.duke.edu/daweb/lexicon.htm.

Goldman, Michael. Decision Traps: Common Decision-Making Problems and Easy-to-Use Solutions. See http://www.refresher.com/amcgtraps.html.

Other Resources

Brousseau, Kenneth; Driver, Michael; Hourihan, Gary; and Larsson, Rikard. "The Seasoned Executive's Decision-Making Style." February 1, 2006. Harvard Business Review.

Change – Decision Making

Instructions

Using the table below and on the next page, refer to the items you listed in the Reflect – Decision Making worksheet and identify specific actions you will take to improve your weaknesses or enhance your strengths in each area. Refer to the Develop and Renew section on the previous pages for action ideas, keeping in mind the needs of your current or aspired position.

You can have multiple actions for each item you intend to focus on. In the first section, list the actions that are specific to the items you listed in the Reflect – Decision Making section. On the following page, list any actions you will take that are general to this competency and are related to more than one scored item. Finally, prioritize your actions based on the need for your current or aspired position. These actions will become part of your Personal Development Plan (PDP) for this competency in Appendix C.

Actions to Improve Weakness or Enhance Strength	Priority

Continue on next page.

Change – Decision Making

Actions to Improve Weakness or Enhance Strength	Priority

Other Actions You Will Take Related to Decision Making (not related to the identified strongest or weakest items)	Priority

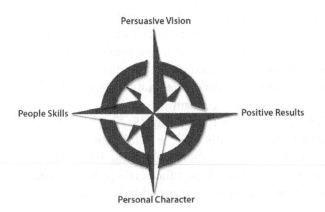

Persuasive Vision

People Skills —— —— Positive Results

Personal Character

CHAPTER 15

Financial Management

(Positive Results)

"Beware of little expenses; a small leak will sink a great ship."
– Benjamin Franklin

Leaders are expected to have financial acumen and know how financial numbers relate to business success. Leaders are also expected to know the big picture of the company's business and be able to correlate their professional objectives to the business objectives of the organization.

Leaders typically have financial responsibilities. Often they are tasked with ensuring that their part of the organization makes a profit or operates within an established budget. Too often people become managers and leaders without any formal training in budgeting and financial management. They are expected to learn these skills on the job as they are promoted. Following this track puts many leaders at risk when they lack understanding of key financial principles.

Finance is an information system. Drawing on the accounting function and its meticulous recording of transactions, finance produces numbers that leaders and managers can use to plan and control operations. These take the form of financial statements, budgets, and forecasts. Financial information gives leaders and managers the numbers they need to make better decisions if they interpret and use these numbers correctly.

For example, financial numbers will tell you which products are profitable and which are not. They will also give you information on which projects are on target to succeed and which may need to be reevaluated. Financial numbers are a metric to measure progress toward a planned goal. They should be looked upon as a tool, not a curse for leaders. They not only point out our shortcomings, but also validate success in operations and in the marketplace.

Astute leaders will, at some point during their career, take a course in finance for non-financial managers. A course such as this provides the fundamental understanding of the financial information needed to be a manager or leader. This type of program also helps you learn to think financially. Leaders need to think financially so they can translate performance into financial terms and assess the financial impacts of their decisions.

Leaders also set the example for financial stewardship. Leaders must be wise in how they spend the organization's money and have low tolerance for waste and financial abuse in their organization. Leaders must ensure that their team understands how and when money is to be spent. If a leader sees waste, fraud, or abuse in how money is handled in the organization, it is their responsibility to report it. But without an understanding of how financial management works, the leader may not recognize mistakes or malfeasance in accounting.

Many leaders must also be responsible for gaining a return on investment (ROI) for their area of responsibility. In this case, it is important that the leader not only build a viable budget, but also spend it wisely with a clear return. Leaders can use financial data to determine how well they are performing. The data will signal, earlier rather than later, when there is a problem with either the upfront planning or the operations. This gives leaders the opportunity to make decisions, adjust and re-plan if needed.

Red Flag Behaviors

- You have no idea what a financial statement is and do not care to learn.
- If you are required to make a budget for your team's efforts, you always add a lot more than you think your team will need.
- When traveling, you often look for ways you can capture some of the expenses for your personal gain.
- You overlook wasteful spending by your peers or team members.
- If you have the opportunity to goof off for a few hours, you take it and enjoy the time.

Case in Point

In his six years at Colson Products, Jeremy was a good employee and rose quickly through the ranks. The company was doing well, but not exceptionally well. Jeremy was asked to be the Chief Executive Officer after learning as much about the business as possible. During his learning period, Jeremy saw a lot of wasteful spending and always wondered how it affected the bottom line for the company. When he became CEO, the wasteful spending over the years became even more apparent. The company was not in good financial shape, and much of it was due to spending practices.

He knew it would not be easy, but he felt obligated to change the way business was being conducted at Colson. First, he reviewed all the contracts with vendors and realized that business was being given to vendors based on relationships and favors, not price. He stopped this practice immediately. When each contract came up, he required a competitive bid to gain the business.

Next, he reviewed all the travel policies. Employees would only be reimbursed for legitimate expenses. In addition, he limited travel to only necessary trips and implemented a meeting software system to enable meetings to be conducted online when possible.

Finally, he realized he needed to change the mindset of all the employees regarding the company's financial situation. He held an all-hands meeting and reviewed the financials in terms everyone could understand so they would realize the situation was precarious. He explained his new rules concerning vendors and travel. He also started a program for team members to suggest money-saving ideas. Implemented ideas earned a cash award for the suggester. In a matter of a few days, he had some additional recommendations and, more importantly, saw a positive change in attitude across the organization.

Notes for the Aspiring Leader

If you want to become more comfortable with financial reports and such, think of them as scorecards. Financial numbers are the language of business and they give you an indication of the performance of the organization and its components. As soon as possible in your career, take a finance for non-financial managers course. This will give you a foundation for understanding the financial information leaders must know.

Assess Your Current Location – Financial Management

(Positive Results)

Instructions: Read each of the skills and behaviors below. As objectively as possible, score yourself for each according to the following scale: 1 = strongly disagree; 2 = disagree; 3 = agree; 4 = strongly agree. If a behavior is not appropriate for your current or aspired position, check the N/A column.

SKILL OR BEHAVIOR	1	2	3	4	N/A
I demonstrate appropriate knowledge of financial management for my position.					
I effectively allocate resources within the organization to reflect my organization's priorities.					
I effectively manage the budget process.					
I strive to continually learn more about financial management.					
I seek methods to improve financial impact.					
I am a wise steward of my organization's financial resources.					
I take responsibility for financial management of my business unit.					
I understand the big picture of my organization's financial strategy.					
I follow my organization's financial processes and procedures.					
I mentor team members to understand financial matters and the impact of their job on the financial welfare of organization.					

Continue on next page.

Assess Your Current Location – Financial Management

(Positive Results)

SKILL OR BEHAVIOR	1	2	3	4	N/A
I am knowledgeable of my organization's procurement and purchasing procedures and processes.					
SCORES FOR FINANCIAL MANAGEMENT (Total check marks in each column and multiply by the heading for the column. Record your scores here.)					

TOTAL SCORE FOR FINANCIAL MANAGEMENT: _____

(Add scores from Columns 1, 2, 3, and 4. Record the total above and on the Master Score Sheet in Appendix A. Also, count the number of N/As and record on the Master Score Sheet.)

Reflect – Financial Management

Scoring Analysis

List Your Four Highest Scored Items (Strengths)

Note: If you have multiple items with the same high score, choose the four items that are most related to your current or aspired position.

Item	Score

List Your Four Lowest Scored Items (Weaknesses)

Note: If you have multiple items with the same low score, choose the four items that are most related to your current or aspired position.

Item	Score

Reflect – Financial Management Questions

Think about the following questions about financial management:

- Why is it every leader's responsibility to understand financial terminology and processes?

- If you are responsible for a budget or the financial performance of your team or department, how can you impress upon your team members or direct reports the importance of financial management?

- What does it mean to say that leaders must be good financial stewards of a company or organization?

- Is proper financial management more important at a for-profit company than at a non-profit organization?

- If you suspect financial mismanagement by your leadership, what steps should you take?

Develop – Financial Management

Develop and Renew

Consider the following development tactics to help improve your skills and behaviors in financial management. Identify which tactics would be valuable to include in your Personal Development Plan (PDP) if you choose to improve in this competency.

- Identify three ways you and your team or department can improve the financial impact of the organization. After identifying and assessing these methods, implement them immediately.

- Are you aware of all your organization's financial systems that impact you or your team? Set an appointment with an expert in your organization to learn more about how these financial systems can help you and your team. Be sure that you understand how each works, its purposes, and how you can use it to the advantage of your team and the organization.

- Identify which areas of financial management are your strengths and which are your weaknesses. Discuss with your manager to learn what additional aspects of financial management you should focus on learning more about.

- Identify three behaviors you will change that will improve your cost/benefit thinking, especially when prioritizing tasks for yourself and others. After identifying these behaviors, develop a plan to implement and begin immediately.

- Identify three members of your team who you think would benefit from mentoring in financial management. Outline a program for them and discuss as a group. Make the mentoring process part of each week's schedule.

- List the financial reporting that is required for your position. How can you accomplish the reporting so that this area is perceived as a strength and not a weakness?

- Does your staff understand the budgeting process? Consider mentoring others through the budget process to help prepare them for the future and gain their support of your budget efforts.

- Be sure that you are in alignment with your manager on what your responsibilities are for the financial management of your business unit. Miscommunication or misunderstanding in this area can lead to great difficulties.

Resources

Books

Arnold, Glen. *Corporate Financial Management*. Pearson, 2012.

Berman, Karen. and Joe. Knight. *Financial Intelligence: A Manager's Guide to Knowing What the Numbers Really Mean*. Cambridge: Harvard Business School Press. 2006.

Block, Stanley; et al. *Foundations of Financial Management*. New York: McGraw-Hill, 2010.

Brigham, Eugene F. and Joel Houston. *Fundamentals of Financial Management*. Cincinnati: South Western College, 2012.

Brooks, Raymond. *Financial Management: Core Concepts*. Prentice Hall, 2011.

Harvard Business School Press. *Harvard Business Essentials: Guide to Finance for Managers*. Cambridge: Harvard Business School Press, 2003.

Kemp, Sid and Eric Dunbar. *Budgeting for Managers*. New York: McGraw-Hill, 2003.

Rao, Ramesh and William Kretlow. *Contemporary Financial Management*. Cincinnati: South-Western, 2011.

Shoffner, H. George et al. *The McGraw-Hill 36-Hour Course: Finance for Non-Financial Managers,* 2010.

Sicilliano, Gene. *Finance for Non-Financial Managers*. New York: McGraw-Hill, 2003.

Siegel, Joel. *Schwann's Outline of Financial Management*. New York: McGraw-Hill, 2009.

Tracy, John. *How to Read a Financial Report: Wringing Vital Signs Out of the Numbers*. New York: Wiley, 2009.

Websites

An excellent article can be found at http://managementhelp.org/businessfinance/index.htm.

Small Business Notes has a comprehensive article on the principles of financial management at http://www.smallbusinessnotes.com/business-finances/financial-management/.

Other Resources

Consider taking a course in Finance for Non-Financial Managers. See the American Management Association courses at http://www.amanet.org. You may also check at your local community college or university.

Change – Financial Management

Instructions

Using the table below and on the next page, refer to the items you listed in the Reflect – Financial Management worksheet and identify specific actions you will take to improve your weaknesses or enhance your strengths in each area. Refer to the Develop and Renew section on the previous pages for action ideas, keeping in mind the needs of your current or aspired position.

You can have multiple actions for each item you intend to focus on. In the first section, list the actions that are specific to the items you listed in the Reflect – Financial Management section. On the following page, list any actions you will take that are general to this competency and are related to more than one scored item. Finally, prioritize your actions based on the need for your current or aspired position. These actions will become part of your Personal Development Plan (PDP) for this competency in Appendix C.

Actions to Improve Weakness or Enhance Strength	Priority

Continue on next page.

Change – Financial Management

Actions to Improve Weakness or Enhance Strength	Priority

Other Actions You Will Take Related to Financial Management (not related to the identified strongest or weakest items)	Priority

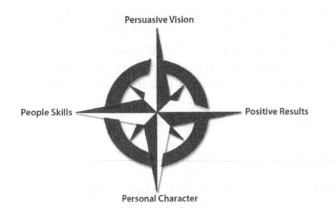

Persuasive Vision

People Skills

Positive Results

Personal Character

CHAPTER 16
Focus on Results

(Positive Results)

"Thoughts lead to feelings. Feelings lead to actions. Actions lead to results."

– T. Harv Eker

Organizations measure leaders on results. Effective leaders get results. It is very easy for leaders to become distracted by the many demands that are placed on them each day. It is easy to take care of things that are routine and simple, while the more difficult achievement-oriented tasks progress slowly. Companies are not interested in how efficiently your office stores supplies; instead, they expect accomplishments. Organizations expect leaders to produce results, and in order to produce results, leaders must focus on the path to achieving them.

When a leader is all about their power and authority or the face time needed for their next promotion, performance suffers. This is not only because they are not performing on task, but also because their lack of focus on what is most important – results – demoralizes the team.

The leader moves the rudder; the people will follow. If the leader models disorganization and a scattered approach, her people will deliver in the same manner. Conversely, a leader focused on results will rally her team to achieve at levels not thought possible.

Robert Pozen (2012) lists specific and practical suggestions on how to increase your productivity at work. He states that in order to be productive, you need to focus on the results you want to achieve, not the time you spend at work.

Pozen sets forth three big ideas to help focus on results:

- Articulate your goals and rank them in order of priority. This helps you align your time allocations with your priorities.
- Focus on the final results. In tracking high-priority projects, quickly formulate tentative conclusions to guide your work.
- Don't sweat the small stuff. Deal with low-priority items in a way that allows you to spend as little time on them as possible.

David Ulrich (1999) posits an interesting definition of effective leadership as it relates to competencies and results. He states that it is not enough to have mastered the leadership competencies; effective leaders must connect the competencies to results. For example, airline pilots should know their company's vision, communicate well, have integrity, and manage change. But, if you are a passenger on the plane your biggest concern is that the pilot gets results – safely landing the plane.

Ulrich provides a formula for effective leadership:

Effective Leadership = Attributes (competencies) X Results

If there is too much focus on results, it drives leaders to do whatever it takes to make short-term performance objectives. Leaders in these firms care more about what is accomplished than about how it is accomplished. They risk the lack of sustainable results. In other firms, the emphasis is almost exclusively on leadership competency development, not paying enough attention to results. Effective leadership requires both emphasis on leadership competencies and results. Balance is the key to success.

Many leaders get confused on the specifics of what their organization expects of them. Be crystal clear regarding the expectations others have for you. Ask clarifying questions to be sure that you are on target. If the picture is clear, develop a plan to achieve your results and stick to it. There will always be competing priorities. Your anchor should always be the plan you have in place to achieve your goals. You should also be able to measure your progress toward results. When setting up your plan, determine when and how you will measure progress. Your focus on your effectiveness will help you measure benchmarks as you accomplish your goals.

Leaders who are responsible to customers should be obsessive about achieving what their customers expect. Set the standard so you will always achieve the outcome customers expect. Strive to always exceed your own standards.

Results in both the professional world and your personal life are intertwined. Leaders must focus on getting results in both environments. This can put a heavy strain on a person and sometimes the leader must be selective in how they deal with everything.

Brian Tracy (2004) says that there are only four things you can do to improve the quality of your life and work:

- You can do *more* of certain things. You can do more of the things that are of greater value to you and bring you greater rewards and satisfaction.
- You can do *less* of certain things. You can deliberately decide to reduce or discontinue activities or behaviors that are not as helpful as others or that can actually be hurtful to you in accomplishing the things you want.
- You can *start* to do things you are not doing at all today. You can make new choices, learn new skills, begin new projects, or change the entire focus of your work or personal life.
- You can *stop* doing certain things altogether. You can stand back and evaluate your life with new eyes. You can then decide to discontinue activities and behaviors that are no longer consistent with what you want and where you want to go.

Focus on results is directly related to time management. Without good time-management skills it is very difficult to achieve results. Consider your time-management skills and behaviors and refer to Chapter 18 to assess how you can gain more time to achieve results. Distractions, scheduling issues, and a larger-than-life to-do list can contribute to a sense of not being able to get enough done to get the results that are needed.

Red Flag Behaviors

- You are always behind in what you must do.
- You have difficulty prioritizing your tasks.
- You do easy, minor-impact tasks to avoid doing the hard things, even though they are more important.
- You do not have goals.
- You have difficulty working with people in other groups or teams in your organization.
- You have no idea what your leadership expects of you.

Case in Point

In a letter Abraham Lincoln offered some advice to Mr. John M.Brockman, who was considering a career in law. He said, "The mode is very simple, though laborious, and tedious. Work, work, work is the main thing." Lincoln was steadfast in his quest for results. No one worked as hard as he. He endured a busy schedule all day with constant meetings and correspondence to consider. As the war continued, he often spent all day and night at the telegraph office near the White House. He would sit for hours waiting to hear the results from the battlefield. On hearing news, he would give advice to his commanders in the field and remain at the office until it was implemented. He ate and slept little. He was constantly building alliances and relationships to achieve his ends, paying particular attention to those who believed differently from him. He sometimes complained of the toil, but he never shied from the effort. This steadfastness and focus led to the results he desired, the end of slavery and the reunification of the union.

Notes for the Aspiring Leader

Get focused on achieving your goals and objectives. List them. Review them daily and take the steps to achieve them. Do not get diverted into spending time on low-priority tasks or make-work activities. Everything you do should be directed toward the success of your organization and yourself.

Assess Your Current Location – Focus on Results

(Positive Results)

Instructions: Read each of the skills and behaviors below. As objectively as possible, score yourself for each according to the following scale: 1 = strongly disagree; 2 = disagree; 3 = agree; 4 = strongly agree. If a behavior is not appropriate for your current or aspired position, check the N/A column.

SKILL OR BEHAVIOR	1	2	3	4	N/A
I demonstrate actions consistent with those of a stakeholder in the organization.					
I understand what is expected of me.					
I clarify expectations when needed.					
I set high standards for myself and others.					
I set challenging but achievable goals for myself and others.					
I deliver results consistently.					
I work across organizational boundaries when appropriate to achieve results.					
I maintain my commitment to goals regardless of the obstacles or frustrations.					
I have a strong sense of urgency about solving problems and getting work done.					
I emphasize results in myself and others.					
I am bottom-line oriented.					
I empower others to achieve results.					
I proactively work to achieve and exceed goals.					

Continue on next page.

Assess Your Current Location – Focus on Results

(Positive Results)

SKILL OR BEHAVIOR	1	2	3	4	N/A
I plan the appropriate steps that will achieve the desired results.					
I monitor progress toward results.					
I delegate tasks to others to achieve results.					
I handle competing priorities well.					
I focus well on the task at hand.					
I manage distractions tactfully and appropriately.					
I guide others back to the appropriate area of focus when needed.					
SCORES FOR FOCUS ON RESULTS (Total check marks in each column and multiply by the heading for the column. Record your scores here.)					

TOTAL SCORE FOR FOCUS ON RESULTS: _____

(Add scores from Columns 1, 2, 3, and 4. Record the total above and on the Master Score Sheet in Appendix A. Also, count the number of N/As and record on the Master Score Sheet.)

Reflect – Focus on Results

Scoring Analysis

List Your Four Highest Scored Items (Strengths)

Note: If you have multiple items with the same high score, choose the four items that are most related to your current or aspired position.

Item	Score

List Your Four Lowest Scored Items (Weaknesses)

Note: If you have multiple items with the same low score, choose the four items that are most related to your current or aspired position.

Item	Score

Reflect – Focus on Results Questions

Think about the following questions about focus on results:

- In order to focus on results, how do you know what the result should be?

- What are some obstacles to staying focused on what you are tasked to do or in taking the steps toward achieving goals?

- Think of someone who is not focused on results. What behaviors do they exhibit to give you this perception?

- Think about the senior leaders in your organization. Why do you think they stay focused on results?

- As a leader, what do you do if you see one of your teammates or direct reports being unfocused? What if they respond by saying, "I don't know what you want; I don't know what your goal is?"

Develop – Focus on Results

Develop and Renew

Consider the following development tactics to help improve your focus on results. Identify which tactics would be valuable to include in your Personal Development Plan (PDP) if you choose to improve in this competency.

- Develop a goal notebook. On each page of the notebook list a personal or professional goal you want to attain. Below each goal, list the reasons for achieving it, steps to achieve, resources needed, and a realistic schedule to achieve the goal. Review weekly and chart your progress. Evaluate whether your goals may be too lofty and require interim goals to achieve to avoid unnecessary frustration.

- Make a list of personal, professional, team, and organizational improvements that need to be made and what role you can play in effecting changes. Share your list of team and organizational improvements with your peers and direct reports. Work together to develop a plan to implement the improvements.

- As a leader, it is important that you model a high level of productivity. Your direct reports, especially, will often assume your behaviors. Consider your responsibilities as a leader to demonstrate high productivity.

- As a leader, how do you instill a sense of initiative in others, particularly your direct reports? Everyone is different and has varying motivators that affect them to seek opportunities and take initiative. Take the time to learn what motivates others to seek opportunities and take initiative, and then work toward leading them to improve.

- What standards have you set for yourself? List them. Which do you have no trouble meeting? Which do you never meet? What are the standards you've set for your team or your direct reports as individuals? List them. Discuss with your team any standards and expectations you have for them.

- Your focus as a leader should be to help your peers and direct reports develop a strong work ethic. List your peers and direct reports. Rank them on how well they work with determination and persistence. Pick two people from this list who need help in this area. Talk with them and learn why they may have a problem in this area. What obstacles do they face that prevent them from working with determination and persistence? What steps can you take that would help them overcome their obstacles?

- Identify some major goals or achievements that you or your team have met over the past year. How have you celebrated the successes?

- Consider how often you delegate tasks and empower others to achieve. You work as part of various teams. The best results occur when delegation and empowerment are integral to a work team.

Resources

Books

Bossidy, Larry and Ram Charan. *Execution: The Discipline of Getting Things Done*. New York: Crown Publishing, 2002.

Costello, Ann. *Getting Results: The Six Disciplines of Performance Management*. CCH, 2008.

Covey, Stephen. *First Things First*. New York: Fireside, 1998.

_____. *The 7 Habits of Highly Effective People*. New York: Free Press, 2004.

Drucker, Peter. *Managing for Results*. New York: Harper Collins, 1993.

Gerson, Richard F. and Robbie Gerson. *Positive Performance Improvement: A New Paradigm for Optimizing Your Workforce*. Palo Alto: Davies-Black Publishing, 2006.

Longenecker, Clinton. *Getting Results: Five Absolutes for High Performance*. New York: Wiley, 2002.

Pozen, Robert. *Extreme Productivity: Boost Your Results, Reduce Your Hours*. New York: Harper, 2012.

Tracy, Brian. *Focal Point: A Proven System to Simplify Your Life, Double Your Productivity, and Achieve All Your Goals*. New York: AMACOM, 2004.

Ulrich, David; et al. *Results-Based Leadership*. Cambridge, MA: Harvard Business School Press, 1999.

Websites

An excellent blog article by Jaclyn Wells can be found at http://www.business-opportunities.biz/2009/03/28/focus-on-results/.

Change – Focus on Results

Instructions

Using the table below and on the next page, refer to the items you listed in the Reflect – Focus on Results worksheet and identify specific actions you will take to improve your weaknesses or enhance your strengths in each area. Refer to the Develop and Renew section on the previous pages for action ideas, keeping in mind the needs of your current or aspired position.

You can have multiple actions for each item you intend to focus on. In the first section, list the actions that are specific to the items you listed in the Reflect – Focus on Results section. On the following page, list any actions you will take that are general to this competency and are related to more than one scored item. Finally, prioritize your actions based on the need for your current or aspired position. These actions will become part of your Personal Development Plan (PDP) for this competency in Appendix C.

Actions to Improve Weakness or Enhance Strength	Priority

Continue on next page.

Change – Focus on Results

Actions to Improve Weakness or Enhance Strength	Priority

Other Actions You Will Take Related to Focus on Results (not related to the identified strongest or weakest items)	Priority

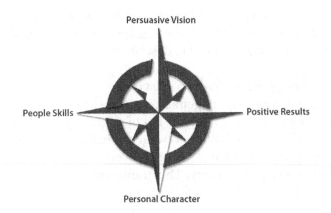

Persuasive Vision

People Skills

Positive Results

Personal Character

CHAPTER 17

Technical Skills

(Positive Results)

"It is possible to fly without motors, but not without knowledge and skill."

– Wilbur Wright

Being an effective leader requires a new set of skills, and many people work hard to learn those skills when they become a leader. Learning these new responsibilities is important in developing new leadership talent. However, prior to becoming a leader, the most important part of an employee's job was their chosen field (which we are referring to as technical skills). Expertise in the technical skills in their chosen field was very important to their success.

Even though leaders must focus on building their skills in the leadership competencies, they must not forget to maintain their skills and knowledge in their chosen field. In today's world, the knowledge base in every field is moving at lightning speed. If a leader does not keep pace, he will lose much of his value to the organization, particularly in his ability to solve problems and mentor direct reports.

Team members are often first to notice whether a leader is staying current in their field or not. If they perceive the leader is current and an active member of their technical community, they will more readily respect the person's decisions. On the other hand, if the expert becomes a leader and only focuses on the business end of things, team members will lose respect and not support the leader's decisions as often. The leader's credibility will suffer.

Successful leaders stay knowledgeable in their field through reading, attending conferences and courses, and spending time with their direct reports who are often more knowledgeable in their field. In addition, leaders contribute to their field through participation in and speaking at conferences. Many write papers that apply the latest advances in their field to practical situations in their company or organization.

Leaders set the example in this area by not only participating themselves in activities that will maintain or expand their technical skills, but also in encouraging and rewarding their peers and direct reports to do the same. Leaders are responsible for the professional development of their direct reports, including encouraging them to continually improve in their technical skills.

The transition from being a technical employee to a manager and leader is often very difficult. Micahel Aucoin (2002) describes this transition for an engineer as follows. The hurdles would be very similar for anyone transitioning to leadership from other fields. He describes:

> We cannot separate engineering from management. The two exist on a continuum, and the transition from engineering to management is a transition from one part of the continuum to another. When we wear the hat of engineer, we practice the management of things. When we transition to wear the hat of manager or leader, we begin to manage people and the elements of work that help or hinder people in their motivation and productivity. This transition requires a major shift in skills.

Managers in technical organizations are generally responsible for three interactive areas of management competency: technical, administrative, and interpersonal. Technical competency is straightforward for the engineer, but there are still challenges here. The new manager must develop a broader view of the scope of technical work and must allow subordinates to take more control of the technical work and decisions.

The administrative elements of management are more challenging. These components include organizing and planning work, and they involve the integration of diverse needs and constraints in the organization. Administrative skills are also relatively straightforward for the engineer to master, but they set a trap. Managers may come to view work as a succession of tasks to be done. They may view supervision of others solely as planning and policing of tasks.

The dimension of management involving interpersonal skills is often the riskiest for the engineer. In essence, the most critical facet of the transition is the shift from the management of things to the management of people. Most engineers are unprepared for the management of people and the new and unique challenges it brings. The engineer must become more social and socially aware (de-geeking).

Many leaders have undertaken this transition, and the new leader should not be wary of moving into a leadership role. If they maintain technical currency and actively learn leadership skills and behaviors, they will join the ranks of leaders who have been successful.

Red Flag Behaviors

- You do not take the time to stay current in your field.
- You no longer go to professional conferences or training sessions.
- Now that you are a leader, you feel you are above technical issues.
- No one seeks you out for advice on a technical matter.

Case in Point

Beth was an excellent software designer, and she was often called upon to present her ideas at technical conferences and meetings. Few people were respected more for their technical skills than Beth. For that reason Jaynell asked Beth to join her startup company as Chief Operating Officer.

Beth was honored by Jaynell's request and did not hesitate to accept her offer. She had one condition, however. Beth knew that for the startup to be successful, she needed to remain at the top of her field. She told Jaynell that she would do her best as COO, but she could not get bogged down in administrative functions or continually developing strategies. She needed to maintain her understanding of what was happening in her field. Jaynell readily agreed to Beth's request, knowing that without Beth continuing to be the best in her field it would effect her contributions as COO and the value to the new company.

Over the next year, Beth attended and presented at many conferences in her field. She listened to the other presenters and considered their ideas. She often heard ideas that would benefit her company and always reported her recommendations to Jaynell. Late in the year, Jaynell suggested that they collaborate on a book that would be the standard in the management of software design. Both were excited about the prospects.

As COO, Beth took an active role in learning from her younger team members at the startup. She realized that it had been a long time since she was in graduate school, and it was important to her to be as adept at design as her best designers on the team. This was recognized by her team members, and they respected her for the efforts to keep current in her field. In return, she was able to assess their ideas with both a technical and business perspective.

Notes for the Aspiring Leader

A career is a life-long learning process. One does not discard all they have learned in a technical field when they become a leader. Rather, they continue to add to their toolbox by maintaining currency in their field and using their new skills in leading others.

Assess Your Current Location – Technical Skills

(Positive Results)

Instructions: Read each of the skills and behaviors below. As objectively as possible, score yourself for each according to the following scale: 1 = strongly disagree; 2 = disagree; 3 = agree; 4 = strongly agree. If a behavior is not appropriate for your current or aspired position, check the N/A column.

SKILL OR BEHAVIOR	1	2	3	4	N/A
I effectively use my technical knowledge to solve problems.					
I continually seek ways to improve my technical knowledge.					
I am a resource to other team members who deal with complex technical issues.					
I am informed on the latest advances in my field.					
I contribute to the body of knowledge in my field by writing papers, speaking at conferences, and contributing to online blogs and forums.					
I take technical training courses if needed to maintain my level of expertise.					
I seek out challenging assignments that will expand my understanding of technical skills and knowledge.					
I know and seek out others who are expert in my field.					
I am sought out to provide expertise in my field to solve problems.					
I seek feedback from others on my technical skills performance.					

Continue on next page.

Assess Your Current Location – Technical Skills

(Positive Results)

	1	2	3	4	N/A
SCORES FOR TECHNICAL SKILLS (Total check marks in each column and multiply by the heading for the column. Record your scores here.)					

TOTAL SCORE FOR TECHNICAL SKILLS: _____

(Add scores from Columns 1, 2, 3, and 4. Record the total above and on the Master Score Sheet in Appendix A. Also, count the number of N/As and record on the Master Score Sheet.)

Reflect – Technical Skills

Scoring Analysis

List Your Four Highest Scored Items (Strengths)

Note: If you have multiple items with the same high score, choose the four items that are most related to your current or aspired position.

Item	Score

List Your Four Lowest Scored Items (Weaknesses)

Note: If you have multiple items with the same low score, choose the four items that are most related to your current or aspired position.

Item	Score

Reflect – Technical Skills Questions

Think about the following questions about technical skills:

- Who are the leaders in your field? If they are in leadership positions, how have they maintained currency in their field?

- What conferences are appropriate for those in your field? Have you attended a conference lately to learn the latest developments in your field?

- Have you met managers or leaders who have not maintained their currency in their field? What effect did this have on their credibility?

- Are there related fields that you should learn about to be a resource to your team or direct reports?

Develop – Technical Skills

Develop and Renew

Consider the following development tactics to help improve your technical skills. Identify which tactics would be valuable to include in your Personal Development Plan (PDP) if you choose to improve in this competency.

- When people become leaders, they must learn and implement a new set of skills. However, they are usually required to maintain and use their technical skills also, regardless of their field.

- Continually seek ways to improve your technical knowledge and skills. As a leader, you may often be called upon to be a resource to other team members who deal with complex technical issues. Many fields, especially high technology, advance very quickly, so it is imperative that effective leaders stay abreast of advances in their field.

- Take steps to proactively contribute to the body of knowledge in your field by writing articles, blogs, or conference papers. This not only contributes to the field, but also establishes your credibility as a leader in the field and helps advance your organization.

- Network and build alliances with others in your field. Knowing others gives you additional resources to tap into when needed to solve problems.

- Set the example to your team that you can not only be an effective leader, but also a leader in your field.

Resources

Books

Aucoin, B. Michael. *From Engineer to Manager: Mastering the Transition*. Norwood, MA: Artech, 2002.

Badawy, Michael. *Developing Managerial Skills in Engineers and Scientists: Succeeding as a Technical Manager*. New York: Van Nostrand Reinhold, 1995.

Bennis, Warren and Robert Thomas. *Geeks and Geezers*. Boston: Harvard Business School Press, 2002.

Glen, Paul. *Leading Geeks: How to Manage and Lead the People Who Deliver Technology*. San Francisco: Jossey-Bass, 2002.

Nazarian, Ara. *Technical Minds: Leading and Getting the Best Work from your Technically-Minded Team.* Charleston, SC: CreateSpace, 2010.

Tobin, Daniel. *Transformational Learning: Renewing Your Company Through Knowledge and Skills.* New York: Wiley, 1996.

Websites

See Steve Pavlina's excellent blog at http://www.stevepavlina.com/blog/2006/08/10-ways-to-improve-your-technical-skills/.

Change – Technical Skills

Instructions

Using the table below and on the next page, refer to the items you listed in the Reflect – Technical Skills worksheet and identify specific actions you will take to improve your weaknesses or enhance your strengths in each area. Refer to the Develop and Renew section on the previous pages for action ideas, keeping in mind the needs of your current or aspired position.

You can have multiple actions for each item you intend to focus on. In the first section, list the actions that are specific to the items you listed in the Reflect – Technical Skills section. On the following page, list any actions you will take that are general to this competency and are related to more than one scored item. Finally, prioritize your actions based on the need for your current or aspired position. These actions will become part of your Personal Development Plan (PDP) for this competency in Appendix C.

Actions to Improve Weakness or Enhance Strength	Priority

Continue on next page.

Change – Technical Skills

Actions to Improve Weakness or Enhance Strength	Priority

Other Actions You Will Take Related to Technical Skills (not related to the identified strongest or weakest items)	Priority

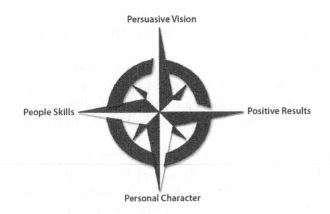

Persuasive Vision

People Skills — Positive Results

Personal Character

CHAPTER 18

Time Management

(Positive Results)

"Lost time is never found again."

– Benjamin Franklin

Time is limited. Once wasted, you can never regain it. Leaders have many demands on their time. Time keeps ticking and they have no control over it. No matter how much power they have, they cannot stop time, they cannot slow it down, nor can they speed it up. Thus, the leader must effectively manage time in order to be most productive in their job.

On the flipside, you can become a time-management fanatic by building time management spreadsheets, creating priority lists and folders, color coding tasks, and separating paperwork into priority piles. This hamster wheel of time fanaticism causes you to waste more time as you seek to micromanage it. Micromanagement is never successful – especially when it comes to time. In addition, time-management techniques can become so complex that you soon give up and return to the comfort of your old time-wasting methods.

Effective time management allows you to make decisions, take ownership of your tasks, and influence the course of your day. It's about creating days that are meaningful and rewarding to you, and feeling a sense of satisfaction in each and every one of your tasks. It's about identifying what is important to you and giving these activities a place on your schedule. It's about helping you feel deeply satisfied at the end of each day.

In his popular new book, *The 4-Hour Workweek*, Tim Ferriss tells us to forget all about time management. He proposes that you should not try to fill every second with some type of busy-work. Rather, you should look at how to become more efficient and eliminate things that keep you from being effective. He gives examples of how many workers - leaders included - spend their days just looking busy and not doing anything toward achieving their goals.

Efficiency is performing a given task (whether important or not) in the most economical manner possible. Being efficient without regard to effectiveness is irresponsible. A perfect example given by Ferriss is the person who checks e-mail 30 times per day and develops an elaborate system of folder rules and sophisticated techniques for ensuring that each of the 30 pieces of mail moves to a folder as quickly as possible. It is efficient (on some perverse level) but not effective.

Meetings are often our biggest time waster. Not only are there typically too many meetings in a person's schedule, but often the meetings consume too much time on non-important issues. The effective time manager only attends meetings that are critical to their job and ensures that the meeting focuses on its agenda. Often an organization's culture must be changed to effectively get meetings under control.

What is most important is to be efficient in those things that lead to your effectiveness. Typically, this involves eliminating or delegating much of what you do so you can focus on achieving your goals. It also means being organized, not only in your time but in your workspace as well. If you spend 10 minutes finding something you need six times each day, you have wasted one hour. Over a week this is five hours that could have been spent being productive. As we become more technological, we think we become more organized. However, the computer desktop and tree of files has replaced the desk full of unorganized paper. In fact, we tend to save more documents now that we can do so electronically. More documents equals more time trying to find the one you need.

Many leaders have difficulty saying no and this is the cause of many time management issues. You should always be aware of your current workload and not take on more than you and your team can handle. Certainly, if a task is your responsibility, you must take it on. But we often take on tasks that should and could be done by others.

Leaders should also take care to make the best use of others' time. Only schedule meetings if necessary, and always consider who should be there. If a person is not essential to the meeting, do not invite them. Be careful to not interrupt others who are busy unless it is important.

In our leadership assessments, we have found that time management is one of the leading difficulties leaders are faced with in their career. The intriguing aspect is that when asked if time management is a problem, almost every leader confesses that it is a struggle for them. Yet few leaders take the initiative to be more effective in their use of time.

Red Flag Behaviors

- You seem to never have enough time to get things done.
- You take work home most days. You also work a lot of weekends.
- When talking with others, you are thinking about what else you must do.
- You always say yes when asked to do something, even though you have a full plate of important tasks.
- You have no outside activities such as a hobby or physical activities.
- You frequently miss deadlines.
- You are often late for meetings.

Case in Point

After being promoted to his leadership position, Ken realized he had a time management problem. He was constantly getting hit with demands and never seemed to get to focus on what he felt was most important. He took work home every evening and spent time every weekend catching up on reading memos and responding to e-mails.

Ken reached out to his colleague, Sandy, who seemed to always have it together. Sandy always had things done on time and she rarely needed to take work home. Sandy helped Ken by training him how to manage an active to do-list. She then mentored him on prioritizing his tasks. She encouraged Ken to structure his day better by only checking e-mail three times a day. Each day she reviewed Ken's task list and schedule.

Sandy knew that part of Ken's problem was meetings. It seemed he was in back-to-back meetings every day and this was not productive. When reviewing his schedule she challenged him to justify his attendance at each meeting. With Sandy's help in this area, he was able to eliminate about 50% of his meetings, giving him more time to focus on his priority tasks.

She also encouraged Ken to not take work home and to exercise daily. She knew Ken had small children, and she encouraged him to spend time with his family each day. The techniques he learned enabled Ken to not only have time to accomplish his important tasks, but also to have the time to take care of himself and his family.

Notes for the Aspiring Leader

Develop time-management habits early in your career as a leader. Choose a system that works for you to keep track of your tasks and the time allocated to completing each. Be organized and regularly assess whether you are wasting time, then make the correction before you create bad habits.

Assess Your Current Location – Time Management

(Positive Results)

Instructions: Read each of the skills and behaviors below. As objectively as possible, score yourself for each according to the following scale: 1 = strongly disagree; 2 = disagree; 3 = agree; 4 = strongly agree. If a behavior is not appropriate for your current or aspired position, check the N/A column.

SKILL OR BEHAVIOR	1	2	3	4	N/A
I alter my schedule as necessary to address pressing concerns.					
I manage meeting agendas appropriately.					
I make the best use of my time.					
I make the best use of others' time.					
I manage meetings according to the communicated schedule.					
I meet deadlines.					
I prioritize my schedule to insure important responsibilities are fulfilled.					
I respond in a timely manner to requests.					
I use time-management techniques and tools to streamline efficiency and productivity.					
I always arrive to meetings or events on time.					
I do tasks according to their criticality and importance without procrastinating.					
I know how much time I spend on various jobs I do.					
I am organized, and it is easy for me to find what I need.					
I manage interruptions well and keep them at a minimum.					

Continue on next page.

Assess Your Current Location – Time Management
(Positive Results)

SKILL OR BEHAVIOR	1	2	3	4	N/A
I leave contingency time in my schedule to deal with the unexpected.					
I say no when asked to do tasks that are not in my area of responsibility when appropriate.					
I do not get distracted from tasks I am working on.					
I delegate time-consuming tasks when appropriate.					
I use goals, plans and measures to guide my efforts.					
I do not make work.					
I use a manageable to-do list focusing on what needs to be done.					
I engage in physical activity each day.					
I only work outside normal hours when necessary.					
I set aside time for planning and scheduling.					
I reward myself after an achievement.					
I am present in the moment whether at work or not at work.					
I do not take work home unless absolutely necessary.					
I monitor team members to ensure they have balance.					
I enjoy both work and non-work activities.					

Continue on next page.

Assess Your Current Location – Time Management

(Positive Results)

SKILL OR BEHAVIOR	1	2	3	4	N/A
I coach colleagues and direct reports with time management issues on how to improve.					
SCORES FOR TIME MANAGEMENT (Total check marks in each column and multiply by the heading for the column. Record your scores here.)					

TOTAL SCORE FOR TIME MANAGEMENT: _____

(Add scores from Columns 1, 2, 3, and 4. Record the total above and on the Master Score Sheet in Appendix A. Also, count the number of N/As and record on the Master Score Sheet.)

Reflect – Time Management

Scoring Analysis

List Your Four Highest Scored Items (Strengths)

Note: If you have multiple items with the same high score, choose the four items that are most related to your current or aspired position.

Item	Score

List Your Four Lowest Scored Items (Weaknesses)

Note: If you have multiple items with the same low score, choose the four items that are most related to your current or aspired position.

Item	Score

Reflect – Time Management Questions

Think about the following questions about time management:

- What time management techniques have you used? What techniques work for you? What techniques have not worked? Why?

- Observe someone who appears to have good time-management skills. What do they do that you don't?

- How would your spouse or children rate your work-life balance?

- Why is it important to exercise daily and have an outside hobby?

- Do you periodically suffer from burn out?

- Do you observe team members who always look busy but seem to never get things done? How can you help them?

Develop – Time Management

Develop and Renew

Consider the following development tactics to help improve in your time management skills and behaviors. Identify which tactics would be valuable to include in your Personal Development Plan (PDP) if you choose to improve in this competency.

- One method of keeping track of requests from others and when you should respond is to maintain a notebook or task list that records the commitments you've made and the date each is due. If you determine you will not meet a deadline, communicate this to the person and note it, along with a new date that you will respond.

- Consider tracking your time for a few days. Then review how you spent your time. Can you identify how much time you wasted? Can you identify when you spent too much time on low-priority items?

- Are you aware of a peer or team member who has difficulty altering their schedule as necessary when faced with pressing concerns? If so, consider mentoring them to improve their behavior in this area. Focus on how they can make better use of their time and be more productive with less stress.

- You must always schedule some open time to address pressing issues and concerns. Try to leave time each day to take care of new issues that arise, or if you take care of those issues as they occur, you can use this time to do your normal activities.

- Think about recent meetings that you either attended or managed. For those you attended that either did not start on time or went beyond the scheduled end time, why did this occur? How did this poor time management affect you? For meetings that you managed, why have you started beyond the start time or ended beyond the scheduled end time?

- Keep track of the amount of time each day and week you spend doing personal, relaxing activities. If you need to find a better balance so that you are not as stressed, consider how you can gain more time for your personal life. List the activities you would like to spend more time doing. Take steps to change your behaviors to adequately take care of yourself.

- Do you have an agenda for every meeting if it is appropriate? Do you solicit input from other attendees for the agenda? Do you set objectives for your meetings as appropriate? Consider these questions and work with other leaders to improve meeting management in your organization.

- Be very careful that e-mail and the internet do not derail you from your objectives. It is easy to justify taking time to respond to e-mails and surf the internet for information. If you see yourself spending time online which negatively affects your productivity, take steps to get it under control. One suggestion is to allot a small amount of time each day for responding to non-critical e-mails and doing internet research. If you schedule the time each day, it will prevent you from becoming derailed from work that is more critical.

- What behaviors work for you to avoid unneeded or unproductive work? Understanding the behaviors that work for you will prevent you from making poor choices.

- How do you track your deadlines? Consider having a method to remind you of upcoming deadlines. What obstacles may be preventing you from meeting deadlines? How can you overcome these obstacles?

Resources

Books

Allen, Joe and David Donaldson. *Learn Time Management in 7 Days: Don't Take Your Time For Granted, It Goes Faster Than You Think*. Amazon, 2012.

Ballantyne, Craig. *Time Management: How to Get More Done in Less Time*. Amazon, 2012.

Chandler, Steve. *Time Warrior: How to Defeat Procrastination, People-Pleasing, Self-Doubt, Over-Commitment, Broken Promises and Chaos*. Anna Maria, FL: Maurice Bassett, 2011.

Emmett, Rita. *The Procrastinator's Handbook: Mastering the Art of Doing It Now*. New York: Walker and Company, 2000.

Ferriss, Timothy. *The 4-Hour Workweek: Escape 9-5, Live Anywhere, and Join the New Rich*. Harmony, 2009.

Harvard Business School Press. *Managing Time: Expert Solutions to Everyday Challenge* (Pocket Mentor Series). Cambridge: Harvard Business School Press, 2006.

Kelsey, Dee and Pam Plumb. *Great Meetings! Great Results*. Portland, ME: Hanson Park Press, Inc., 2004.

Mackenzie, Alec and Pat Nickerson. *The Time Trap: The Classic Book on Time Management*. New York: AMACOM, 2009.

McDonald, Ben and Sidney McDonald. *Time Management: The SID Way*. Boise, ID: BenchMark Learning, 2011.

Molloy, Andrea. *Stop Living Your Job, Start Living Your Life: 85 Simple Strategies to Achieve Work/Life Balance.* Berkeley, CA: Ulysses Press, 2005.

Morgenstern, Julie. *Time Management from the Inside Out: The Foolproof System for Taking Control of Your Schedule – and You Life.* New York: Holt Paperbacks, 2004.

_____. *Never Check E-Mail in the Morning: And Other Unexpected Strategies for Making Your Work Life Work.* Touchstone, 2005.

Panella, Vince. *The 26 Hour Day: How to Gain at Least Two Hours a Day With Time Control.* Franklin Lakes, NJ: Career Press, 2002.

Roesch, Roberta. Time *Management for Busy People.* New York: McGraw-Hill, 1998.

Silber, Lee. *Time Management for the Creative Person.* New York: Three Rivers Press, 1998.

Tracy, Brian. *Eat That Frog!: 21 Great Ways to Stop Procrastinating and Get More Done in Less Time.* San Francisco: Berrett-Koehler, 2001.

_____. *Time Power: A Proven System for Getting More Done in Less Time Than You Ever Thought Possible.* New York: AMACOM, 2004.

Websites

Wikipedia offers an excellent description of time management principles at: http://en.wikipedia.org/wiki/Time_management.

MindTools.com. http://www.mindtools.com. Tools and resources to help improve time management skills.

Other Resources

We have used and recommend The Pomodoro Technique to help manage your time. See their information at http://www.pomodorotechnique.com/.

Bruch, Heike. and Ghoshal, Sumantra. Beware the Busy Manager. Harvard Business Review. February 1, 2002. http://harvardbusinessonline.hbsp.harvard.edu/b01/en/common/item_detail.jhtml?id=R0202D.

Change – Time Management

Instructions

Using the table below and on the next page, refer to the items you listed in the Reflect – Time Management worksheet and identify specific actions you will take to improve your weaknesses or enhance your strengths in each area. Refer to the Develop and Renew section on the previous pages for action ideas, keeping in mind the needs of your current or aspired position.

You can have multiple actions for each item you intend to focus on. In the first section, list the actions that are specific to the items you listed in the Reflect – Time Management section. On the following page, list any actions you will take that are general to this competency and are related to more than one scored item. Finally, prioritize your actions based on the need for your current or aspired position. These actions will become part of your Personal Development Plan (PDP) for this competency in Appendix C.

Actions to Improve Weakness or Enhance Strength	Priority

Continue on next page.

Change – Time Management

Actions to Improve Weakness or Enhance Strength	Priority

Other Actions You Will Take Related to Time Management (not related to the identified strongest or weakest items)	Priority

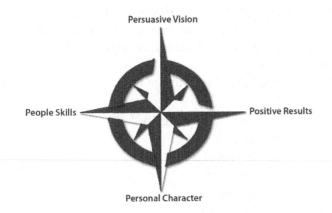

Persuasive Vision

People Skills — Positive Results

Personal Character

CHAPTER 19

Courage

(Personal Character)

"Success is not final, failure is not fatal; it is the courage to continue that counts."

– Winston Churchill

Courage is defined (Wikipedia) as the ability to confront fear, pain, danger, uncertainty, or intimidation. Physical courage is courage in the face of physical pain, hardship, death, or threat of death. Moral courage is the ability to act rightly in the face of popular opposition, shame, scandal, or discouragement.

It is easy to think of those who face physical courage – first responders, soldiers, and others who put their lives on the line. Leaders are most often faced with opportunities to display moral courage – making tough decisions, accepting responsibility for costly mistakes, or needing to restructure an organization to get better results.

Followers expect their leaders to act courageously. They expect them to do the right thing, no matter how difficult the circumstances. Courageous leadership creates loyalty both within the organization and with those externally such as customers, shareholders, and vendors.

A leader with courage will face the obstacles to success. If a team has a problem to be solved or a decision to be made, they need to know that their leader will participate, lead, and show resolve. Some of the most difficult decisions involve people, and a leader with courage will not shirk their responsibility to conduct difficult conversations regarding employee performance. But the leader will be prepared for a difficult conversation and exhibit the right combination of authority and empathy in the situation.

Courageous leaders are determined to achieve success with integrity. Sometimes it takes courage to make decisions with integrity, even though the decision may have a short-term negative effect. The courageous leader will look at the long term, know what is right, and do it, regardless of how people may view them. As General Norman Schwarzkopf has said, "The truth of the matter is that you always know the right thing to do; the hard part is doing it."

A courageous leader does not charge ahead without thinking things through, however. Risks must be assessed and the effects of a change need to be considered. But, when these things are done, the courageous leader takes action and engages others to follow.

Principled conduct under pressure is a simple concept. It has two working parts: (1) establishment of high core values, and (2) courageous behaviors in alignment with those core values. Principled leaders solve moral problems. They have the courage to act rightly. They consistently demonstrate principled conduct under pressure.

Warrell (2008) describes courage in twelve "acts." These are the courage to:

- Take responsibility
- Challenge your stories
- Speak up
- Take action
- Say no
- Live with an open heart

- Live with integrity
- Dream bigger
- Be yourself
- Persevere
- Let go
- Be a leader

Study courageous leaders from history. You will learn that it is not easy to be courageous. Physical courage is very difficult and it is exemplified by the firefighters and police who ran into the World Trade Center towers on 9/11, knowing that there would be a good chance they would not return. But their job required them to use their courage to help others.

Moral courage is more often needed by corporate or educational leaders. We can easily think of leaders who fell because of a lack of moral courage to do the right thing. But there are countless examples of leaders in business and education who dream big, invest their financial security, and take action – dealing with ethical issues daily in their quest.

Red Flag Behaviors

- You are fearful of making decisions.
- You focus on today and avoid thinking of the future because it is uncertain.
- You look to others for guidance in difficult situations.
- You ignore issues that require courage.
- You change your mind a lot when making decisions; you don't display conviction.
- When something goes wrong, you search for someone to blame.
- You avoid difficult conversations or confrontations.
- You are close-minded because you do not have the courage to look at alternative ideas or solutions.

Case in Point

Courage manifests itself in many leaders – our initial thought is of the men and women in uniform who leave their families to undertake an uncertain task in the face of peril. I (Ben) immediately think of the leaders like Senator John McCain who were prisoners of war held in North Vietnam. It took extraordinary courage to suffer for years in solitary confinement and undergo frequent torture at the hands of their captors. Many did not survive, and others were permanently disabled. They also did not know whether their country was doing anything to change their plight, only hearing the news their captors wished them to hear. Even in this environment, leaders emerged who established rules, set up a communications system, and encouraged those who were having difficulty getting through their torture, uncertainty, and loneliness.

But the leader who consistently exhibited great courage is Abraham Lincoln. In an 1864 meeting at the White House, Lincoln had been warned by Albert Hodges, a Kentucky newspaper editor that there was "much dissatisfaction" in his state about the president's enlistment of slaves as soldiers. Hodges admired Lincoln's explanation so much that he asked the president to consecrate it in a formal letter. This letter stated, "I am naturally anti-slavery. If slavery is not wrong, nothing is wrong. And yet, I have never understood that the Presidency conferred upon me an unrestricted right to act officially upon this judgment and feeling. It was in the oath I took that I would, to the best of my ability, preserve, protect, and defend the Constitution of the United States. Right or wrong, I assumed this ground and now I avow it. I could not feel that I had even tried to preserve the constitution, if, to save slavery, or any minor matter, I should permit the wreck of government, country, and Constitution all together."

Lincoln exhibited courage many times during his tenure, but his unwavering opposition to slavery in the midst of a war that was tearing his country apart required strong and consistent courage.

Notes for the Aspiring Leader

Spend some time reading about courageous leaders in history. Even more appropriate, find some living legends that may have fought in battles and talk to them about courage. You will learn that the issues you face as a leader are miniscule compared to those faced by leaders in battle.

Assess Your Current Location – Courage

(Personal Character)

Instructions: Read each of the skills and behaviors below. As objectively as possible, score yourself for each according to the following scale: 1 = strongly disagree; 2 = disagree; 3 = agree; 4 = strongly agree. If a behavior is not appropriate for your current or aspired position, check the N/A column.

SKILL OR BEHAVIOR	1	2	3	4	N/A
I can state the benefits courage brings to a leader.					
I recognize my fear internally but do not show it outwardly to others.					
I am adept at seeing the risks in a difficult situation.					
I evaluate situations and take steps to mitigate risks.					
I participate in difficult conversations or situations when needed.					
I demonstrate confidence to others when facing uncertainty in difficult situations.					
I take command in difficult situations.					
I do not worry about trivial matters.					
I focus my attention on the greatest need.					
When I move forward with a decision, I do so with outward conviction.					
I do not avoid confrontations with others when necessary.					
I push the limits on my courage to grow whether in business or my personal life.					
I do not hesitate to bring appropriate issues to my superiors.					

Continue on next page.

Assess Your Current Location – Courage
(Personal Character)

SKILL OR BEHAVIOR	1	2	3	4	N/A
I know when to say no and do so when needed.					
I accept responsibility for poor performance in my group, team, or organization as appropriate.					
I speak up appropriately when I disagree with a position or strategy.					
SCORES FOR COURAGE (Total check marks in each column and multiply by the heading for the column. Record your scores here.)					

TOTAL SCORE FOR COURAGE: _____

(Add scores from Columns 1, 2, 3, and 4. Record the total above and on the Master Score Sheet in Appendix A. Also, count the number of N/As and record on the Master Score Sheet.)

Reflect – Courage

Scoring Analysis

List Your Four Highest Scored Items (Strengths)

Note: If you have multiple items with the same high score, choose the four items that are most related to your current or aspired position.

Item	Score

List Your Four Lowest Scored Items (Weaknesses)

Note: If you have multiple items with the same low score, choose the four items that are most related to your current or aspired position.

Item	Score

Reflect – Courage Questions

Think about the following questions about courage:

- What does courage in the workplace mean to you?

- Think of a leader you would describe as courageous. What attributes does the person have that cause you to describe them as courageous?

- Do you know any leaders who lack courage? What effects do you see as a result?

- Do you avoid difficult conversations?

- Can a person have courage without integrity?

- Do you struggle when you have to deliver bad news to your boss? What about to your direct reports?

Develop – Courage

Develop and Renew

Consider the following development tactics to help improve your courage. Identify which tactics would be valuable to include in your Personal Development Plan (PDP) if you choose to improve in this competency.

- A courageous leader speaks up, even when others may judge them harshly. If you are right (and be sure you are right), don't hesitate to present your case, even if it will be unpopular. Know when to speak up and when to question the decisions of others.

- Think about how you would give feedback to your boss or someone else in a position of authority. Our feedback model is to state what you observe, describe the effects of the behavior, and provide a recommendation.

- Do you seek feedback on your performance? It often requires courage to ask others how they perceive you and your performance. You should actively seek feedback from your leader, peers, direct reports, and customers.

- How do you receive feedback? It should be received as a gift that you will learn from and improve.

- How do you react to those who disagree with you? Develop your listening skills and open your mind to how others feel or see a situation.

- Don't hesitate to be the devil's advocate in a brainstorming session or in a meeting that is discussing options to take. This encourages everyone to think more clearly about a situation.

- Courageous leaders take the high road, even when it is difficult. Do you have a set of principles that guide your behavior?

- Don't hesitate to give others credit, even when you are the one most responsible for the good result.

- Review the processes and procedures in your group. A courageous leader does not hesitate to make changes if needed.

- Do you admit mistakes? Courageous leaders learn from their mistakes and are not hesitant to admit them to others when necessary.

- When you choose a course of action, pursue it with zest, confidence, and resolve. Show others the benefits of pursuing the course and gain their confidence and commitment.

Resources

Books

Chaleff, Ira. *The Courageous Follower: Standing Up to and for Our Leaders*. San Francisco: Berrett Koehler, 2003.

Cottrell, David. *Leadership Courage*. Flower Mound, TX: The Walk the Talk Company, 2005.

Harrison, Elle. *Wild Courage: A Journey of Transformation for You and Your Business*. London, 2011.

Lee, Gus and Diane Elliott-Lee. *Courage: The Backbone of Leadership*. San Francisco: Jossey-Bass, 2006.

Maxwell, John. *The Right to Lead: Learning Leadership Through Character and Courage*. Nashville, TN: Thomas Nelson, 2010.

Staub, Robert. *The Heart of Leadership: 12 Practices of Courageous Leaders*. Staub Leadership Consultants, 2007.

Stutz, Phil and Barry Michels. *The Tools: Transform Your Problems into Courage, Confidence, and Creativity*. New York: Spiegel & Grau, 2012.

Sullenberger, Chesley. *Making a Difference: Stories of Vision and Courage From America's Leaders*. New York: Morrow, 2012.

Terry, Robert. *Authentic Leadership: Courage in Action*. San Francisco: Jossey-Bass, 1993.

Treasurer, Bill. *Courage Goes to Work: How to Build Backbones, Boost Performance, and Get Results*. San Francisco: Berrett-Koehler, 2008.

Warrell, Margie. *Find Your Courage: 12 Acts for Becoming Fearless at Work and in Life*. New York: McGraw-Hill, 2008.

Other Resources

Forbes presents an interesting article on how courage helped Apple be successful at http://www.forbes.com/sites/carminegallo/2012/08/21/7-courageous-ways-apple-became-americas-most-valuable-company/.

See the article titled, "Courage is the Key to Great Leadership" on the Entrepreneur's Organization site at: http://www.eonetwork.org/knowledgebase/specialfeatures/pages/courageisthekeytogreatleadership.aspx.

Change – Courage

Instructions

Using the table below and on the next page, refer to the items you listed in the Reflect – Courage worksheet and identify specific actions you will take to improve your weaknesses or enhance your strengths in each area. Refer to the Develop and Renew section on the previous pages for action ideas, keeping in mind the needs of your current or aspired position.

You can have multiple actions for each item you intend to focus on. In the first section, list the actions that are specific to the items you listed in the Reflect – Courage section. On the following page, list any actions you will take that are general to this competency and are related to more than one scored item. Finally, prioritize your actions based on the need for your current or aspired position. These actions will become part of your Personal Development Plan (PDP) for this competency in Appendix C.

Actions to Improve Weakness or Enhance Strength	Priority

Continue on next page.

Change – Courage

Actions to Improve Weakness or Enhance Strength	Priority

Other Actions You Will Take Related to Courage (not related to the identified strongest or weakest items)	Priority

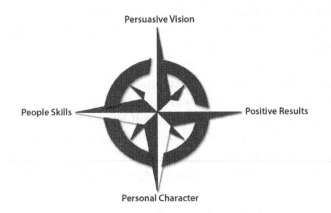

Persuasive Vision

People Skills

Positive Results

Personal Character

CHAPTER 20

Credibility

(Personal Character)

*"The more you are willing to accept responsibility for your actions,
the more credibility you will have"*
– Brian Koslow

Any discussion of leadership must address the issue of credibility, for without credibility a leader will have no willing followers. Credibility does not just mean the number of degrees you have attained, or even the number of years of experience. Credibility comes from others and their attitude toward you based on your actions.

There are many components to credibility, but it is similar to trust – it may take a long time to build, but it can be lost in a nanosecond. People want to believe in their leaders, trust their words, and most of all, see a match between their words and their actions. The loyalty, commitment, energy, and productivity of followers depend on the credibility of the leader. Decision making also plays a role in credibility. If a leader consistently makes poor decisions or avoids making decisions, credibility suffers. On the other hand, if a leader makes wise decisions after assessing all information, credibility is enhanced.

Leaders must focus on developing and maintaining both their professional credibility and personal credibility. Professional credibility is much easier to maintain than personal credibility. Personal credibility grows when a person's actions are in alignment with what they say. When there is a gap between what a leader says and does, personal credibility is undermined.

An example of this is the medical profession. Have you ever been in a doctor's office and while waiting for the doctor searched out her diplomas hanging on the wall? When you spot the diplomas, you note what schools she graduated from. If they are excellent schools you are more assured in your mind that you will be taken care of well. Then you may wonder if your doctor finished first or last in her class. Alternatively, if you never heard of the schools, you begin to have doubts about the doctor's professional credibility. These doubts, however, can be dismissed if, in the first few minutes, she establishes personal credibility by being friendly, demonstrating concern, and asking insightful questions.

Maynard Brusman has described six ingredients of credibility. (Working Resources Newsletter, Vol. V, No. 8.). Notice that five of the six ingredients are determinants of personal credibility and only one (competence) describes professional credibility.

- Character – Leaders must demonstrate integrity, honesty, respect, and trust.
- Conviction – Leaders must show passion and commitment toward their vision.
- Care – Leaders show concern for others' personal and professional well-being.
- Courage – Leaders must be willing to stand up for their beliefs, challenge others, admit mistakes, and change their own behavior when necessary.
- Composure – Leaders display the appropriate emotional reactions, especially in difficult circumstances.
- Competence – Leaders must be accomplished in hard skills (technical and content expertise) and soft skills (interpersonal relationships, communications, and teamwork).

People may initially assume credibility, but it can be damaged in a short period of time. For example, a college professor initially has credibility due to his degrees. However, if he then demonstrates poor teacher behaviors, his credibility suffers.

Sandy Allgeier (2009) lists seven steps to influence credibility:

- Know your stuff
- Keep commitments
- Honor confidences and avoid gossip
- Know yourself – the good, the bad, and the ugly
- Choose to value others – the good and yes, the bad and the ugly
- Ask more and listen most
- Create credible interactions

Having high credibility is a key component of leadership success. With it, you will have the following needed to achieve your objectives and goals. Without it, you will soon find yourself alone, awash in failure.

Red Flag Behaviors

- You brag about your accomplishments.
- You flaunt your credibility by constantly mentioning your education.
- You have poor listening skills. When listening to others your mind is elsewhere and your body language betrays you.
- You are judgmental of others. You fail to value others' contributions.
- You are not aware of your true strengths and weaknesses.
- You display your emotions in many situations, such as anger, disappointment, and frustration.

Case in Point

Carrie was anxious to start her new leadership position at Coddem Corporation. She knew, however, that she would be watched closely in the first few days and weeks, especially by her direct reports.

She began her first day with a team meeting, and then spent a few days getting to know her team. In her informal discussions, she answered any questions the team members had for her. She focused on giving examples from her experience and demonstrating to them that she knew what she was doing. At the same time, she learned as much as possible about the people and organization by asking questions and demonstrating excellent listening skills.

When the first crisis occurred, she remained calm and dealt with the issues each team member struggled with and provided the needed resources. She collaborated with her senior leadership and communicated as much as possible with her team about what was happening. These actions helped her quickly establish professional and personal credibility.

Notes for the Aspiring Leader

Realize that it takes time to establish credibility and people will be skeptical of new leaders. Listen and learn from others. When you see opportunities to demonstrate your skill or knowledge, do so, but in a humble manner.

Assessing Your Current Location – Credibility

(Personal Character)

Instructions: Read each of the skills and behaviors below. As objectively as possible, score yourself for each according to the following scale: 1 = strongly disagree; 2 = disagree; 3 = agree; 4 = strongly agree. If a behavior is not appropriate for your current or aspired position, check the N/A column.

SKILL OR BEHAVIOR	1	2	3	4	N/A
I work to continuously improve my leadership skills and behaviors.					
I have a good knowledge of my strengths and weaknesses.					
I am truthful in all dealings with others.					
I am honest and forthcoming when I make a mistake.					
I model the behaviors I expect others to demonstrate.					
I maintain confidentiality of information when appropriate.					
I show passion and commitment to goals and vision.					
I consistently work to develop trust with others.					
I show genuine concern for others' personal and professional well-being.					
I remain emotionally centered, even when under significant stress.					
I follow through on promises and commitments.					
I base my decisions on facts and not emotion, hearsay, or personal bias.					

Continue on next page.

Assessing Your Current Location – Credibility

(Personal Character)

SKILL OR BEHAVIOR	1	2	3	4	N/A
My actions are consistent with my words.					
SCORES FOR CREDIBILITY (Total check marks in each column and multiply by the heading for the column. Record your scores here.)					

TOTAL SCORE FOR CREDIBILITY: _____

(Add scores from Columns 1, 2, 3, and 4. Record the total above and on the Master Score Sheet in Appendix A. Also, count the number of N/As and record on the Master Score Sheet.)

Reflect – Credibility

Scoring Analysis

List Your Four Highest Scored Items (Strengths)

Note: If you have multiple items with the same high score, choose the four items that are most related to your current or aspired position.

Item	Score

List Your Four Lowest Scored Items (Weaknesses)

Note: If you have multiple items with the same low score, choose the four items that are most related to your current or aspired position.

Item	Score

Reflect – Credibility Questions

Think about the following questions about credibility:

- What attributes do you have that bring you credibility with your peers and direct reports?

- List some leaders who have lost credibility. What happened?

- If a leader loses credibility, what should they do to restore it?

- Have you ever worked for a leader you did not find personally or professionally credible? What was the experience like for you?

- What role does credibility play in decision making?

- Do you find a leader credible if they gossip to you about others when you are having a one-on-one conversation?

- What is the role of consistency in building and maintaining credibility?

Develop – Credibility

Develop and Renew

Consider the following development tactics to help improve your credibility. Identify which tactics would be valuable to include in your Personal Development Plan (PDP) if you choose to improve in this competency.

- Know yourself. What are your strengths and weaknesses? How will you work to enhance your strengths and mitigate your weaknesses? Buying this book and working through the self assessment for each competency is a good start. Be sure to follow through in your areas of weakness and take steps to improve.

- Constantly work to improve yourself. Take courses, talk to experts, and ask the right questions. Demonstrate you have a love of learning and jump at opportunities to improve through courses, workshops, and professional meetings. Modeling behaviors that show you want to learn and get better in your job is infectious and will motivate others on your team to improve as well.

- Always tell the truth. If others perceive you are not telling the truth, your credibility will suffer substantially. If asked for confidential information or information not to be released yet, be transparent and tell the person you are not at liberty to disclose the information.

- Walk the talk! You instantly lose credibility if you do not. Don't expect others to adhere to standards that you won't follow yourself. In our coaching practice, we sometimes uncover leaders' behavior that is not consistent with the expectations they have of others. We immediately begin to work with the leader on this issue because without credibility it is difficult to work on any other area involving working with a team. For example, if you want everyone in the office each day by 8:00 a.m., YOU must be there before 8:00 a.m.

- Think about the following quote from Frank Outlaw, the supermarket clerk who founded BiLo Supermarkets:

  > Watch your thoughts, they become words;
  > Watch your words, they become actions;
  > Watch your actions, they become habits;
  > Watch your habits, they become character;
  > Watch your character, it becomes your destiny.

- Be convicted and show passion and commitment toward your vision. If you don't have conviction and passion toward what is important, your followers will have difficulty generating conviction and passion.

- Consistently work to develop trust in others. We recommend that you spend time with the Trust competency development recommendations. Without trust, you cannot have credibility.

- Show concern for other's personal and professional well-being. It is important that you are authentic and sincere in your concern. Credibility is damaged when concern is perceived as artificial or insincere.

- Stand up for your beliefs and those of your subordinates (when right). When a subordinate is in a tough place because of a decision they made or a situation they are in, your responsibility is to do what you can to help the person. If they are right in their position, you should lead them through it and be their advocate in your organization.

- Admit your mistakes and present the corrective action you will take to ensure that it will not happen again. Few things damage credibility more than making a mistake and blaming others. Followers expect transparency and honesty. It is important to admit your mistakes and provide others with any corrective action you will take.

- Be emotionally centered, especially in difficult circumstances. People look to their leaders to see how they should react in difficult situations. If bad news is announced, it is important that the leaders maintain their composure and appear to be solid. If you have anger or disagreement about a difficult circumstance, do not display your anger. Keep your emotions in check and then follow the right path to disagree with the situation by discussing with other leaders or the person responsible.

- Credibility crumbles without integrity. ALWAYS act with integrity. We can pretend to be honest, genuine, and competent for a time, but the pressure of problems always reveals our true character.

Resources

Books

Allgeier, Sandra. *The Personal Credibility Factor: How to Get It, Keep It, and Get It Back If You've Lost It.* London: FT Press, 2009.

Alter, Cara Hale. *The Credibility Code: How to Project Confidence and Competence When It Matters Most.* Meritus, 2012.

Cope, Kevin. *Seeing the Big Picture: Business Acumen to Build Your Credibility, Career, and Company.* Austin, TX: Greenleaf, 2012.

Figliuolo, Mike. *One Piece of Paper: The Simple Approach to Powerful, Personal Leadership*. San Francisco: Jossey-Bass, 2011.

Hurley, Robert. *The Decision to Trust: How Leaders Create High Trust Organizations*. San Francisco: Jossey-Bass, 2011.

Klann, G. *Building Character: Strengthening the Heart of Good Leadership*. San Francisco: Jossey-Bass, 2006.

Kouzes, James M., and Posner, Barry Z. *Credibility: How Leaders Gain and Lose it, Why People Demand It*. San Francisco: Jossey-Bass, 2011.

Other Resources

See the following article on the LeaderToday.org site: http://leadertoday.org/faq/credibility.htm.

An excellent article on credibility in leaders can be found at http://wildfiremag.com/command/credible_leader/.

Under 30 CEO offers an excellent article on how to grow your credibility at http://under30ceo.com/59-ways-to-grow-your-credibility-and-look-experienced/.

Change – Credibility

Instructions

Using the table below and on the next page, refer to the items you listed in the Reflect – Credibility worksheet and identify specific actions you will take to improve your weaknesses or enhance your strengths in each area. Refer to the Develop and Renew section on the previous pages for action ideas, keeping in mind the needs of your current or aspired position.

You can have multiple actions for each item you intend to focus on. In the first section, list the actions that are specific to the items you listed in the Reflect – Credibility section. On the following page, list any actions you will take that are general to this competency and are related to more than one scored item. Finally, prioritize your actions based on the need for your current or aspired position. These actions will become part of your Personal Development Plan (PDP) for this competency in Appendix C.

Actions to Improve Weakness or Enhance Strength	Priority

Continue on next page.

Change – Credibility

Actions to Improve Weakness or Enhance Strength	Priority

Other Actions You Will Take Related to Credibility (not related to the identified strongest or weakest items)	Priority

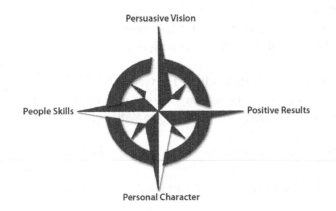

Persuasive Vision

People Skills — Positive Results

Personal Character

CHAPTER 21

Followership

(Personal Character)

"We cannot all be masters, nor all masters can be truly followed"

– William Shakespeare

A follower is anyone that is required to be directed by another person for the benefit of the organization or project. We are all followers and accountable to someone. The most effective leaders know when to lead and when to follow, and sometimes these two roles operate simultaneously. For example, a leader may be directing a team of subordinates toward the successful completion of the project. At the same time, the leader follows the direction of their immediate supervisor concerning schedule, budget, quality and other issues. Perhaps the leader is also following other leaders who are stakeholders in the project.

Excellent followership is also required in non-profit and governmental organizations. Leaders in these organizations are accountable to their Board of Trustees or to their electorate. These leaders are expected to follow the direction of their body of voters and if they fail to do so they lose credibility and likely reelection to their leadership position.

Followership describes how well we trust our leaders and our organization and carry out the actions to achieve the mission and goals of the organization. It is not simply following orders. A good follower also contributes to the organization by setting an example for others, giving feedback to other leaders, and asking the right questions when appropriate to understand the situation.

Some leaders may have the final decision on a matter, and at other times they must gain the approval of other leaders and/or their immediate supervisor. Or a leader may delegate decision making on a part of a project to members of his team. After delegating, the leader becomes a follower of the decisions that the team makes.

Following is not passive. It is an agreement to yield to another person or group. Most of the time the agreement is inherent in the organizational structure – everyone has a boss. Other times being a follower is a choice, such as in the example in the previous paragraph.

Followership is a subject that is often overlooked because it is generally associated with weakness, servitude, or loss of identity. However, true leadership and followership are intimately related. Every great leader must be a great follower and a strong following is proof of strong leadership.

An effective follower believes in their organization and its leaders. They accept the mission and strategic plans of the organization. They communicate those plans and requirements to their teams and inspire them to be their best for the organization. They follow up with projects and ensure that their team members are good followers as well.

Robert Kelley, in "The Power of Followership" (1992), describes five styles of followers:

- Sheep. This style of follower is passive and looks to the leader to think for them and motivate them.

- The Yes People. These followers are always on the leader's side but still looking to the leader for thinking, direction, and vision.

- The Alienated. These followers think for themselves but have a lot of negative energy. They always have reasons not to do something. They are always skeptical and cynical about where things are going.

- The Pragmatics. These followers sit on the fence and see which way the wind blows, then they get on board.

- The Star Followers. They think for themselves. They are very active and high in positive energy. But they do not accept the leader's decision without their own independent evaluation of its soundness. They challenge if they disagree, but offer constructive, helpful alternatives.

Kelley's categories are a handy way of thinking about how we follow our leaders. As a leader, you can also assess your team and determine which category your followers fall into. From there, you can determine where you may need to coach your team members to be better followers (Star Followers).

Leaders sometimes forget that they are followers and are openly critical of their leadership's activities (the alienated). They sometimes vent their frustration with an action or policy in front of their peers or team members. This is not being a good follower in a leadership role. If a follower questions a policy, procedure, or project, they have an obligation to bring their concerns to their leadership in a thoughtful and respectful manner (the star follower style). This usually enables them to gain more information and understanding of the situation.

Leaders as followers are not hasty in their judgment of tasks, policies or procedures that come from above. They seek out information from their leaders that helps them understand a situation; then they can pass on information that will bring understanding to the team.

Followers need to know what is expected of them. If you are unclear about what is expected of you by your leadership, schedule a meeting to discuss expectations. By the same token, are your followers clear on your expectations of them? We recommend having a conversation with each direct report to clarify your expectations and answer any questions they may have in this area. It is also important to ask your followers what they expect of you. Having clarity in this area is important to both leaders and followers.

Latour and Rast, in their excellent paper, state that, "Developing dynamic followership is a discipline. It is jointly an art and a science requiring skill and conceptualization of roles in innovative ways – one perhaps more essential to mission success than leadership development. Without followership, a leader at any level will fail to produce effective institutions. Valuing followers and their development is the first step toward cultivating effective, transformational leaders."

Red Flag Behaviors

- You get angry at your leaders over issues and show the anger to your team.
- You do not know what is expected from you in your position.
- You challenge your leaders with emotion and at inappropriate times and places.
- You withhold information from your leaders.
- You have difficulty accepting direction from above.
- You do not have confidence in your leadership.
- You encourage your team members to disagree with your leadership on issues.

Case in Point

Being a good follower does not mean you blindly follow. There are situations where a good follower must influence their leaders, and there are even situations where the follower must take a stand in opposition to their leadership.

David was the manager of a project team at Karsten Industries. He had an excellent relationship with his boss, Carl. Over the years they developed the relationship and worked well together. Carl provided the support that David needed on all his projects. They even socialized through frequent lunches together and met monthly at a local pub for a few beers.

But David increasingly felt something was wrong. Although he respected Carl and followed his guidance on the projects he was managing, something wasn't right. David delved into the accounts for the project and realized that Carl was getting kickbacks from three vendors who supplied the project. Although the vendors were doing a good job, it was clear Carl selected them for his personal financial gain.

David did not know what to do, but finally realized he needed to confront Carl. In a private meeting, David disclosed his findings. Carl was initially angry and accused David of betraying him. David persevered and finally Carl calmed down and became very emotional. He disclosed that he faced some incredible debts that he had to pay off, and he found his actions were the easiest way to do it. He pleaded with David to ignore what happened, but David could not. He convinced Carl to go to Human Resources and get guidance on what to do. David agreed to accompany him and help in any way possible.

Notes for the Aspiring Leader

Seek out strong leaders to emulate. Ask them if they will mentor you in the skills and behaviors that are their strengths. Build a relationship with your chosen leaders/mentors and seek their advice on your career development and professional growth. Learn as much as possible about your organization so that you can fully support its goals.

Assess Your Current Location – Followership

(Personal Character)

Instructions: Read each of the skills and behaviors below. As objectively as possible, score yourself for each according to the following scale: 1 = strongly disagree; 2 = disagree; 3 = agree; 4 = strongly agree. If a behavior is not appropriate for your current or aspired position, check the N/A column.

SKILL OR BEHAVIOR	1	2	3	4	N/A
I accept directions from above.					
I can seamlessly move from my role as a leader to one of a follower when the situation requires.					
I support my organization's leaders.					
When I have a disagreement with a leader, I discuss it with them in private.					
I demonstrate personal confidence when appearing before senior leaders.					
I challenge my leaders when appropriate, but I do it with respect and accept their final decisions.					
If I make a difficult or impactful decision I run it by my leaders for confirmation before announcing.					
I can determine the best way to get things done with my leaders by talking their language and responding to their needs.					
I give my leaders as much information as needed for their decisions and planning.					
I keep my leaders informed of progress on initiatives.					
I strive to teach my team members to be effective followers.					
I work to gain my leaders' trust.					

Continue on next page.

Assess Your Current Location – Followership

(Personal Character)

	1	2	3	4	N/A
SCORES FOR FOLLOWERSHIP (Total check marks in each column and multiply by the heading for the column. Record your scores here.)					

TOTAL SCORE FOR FOLLOWERSHIP: _____

(Add scores from Columns 1, 2, 3, and 4. Record the total above and on the Master Score Sheet in Appendix A. Also, count the number of N/As and record on the Master Score Sheet.)

Reflect – Followership

Scoring Analysis

List Your Four Highest Scored Items (Strengths)

Note: If you have multiple items with the same high score, choose the four items that are most related to your current or aspired position.

Item	Score

List Your Four Lowest Scored Items (Weaknesses)

Note: If you have multiple items with the same low score, choose the four items that are most related to your current or aspired position.

Item	Score

Reflect – Followership Questions

Think about the following questions about followership:

- Who do you follow in your work life? What about outside of work? Do you follow a spiritual or political leader?

- Have you ever disagreed with your leaders about a decision or problem? How did you handle the disagreement?

- How do you interact with your leaders? Are you respectful or disrespectful?

- How could you effectively teach your direct reports to be good followers?

- What makes it difficult to be a good follower?

- What is the difference between being a good follower and one who (as commonly called) is sucking up?

Develop – Followership

Develop and Renew

Consider the following development tactics to help improve your followership skills and behaviors. Identify which tactics would be valuable to include in your Personal Development Plan (PDP) if you choose to improve in this competency.

- All leaders are also followers. If you have trouble accepting direction from above or dealing with your superiors, consider that although you are a leader, you must also model excellent follower behaviors.

- Show support for your leaders, especially when you are providing guidance to your direct reports. If you have an issue with a leader's decision or a directive coming down from above, discuss the issue with the appropriate leader(s) and do not complain in front of your direct reports.

- Challenge your leaders respectfully, and accept their final decisions. Learn to effectively stand up to your leadership when necessary, using appropriate influencing tactics. Prepare for this type of conversation. Be open to their response because their decisions may be based on information you are not aware of.

- Get to know your leaders. By knowing them you can often anticipate their position, needs, and actions.

- Be proactive in giving information to your leaders. If a project is having difficulties, seek the advice of your leaders or, at a minimum, keep them informed about what you are doing to rectify the situation. Be sure you provide enough information to your leaders so they can make informed decisions.

- Work to gain the trust of your leaders by communicating well, being honest and transparent, and listening to them in discussions.

- Take the responsibility to teach your direct reports to be good followers of all those who are in higher positions. The best method to do this is to model excellent follower behaviors yourself.

- Learn as much as you can about your organization, and support its strategies and mission.

Resources

Books

Capon, Claire. *Understanding Organizational Context*. Upper Saddle River, NJ: Prentice Hall, 2002.

Chaleff, Ira. *The Courageous Follower: Standing Up to and For Our Leaders*. San Francisco: Berrett-Koehler, 2003.

Goffee, Rob and Gareth Jones. *Authentic Followership: Being a More Effective Leader*. Cambridge: Harvard University Press, 2009.

Kellerman, Barbara. *Followership: How Followers are Creating Change and Changing Leaders*. Cambridge: Harvard Business Journal Press, 2008.

Lundin, Stephen C. and Lynne Lancaster. *The Importance of Followership: Developing Followers in Organizational Work*. Bethesda, MD: World Future Society, 2005.

Madden, Kurt and Kris Madden. *The Synergetic Follower: Changing Our World Without Being the Leader*. Charleston, SC: CreateSpace, 2011.

Omokhai, Imoukhuede. *Discovering Followership: Learn the Secrets of Walking Behind and Still Staying Ahead*. Estes Park, CO: Summit House Publishers, 2011.

Riggio, Ronald. *The Art of Followership: How Great Followers Create Great Leaders and Organizations*. San Francisco: Jossey-Bass, 2008.

Ros, Jay. *How to Manage Your Boss: Developing the Perfect Working Relationship*. London: Financial Times Management, 2002.

Sviatoslav, Steve. *Beyond Leadership to Followership*. Trafford Publishing, 2006.

Websites

See the links in the ChangingMinds.org website at
http://changingminds.org/disciplines/leadership/followership/followership.htm.

Other Resources

An excellent article on the ten rules of good followership and leadership can be found at
http://www.au.af.mil/au/awc/awcgate/au-24/meilinger.pdf.

Latour, Sharon and Vicki Rast. Dynamic Followership: Prerequisite for Effective Leadership.
HTTP://www.airpower.maxwell.af.mil/airchronicles/apj/apj04/win 04/LATO ur.html #Latour.

236

Change – Followership

Instructions

Using the table below and on the next page, refer to the items you listed in the Reflect – Followership worksheet and identify specific actions you will take to improve your weaknesses or enhance your strengths in each area. Refer to the Develop and Renew section on the previous pages for action ideas, keeping in mind the needs of your current or aspired position.

You can have multiple actions for each item you intend to focus on. In the first section, list the actions that are specific to the items you listed in the Reflect – Followership section. On the following page, list any actions you will take that are general to this competency and are related to more than one scored item. Finally, prioritize your actions based on the need for your current or aspired position. These actions will become part of your Personal Development Plan (PDP) for this competency in Appendix C.

Actions to Improve Weakness or Enhance Strength	Priority

Continue on next page.

Change Followership

Actions to Improve Weakness or Enhance Strength	Priority

Other Actions You Will Take Related to Followership (not related to the identified strongest or weakest items)	Priority

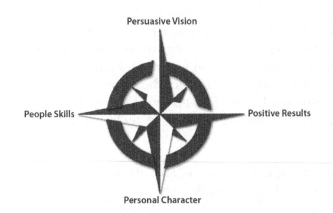

Persuasive Vision

People Skills — Positive Results

Personal Character

CHAPTER 22

Initiative

(Personal Character)

"Without initiative, leaders are simply workers in leadership positions."

– Bo Bennett

Mary Kay Ash, the entrepreneur who founded the cosmetics empire of her own name, once said, "There are three types of people in the world: those who make things happen, those who watch things happen, and those who wonder what happened." Leaders make things happen. They must. Moreover, leaders make things happen by demonstrating initiative.

Initiative is defined as an introductory act or step; leading action. Another definition is taking action even though someone has not given you orders to do so. It means meeting new and unexpected situations with prompt action. It includes using resourcefulness to get something done without the normal material or methods available to you. Initiative involves a decision to do something. This does not mean completing the effort, which may be done by others; but it does mean that the leader takes the initial steps.

Initiative is often misunderstood because it is not about meeting performance goals. Its about going the extra mile. Initiative is about identifying a need and championing a solution for the benefit of the organization without being asked to do so. There is no magic to initiative, just a sense of responsibility for the organization's well-being. Initiative is about taking steps to make the organization better, not about wasting time tackling unimportant matters. To make the distinction, try determining the impact a certain action would make on team performance or the company's bottom line.

Personal initiative can have rewards, and few leaders progress far in their career without initiative. Nevertheless, initiative can also be risky. Some initiatives a leader undertakes may be wrong or not gain the expected results. This can be especially disheartening to young leaders. However, when the leader takes assessed risks and uses initiative, the results are often positive and outweigh the potential negative.

To take initiative you must first see the opportunity and the potential reward. You may not always have the resources available, but when using initiative, you take the steps forward and figure out how to overcome the obstacles as you go. Don't wait for things to happen; make them happen. This does not mean you do not seek your leader's approval for your initiative. You don't want to be seen as pursuing an unsanctioned activity that is not right for the organization. Prepare an outline of your idea and review it with your leaders for approval to proceed.

Art Petty, in his leadership blog (www.artpetty.com), lists seven steps to get from the whiteboard to action. The steps are:

1. Set the stage for action by creating a charter for your initiative. This gives context for the importance, highlights expected outcomes, and sets accountability.
2. Move forward as if you are leading a series of sprints, not asking the team to run a marathon.
3. Mix things up by inviting outside viewpoints into meetings.
4. Create the right balance of homework and sub-team activities (prioritization).
5. Recruit extended talent.
6. Be careful on the number of major initiatives you introduce to your team at one time.
7. Cultivate a culture of experimentation (See Creativity on page 31).

Initiative is related to several other competencies such as Creativity, Decision Making, Problem Solving, Integrity, and Focus on Results. People who do not demonstrate initiative also often have problems in these areas as well. Those with initiative will focus on their goal and not let hurdles get in their way. They see problems and solve them routinely.

Red Flag Behaviors

- You do the minimal amount of work required in your position.
- You are resistant to change.
- When things go wrong, you blame others and do not take ownership.
- You are apathetic about your responsibilities.
- You do not put forth ideas to improve processes, quality, or the work environment.
- You do not address problems in your work environment.
- You do not pursue others' ideas; rather, you discount them.
- You are not involved in any continuous learning or improvement programs.

Case in Point

The example of Fred Smith, founder of FedEx, is appropriate for this competency. While serving in Vietnam, Smith thought a lot about how to move supplies throughout the country. Upon his return, he went to college and in his dissertation, he wrote about his concept of having a hub location for air cargo transportation. Others did not think much of his concept, but that didn't stop him. He used initiative and found some other dreamers who helped him put together the financial means to get started and the rest is history. He built the world's largest package-distribution system, and his concept is now common throughout the industry.

Even most passenger airlines have adopted his system, having hubs in key cities across the country. People from smaller cities funnel into hubs (on fuel-efficient smaller aircraft) and then disperse from the hub to another small city or another hub.

Notes for the Aspiring Leader

Showing initiative is one of the best ways to get ahead in any organization. However, your initiative must be well thought out and provide true benefits to the organization. Learn your leader's needs, and seek to meet those needs before being asked or reminded. Quickly establish that you are one who can work without supervision.

Assess Your Current Location – Initiative

(Personal Character)

Instructions: Read each of the skills and behaviors below. As objectively as possible, score yourself for each according to the following scale: 1 = strongly disagree; 2 = disagree; 3 = agree; 4 = strongly agree. If a behavior is not appropriate for your current or aspired position, check the N/A column.

SKILL OR BEHAVIOR	1	2	3	4	N/A
I formulate ideas to further organizational goals and initiate their implementation.					
I assume ownership of assigned tasks and responsibilities.					
I proactively address problems within the organization in a positive manner.					
I take personal responsibility for getting the job done while involving others as appropriate.					
I proactively encourage others to expand their boundaries and take risks.					
I assess and mitigate risks when pursuing ideas.					
I tackle important or difficult tasks without hesitation.					
I assess the availability of resources when initiating a project.					
I begin new tasks before being told.					
I take on extra tasks, such as helping others when needed.					
I am trusted to work without close supervision.					
I demonstrate a commitment to life-long learning.					
I correct mistakes or address problems as I see them.					

Continue on next page.

Assess Your Current Location – Initiative

(Personal Character)

SKILL OR BEHAVIOR	1	2	3	4	N/A
I seek opportunities to demonstrate initiative.					
I assess the potential benefits of each initiative.					
SCORES FOR INITIATIVE (Total check marks in each column and multiply by the heading for the column. Record your scores here.)					

TOTAL SCORE FOR INITIATIVE: _____

(Add scores from Columns 1, 2, 3, and 4. Record the total above and on the Master Score Sheet in Appendix A. Also, count the number of N/As and record on the Master Score Sheet.)

Reflect – Initiative

Scoring Analysis

List Your Four Highest Scored Items (Strengths)

Note: If you have multiple items with the same high score, choose the four items that are most related to your current or aspired position.

Item	Score

List Your Four Lowest Scored Items (Weaknesses)

Note: If you have multiple items with the same low score, choose the four items that are most related to your current or aspired position.

Item	Score

Reflect – Initiative Questions

Think about the following questions about initiative:

- What are some of the obstacles that you may personally encounter that hinder your initiative?

- Have you ever worked for a leader who did not demonstrate initiative? What effect did this have on you?

- What must a leader do to reinforce the initiative of followers?

- What can you do if your direct reports are not demonstrating initiative?

- What is the difference between initiative and looking busy?

- Why do people who have initiative demonstrate a love of learning?

Develop – Initiative

Develop and Renew

Consider the following development tactics to help improve your initiative. Identify which tactics would be valuable to include in your Personal Development Plan (PDP) if you choose to improve in this competency.

- List the factors that motivate you. What drives you to do a good job?

- Look for ways to make things better. What ideas do you have that could improve conditions or quality?

- As a leader, it is important to demonstrate the value of working with others to achieve the organization's goals. If you have team members who are uncooperative with others, take steps to correct this behavior in the team member. You and your peer leaders should work toward a culture of cooperation between individuals and teams.

- List your tasks and responsibilities. What does ownership of each mean to you? Do you accept all responsibilities that come with your position? Are you proactive in taking ownership of tasks and projects? How do you react when there is a problem with one of your tasks or responsibilities?

- What processes or procedures have you identified that could be streamlined that you have not taken action on yet? What are the obstacles that prevent you from pursuing these initiatives? List the initiatives and obstacles and determine the next steps to move the initiative forward.

- What does it mean to you to stretch yourself beyond your normal tasks? Consider your team members. Who stretches to achieve more? How can you help those who only do the minimum to do more?

- High-performing organizations have a culture that encourages people to do more than is required. People build their own challenges and step up to achieve their goals and more. Talk with your peer leaders about how your organization can nurture this culture.

- Consider the ideas you have had that would benefit the organization. Have you been proactive about formulating and implementing them? List the ideas you have that would further your organization's goals. Identify the next steps to begin initiating each.

Resources

Books

Bossidy, Larry et al. *Execution: The Discipline of Getting Things Done.* New York: Crown Business Publishers, 2002.

Covey, Stephen R. *The Seven Habits of Highly Effective People: Powerful Lessons in Personal Change.* New York: The Free Press, 1989.

Deci, Edward. and Richard. Flaste. *Why We Do What We Do: Understanding Self-Motivation.* New York: Penguin, 1996.

Duke Corporate Education. *Staying Focused on Goals and Priorities: Leading from the Center.* New York: Kaplan Business, 2005.

Hickman, Craig; et al. *The Oz Principle: Getting Results through Individual and Organizational Accountability.* New York: Portfolio Hardcover, 2004.

Harvard Business School Press. Harvard Business Essentials: *Performance Management: Measure and Improve the Effectiveness of Your Employees.* Cambridge: Harvard Business School Press, 2006.

Kotler, Philip; et al. *Good Works!: Marketing and Corporate Initiatives that Build a Better World…and the Bottom Line.* New York: Wiley, 2012.

Nelson, Bob. *1001 Ways to Take Initiative at Work.* New York: Workman, 1999.

Pfeffer, Jeffrey and Robert Sutton. *The Knowing-Doing Gap: How Smart Companies Turn Knowledge Into Action.* Boston: Harvard Business School Press, 2000.

Change – Initiative

Instructions

Using the table below and on the next page, refer to the items you listed in the Reflect – Initiative worksheet and identify specific actions you will take to improve your weaknesses or enhance your strengths in each area. Refer to the Develop and Renew section on the previous pages for action ideas, keeping in mind the needs of your current or aspired position.

You can have multiple actions for each item you intend to focus on. In the first section, list the actions that are specific to the items you listed in the Reflect – Initiative section. On the following page, list any actions you will take that are general to this competency and are related to more than one scored item. Finally, prioritize your actions based on the need for your current or aspired position. These actions will become part of your Personal Development Plan (PDP) for this competency in Appendix C.

Actions to Improve Weakness or Enhance Strength	Priority

Continue on next page.

Change – Initiative

Actions to Improve Weakness or Enhance Strength	Priority

Other Actions You Will Take Related to Initiative (not related to the identified strongest or weakest items)	Priority

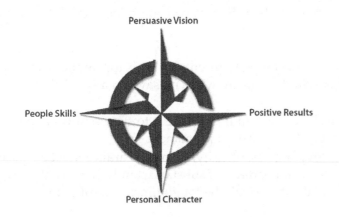

Persuasive Vision

People Skills — Positive Results

Personal Character

CHAPTER 23

Integrity

(Personal Character)

> *"Real integrity is doing the right thing, knowing that nobody's going to know whether you did it or not."*
> – Oprah Winfrey

Integrity is the foundation of every successful organization. In addition, since people build an organization, the integrity of a business is only as good as that of its people. A failure of integrity poisons an organization, and everyone suffers. Acting with integrity is a choice that each leader needs to make. For many, it is an easy choice and they do the right thing. For others, competing issues such as money, power, and prestige, can make the decision hard, and some leaders make the wrong choice. If competing issues are more important than integrity, it is likely that decisions and actions will be done without integrity.

Integrity is defined as steadfast adherence to a strict moral or ethical code, moral soundness, honesty, and freedom from corrupting influence or motive. Leaders are expected to be honest and trustworthy. They are expected to do the right thing, even if it causes the organization some short-term pain or fewer profits. In some cases, if senior leadership consistently acts without integrity, lower-level leaders become concerned and may even feel the need to leave the organization.

Your personal integrity is of paramount importance to your career. If people feel you are not honest, cannot be trusted, or engage in unethical behaviors, you will lose your best followers. In particular, leaders are expected to maintain the privacy of information, including both personal and confidential information about the company or employees. If this trust is breached, the leader will lose the ability to effectively lead in the organization. Other behaviors that demonstrate a lack of integrity include cheating, accepting bribes, laziness, manipulation, intimidation, and a lack of transparency.

As a leader, you have a responsibility to not only operate with integrity yourself, but to insure your team members do as well. Sometimes people don't know better and make a mistake. The leader must be firm in handling these situations, but if possible, give the individual the opportunity to learn from the mistake. Clearly, however, there are many types of behavior that cannot be tolerated and are grounds for dismissal.

General Ronald Fogleman, former Chief of Staff of the U.S. Air Force, describes the characteristics of integrity as:

- **Sincerity**. Sincerity is behavior that is unfeigned and presents no false appearances. In other words, you do what you say you will do; you are who you say you are, in all circumstances.
- **Consistency**. A leader's behavior must be consistent if he or she is to successfully shape an organization. A single breach of integrity can leave a permanent scar.
- **Substance**. You must have more than an image of integrity; your appearance must be based on substance. Leaders who have the appearance of substance but lack internal integrity will not have the strength to make it through the tough times and difficult decisions.
- **Being a Good Finisher**. Leaders show their integrity by performing all tasks to the maximum extent of their ability. They do not cut corners or shirk their responsibilities. They get results with honor.

Fogleman believes that leaders build a lifestyle of integrity one step at a time. Individual acts of integrity lead to a habit of integrity, and individual habits lead to a way of life.

A leader needs to apply integrity to everything they do. It is especially important that integrity be evident to customers. If a customer detects any sign of a lack of integrity, they will take their business elsewhere. For example, many people do not feel sales people have integrity. However, we believe differently because without integrity, a sales person will not succeed in the long run.

The integrity of an organization's leaders is the foundation of every successful business, from one end of the organization to the other. As a leader, you are responsible for creating a culture of integrity in your organization, and it begins with your own behaviors and standards of conduct.

Red Flag Behaviors

- You make decision and take actions based on the wrong reasons – money, power, prestige, or retaliation.
- You overlook unethical behavior in others.
- You gossip and disclose personal information about others that should be confidential.
- You bend the truth at times to seal a deal with a customer or placate an employee.
- You are disrespectful of others.
- You blame others for your mistakes.
- You engage in theft of your organization's property or that of others in the organization.

Case in Point

Leaders must constantly be aware that their actions are being watched – by those above them, their direct reports, customers, and even the public. Rarely can an individual operate out of integrity and get away with it.

Bill was the manager of a large contract to a foreign government. The contract was administered by the U.S. Government, but the end customer was another country. It was clear that Bill's company was to operate according to the U.S. Government regulations for quality, delivery, standards, and expenses. Bill was required to travel to the end customer's location frequently. After a period of time, he began to let his travel expenses go beyond the legal boundaries. He flew first class, justifying the expense that the flights were over eight hours. He entertained in his hotel suite frequently. He often bought gifts for family and friends while traveling.

No one noticed for a while, because everyone was busy doing the project's work. Bill was doing an excellent job managing the contract, so no one purposely looked for irregularities. Bill became more brazen in his dealings overseas. He began to meet with some shady characters on his travels and set up a side business importing artwork to the U.S. Much of it ended up in his house or given as gifts.

He was paid well for transporting the artwork through a particular expeditor. Soon, U.S. Customs became interested in the expeditor and, in a sting operation, they arrested Bill when he arrived at the expeditor to pick up his most recent shipment of artwork.

Bill claimed he did not know the artwork was used to smuggle drugs into the country. After Bill's arrest, the government audited his company and found many irregularities related to Bill's travel. The contract was cancelled immediately and the senior leadership of the company was forced to resign under the cloud of suspicion and crimes that were committed by Bill.

Notes for the Aspiring Leader

Your reputation is a valuable asset, or it can be a career-ending liability. You must choose from the beginning whether to develop and be consistent in integrity or not. Don't compromise your reputation by acting out of integrity. Do the right thing – all the time – and integrity will become a habit and the basis for an excellent reputation.

Assess Your Current Location – Integrity

(Personal Character)

Instructions: Read each of the skills and behaviors below. As objectively as possible, score yourself for each according to the following scale: 1 = strongly disagree; 2 = disagree; 3 = agree; 4 = strongly agree. If a behavior is not appropriate for your current or aspired position, check the N/A column.

SKILL OR BEHAVIOR	1	2	3	4	N/A
I accept personal responsibility for mistakes.					
I create an environment that fosters honesty and truthfulness.					
I demonstrate fairness to others.					
I demonstrate the highest ethical standards.					
I demonstrate truthfulness and honesty in all actions and communications.					
I am perceptive of ethical issues and provide guidance on those issues across organizational constituencies.					
I earn my pay and work hard.					
I treat others with respect and dignity.					
I make decisions based on what is right for the organization and not on my personal benefit.					
I am concerned about the reputation of the organization and my self.					
I am sensitive to issues and their effects.					
I do not manipulate others to get what I want.					
I am honest and transparent with employees and customers.					

Continue on next page.

Assess Your Current Location – Integrity

(Personal Character)

SKILL OR BEHAVIOR	1	2	3	4	N/A
I take immediate and appropriate action to address unethical behavior in others.					
I demonstrate proper discretion of confidential information.					
SCORES FOR INTEGRITY (Total check marks in each column and multiply by the heading for the column. Record your scores here.)					

TOTAL SCORE FOR INTEGRITY: _____

(Add scores from Columns 1, 2, 3, and 4. Record the total above and on the Master Score Sheet in Appendix A. Also, count the number of N/As and record on the Master Score Sheet.)

Reflect – Integrity

Scoring Analysis

List Your Four Highest Scored Items (Strengths)

Note: If you have multiple items with the same high score, choose the four items that are most related to your current or aspired position.

Item	Score

List Your Four Lowest Scored Items (Weaknesses)

Note: If you have multiple items with the same low score, choose the four items that are most related to your current or aspired position.

Item	Score

Reflect – Integrity Questions

Think about the following questions about integrity:

- What can you say about yourself that would lead to others describing you as having strong integrity?

- Have you done anything in the past that, if others knew, would damage your integrity? What can you learn from instances such as this?

- Do you have difficulty following a leader who does not demonstrate good integrity?

- What do you think you should do if you observe a leader who is violating a company policy?

- Are there degrees of integrity? In other words, are there differences between taking home a box of paper clips, telling a co-worker confidential salary information, or lying to a customer?

Develop – Integrity

Develop and Renew

Consider the following development tactics to help improve your integrity. Identify which tactics would be valuable to include in your Personal Development Plan (PDP) if you choose to improve in this competency.

- Think of instances when you may not have been fully truthful in your statements or actions. What would the result have been if you had been honest in the situation? What behaviors should you change in this area? List them and develop an action plan to immediately improve in this important area.

- Can you list the ethical standards for your position? Consider listing them and posting in a prominent place in your work area. Not only will this remind you of your standards but it will demonstrate to others that you take them seriously.

- Review your behaviors toward others. What behaviors could you change that would demonstrate you are fair to others? List these behaviors and monitor your performance in this area.

- Have you ever been the victim of someone's indiscretion? Perhaps someone told another person your salary information. How did it make you feel? Hopefully it reminded you of the importance of being discrete with confidential information.

- Review the types of information you encounter in your position. Which information should be held in confidence? Which information can be shared with others? Make this list, and if you have any confusion or uncertainty, discuss with your supervisor.

- Identify the trusting relationships you have. Identify those relationships that suffer from mistrust. What characterizes the differences in the relationships? How can you change your behaviors to repair any relationships that suffer from mistrust? What behaviors will you change in the future to establish and maintain trusting relationships?

- Have there been times when you blamed others for mistakes you have made? Have you ostracized and punished a team member for a mistake that would not have been made if you had adequately supervised the person? Think about your behaviors in this area. What behaviors can you change that would lead to a better environment for everyone and lead to an open discussion of mistakes as learning experiences.

- Identify times when you have not delivered a consistent message to others in the organization. Why didn't you deliver a consistent message? What were the effects? List the behaviors you would change to improve in this area.

258

Resources

Books

Badaracco, Joseph L. Jr. *Leading Quietly: An Unorthodox Guide to Doing the Right Thing.* Cambridge: Harvard Business School Press, 2002.

Baum, Herb. and Tammy. King. *The Transparent Leader.* New York: Harper Collins, 2005.

Blanchard, Ken. and Michael. O'Connor. *Managing by Values: How to Put Your Values Into Action for Extraordinary Results.* San Francisco: Berrett-Koehler, 2000.

Boxx, Rick. *How to Prosper in Business Without Sacrificing Integrity.* Cross Training Publishing, 2003.

Cloud, Henry. *Integrity: The Courage to Meet the Demands of Reality.* New York: Harper Business, 2009.

Collins, Denis. *Essentials of Business Ethics: Creating an Organization of High Integrity and Superior Performance.* San Francisco: Wiley, 2009.

Damon, William. *The Moral Advantage: How to Succeed in Business by Doing the Right Thing.* San Francisco, Berrett-Koehler, 2004.

Dickhart, Gary. *The Power of Integrity: An Ethical Approach to Business Management.* Charleston, SC: CreateSpace, 2012.

Erickson, Gary and Lois Lorentzen. *Raising the Bar: Integrity and Passion in Life and Business.* San Francisco: Jossey-Bass, 2012.

Gardner, Howard. *Responsibility at Work: How Leading Professionals Act (Or Don't Act) Responsibly.* San Francisco: Jossey-Bass, 2007.

Gostick, Adrian and Dana Telford. *The Integrity Advantage: How Taking the High Road Creates a Competitive Advantage in Business.* Gibbs Smith, 2003.

Hartley, Robert F. *Business Ethics: Mistakes and Successes.* New York: Wiley, 2005.

Hayes, Merwyn and Michael Comer. *Start With Humility: Lessons From America's Quiet CEOs on How to Build Trust and Inspire Followers.* The Greenleaf Center for Servant Leadership, 2010.

Heineman, Ben. *High Performance with High Integrity.* Cambridge: Harvard Business School Press, 2008.

Johnson, Larry and Bob Phillips. *Absolute Honesty: Building a Corporate Culture that Values Straight Talk and Rewards Integrity.* New York: AMACOM, 2004.

Killinger, Barbara. *Integrity: Doing the Right Thing for the Right Reason.* London: McGill-Queens University Press, 2007.

Klann, George. *Building Character: Strengthening the Heart of Good Leadership.* San Francisco: Jossey-Bass, 2006.

Kolp, Alan. and Peter Rea. *Leading with Integrity: Character-Based Leadership.* Mason, OH: Atomic Dog Publishing, 2005.

Kraemer, Harry. *From Values to Action: The Four Principles of Values-Based Leadership.* San Francisco: Jossey-Bass, 2011.

Lead Change Group. *The Character-Based Leader: Instigating a Leadership Revolution…One Person at a Time.* Dog Ear Publishing, 2012.

Rea, Scott. and Kenman. Wong. *Beyond Integrity: A Judeo-Christian Approach to Business Ethics.* Grand Rapids, MI: Zondervan, 2004.

Tichy, Noel. *The Ethical Challenge: How to Lead with Unyielding Integrity.* San Francisco: Jossey-Bass, 2003.

Watson, Charles E. *How Honesty Pays: Restoring Integrity to the Workplace.* Praeger, 2005.

Watts, Al. *Navigating Integrity.* Minneapolis: Brio Press, 2011.

Other Resources

An excellent article on business integrity can be found at http://www.webpronews.com/the-principles-of-business-integrity-2004-07.

An article on integrity for entrepreneurs can be found at http://blog.startupprofessionals.com/2012/03/5-ways-to-see-if-your-business.html.

Change – Integrity

Instructions

Using the table below and on the next page, refer to the items you listed in the Reflect – Integrity worksheet and identify specific actions you will take to improve your weaknesses or enhance your strengths in each area. Refer to the Develop and Renew section on the previous pages for action ideas, keeping in mind the needs of your current or aspired position.

You can have multiple actions for each item you intend to focus on. In the first section, list the actions that are specific to the items you listed in the Reflect – Integrity section. On the following page, list any actions you will take that are general to this competency and are related to more than one scored item. Finally, prioritize your actions based on the need for your current or aspired position. These actions will become part of your Personal Development Plan (PDP) for this competency in Appendix C.

Actions to Improve Weakness or Enhance Strength	Priority

Continue on next page.

Change – Integrity

Actions to Improve Weakness or Enhance Strength	Priority

Other Actions You Will Take Related to Integrity (not related to the identified strongest or weakest items)	Priority

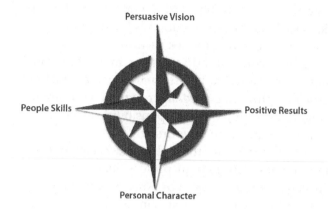

Persuasive Vision

People Skills — Positive Results

Personal Character

CHAPTER 24

Stress Management

(Personal Character)

"Its not stress that kills us, it is our reaction to it."

– Hans Selye

Stress is a constant part of life, and work often exacerbates a person's stress level. It is critical that leaders manage their stress level so their performance is strong. It is also important that leaders demonstrate to their peers and teams that they are managing their stress well.

When a leader exhibits an unhealthy level of stress, it affects their performance and the stress of those around her. If the leader is worried and exhibits behaviors that convey their fear and uncertainty, team members will follow suit and it will affect their behaviors and possibly create a culture of unhealthy stress within the organization.

You can manage stress by being organized, knowing how to achieve goals, and keeping things in perspective. We encourage leaders to be calm, especially in front of their peers and teams. If a leader is overly concerned and needs to vent some anger or frustration, they need to find a trusted partner who is a peer or above, someone who will allow them to voice their concerns without judgment. This is often all that is needed to reduce the stress level in an individual.

Poor stress management can also lead to health problems. Leaders need to be aware of their health, take steps to improve it (such as exercise), and watch for signs in their team members that stress is having a negative effect. Leaders should mentor team members who have difficulty managing stress by coaching them in relaxation techniques and listening to their concerns.

Leaders need to have work-life balance. This does not mean that you should balance your time equally – 8 hours of work must be balanced with 8 hours of home activities. It means you should strive to have a reasonable balance for *you*. Strive to have off-work time that is meaningful and free from the pressures of work. Every situation is different – some people have families, some engage in sports or fitness activities, some have more calming activities such as reading. Find something you are passionate about and invest your time into it.

At the same time, your off-work activities can be so hectic that they add to your stress at work. A study done by AT&T has shown that in situations such as this, the solution is to add more structure to your off-duty time. For example, if you are successful at work because you prioritize your tasks and delegate many to subordinates, think how you could do the same in your personal life. If you have home management responsibilities, how could you prioritize them? What tasks could you delegate to others – perhaps you can pay a neighborhood teenager to mow your lawn once a week. This would give you more time to devote to getting other responsibilities completed that only you can do. Or it will give you time to relax and take care of yourself.

Learn to say NO. It often seems that the most stressed people are those that take on every task that comes their way. Think about what you can say no to – both in your professional and personal lives. Do people take advantage of you because you don't say no? Are you agreeing to take on more unnecessary work at the expense of spending time with your family? This is a sign that stress is getting the best of you.

Much of stress relief comes from planning ahead and organizing yourself. Take the time to plan each week and each day. But know that you must be flexible and change your schedule when the need arises. This type of change to a schedule can be very stressful, but if you know in advance that it may happen and tell yourself that you will be flexible and adapt to the situation, stress is reduced.

Stress can grow from a variety of situations, people, or problems. It is important to remember when managing stress that we cannot control every situation, person, or problem. It is wise to identify those things you can control and take positive steps to do so. But it is equally important to understand what situations you cannot control and focus your energy elsewhere rather than dwell on situations outside your control.

Worry also induces stress. Think about what is worrying you. What can you do about each situation? If you can't do anything about it, don't spend time worrying about it. If you can attack a problem that is causing you worry (and stress), by all means take the time and effort to deal with the problem. Often, just doing something toward solving a problem or addressing a worry lowers stress.

If stress is a problem for you, review the chapters for Time Management (page 189), Planning (page 79), and Problem Solving (page 367).

Red Flag Behaviors

- You dread going to work or home each day because of overwhelming problems.
- You are often ill and sense that you are not in good physical condition.
- You frequently take work home and spend free time doing work that could have been accomplished at your place of business.
- You fail to plan each day or week and go from task to task focusing on what is in front of you.
- You often lose your temper.
- You worry about work at home, and you worry about your home life at work.
- You do not accept feedback or criticism well.

Case in Point

The doctor's assessment was serious. If Marc did not get a handle on his stress level, his chances for a heart attack would continue to climb. On top of that, Marc knew his stress affected his work performance and his marriage. Marc took his work performance and marriage seriously, along with his health. He realized that he needed to change his behaviors.

The doctor gave him some tips, such as watching his diet and exercising daily. Marc talked with his wife, and she promised to do what she could to help his diet and to give him positive reinforcement when he ate well. Together they joined the local health club and began to go each morning before work. Marc enjoyed his workouts, and they soon became a habit.

After the doctor's assessment, Marc talked to his boss, Julie. He told her that he loved his job, perhaps too much. He asked for her help in getting his work stress under control. Julie was aware that Marc took too much on and did not delegate much. She was careful to not take important projects from Marc, thereby damaging his esteem. Rather, she agreed to mentor him in techniques to manage his workload. She began by reviewing his responsibilities and pointing out those he could (and should) delegate to his team members. Marc would remember what she said at this point: "Marc, you are a leader now; let others do the work so you can manage them, support them, and provide resources to them – THAT is your job."

Additionally, Julie encouraged Marc to take short walks during the day to refresh himself and gather his thoughts. Julie also supported his workout schedule and told him that he should not rush his schedule to be at work early every day. Over the next few months, Marc could feel his stress level decrease. He was also more mentally alert and able to focus on the tasks at hand. His team was doing well with their new responsibilities, and he received positive feedback from the team on his new style.

On the home front, he felt that he was pulling his marriage back from the brink. He spent his evenings with his wife working on projects or visiting friends. His wife supported him well and could tell a difference in his attitude and physical abilities.

When Marc returned to the doctor after six months, she was amazed that his condition was greatly improved. His heart was stronger, his blood pressure was under control, and he was much more relaxed. Dr. Simpson congratulated Marc and told him to keep his new behaviors.

Notes for the Aspiring Leader

Simply aspiring to be a leader can be a stressful situation – so much to learn and so many opportunities to consider. By systematically developing your leadership skills and behaviors you can reduce your stress level so that it does not negatively impact your performance. Develop stress reduction habits early in your career so you can rely on them in the future.

Assess Your Current Location – Stress Management

(Personal Character)

Instructions: Read each of the skills and behaviors below. As objectively as possible, score yourself for each according to the following scale: 1 = strongly disagree; 2 = disagree; 3 = agree; 4 = strongly agree. If a behavior is not appropriate for your current or aspired position, check the N/A column.

SKILL OR BEHAVIOR	1	2	3	4	N/A
I remain calm in stressful situations.					
I can effectively handle multiple tasks at once.					
I control my response when being criticized or provoked.					
I display an appropriate sense of humor when dealing with difficult circumstances.					
I participate in an outside activity such as a hobby or exercise.					
I am careful not to display outward signs of stress to subordinates.					
I take time each day to think about my goals and my progress toward achieving them.					
I know what types of situations cause me the most stress.					
My behavior, when I am under stress, is a good model for my team to follow.					
I plan my day each morning.					
I do not become stressed if my plans are derailed.					
If I have stress from my personal life, I am able to compartmentalize it from my work situations.					

Continue on next page.

Assess Your Current Location – Stress Management

(Personal Character)

SKILL OR BEHAVIOR	1	2	3	4	N/A
I take adequate time to eat meals, especially lunch or other work-time meal.					
SCORES FOR STRESS MANAGEMENT (Total check marks in each column and multiply by the heading for the column. Record your scores here.)					

TOTAL SCORE FOR STRESS MANAGEMENT: _____

(Add scores from Columns 1, 2, 3, and 4. Record the total above and on the Master Score Sheet in Appendix A. Also, count the number of N/As and record on the Master Score Sheet.)

Reflect – Stress Management

Scoring Analysis

List Your Four Highest Scored Items (Strengths)

Note: If you have multiple items with the same high score, choose the four items that are most related to your current or aspired position.

Item	Score

List Your Four Lowest Scored Items (Weaknesses)

Note: If you have multiple items with the same low score, choose the four items that are most related to your current or aspired position.

Item	Score

Reflect – Stress Management Questions

Think about the following questions about stress management:

- What causes you more stress, your work world or your non-work life? Do you let stress from one area impact the other?

- Do you suffer from stress more at particular times of the day or year? Are you more stressed in some situations than others?

- Do you feel stressed when you are in the presence of, or working with, certain people?

- Do you practice any stress-reducing techniques that work for you?

- When you are very stressed, how is it manifested in your behaviors?

Develop – Stress Management

Develop and Renew

Consider the following development tactics to help improve your stress management. Identify which tactics would be valuable to include in your Personal Development Plan (PDP) if you choose to improve in this competency.

- Stress is inherent in every job and almost every part of life. It is important that leaders know how to manage their stress level so they can function well and not add to the stress of others. If you are under a lot of stress, take steps to resolve the issues that are causing it.

- Look for the signs that your stress level is impacting your performance. Do you frequently lose your temper? Are you dismissive of others? Are you working harder but getting fewer results? Do you react poorly in difficult situations? Are you getting sufficient sleep and exercise?

- Recognize what types of situations cause you stress. If you can recognize these situations, you can keep a rein on your emotions and look for a way to get through the situation without increasing your stress level substantially.

- Get organized. Set your goals and make progress toward them each day. Work to limit interruptions and inappropriate meetings that consume time. Leaders who are organized are less susceptible to increased stress.

- If you feel your stress level rising, take a break if possible. Go for a walk.

- Monitor your behaviors when under a lot of stress. Your team is watching you, and if you model good behaviors when under stress, they will attempt to do so as well.

- If you are under a lot of stress in your personal life, consider how to compartmentalize your problems. When you arrive at work, tell yourself that you will return to your personal problems when work is completed. If your personal stress level is very high, be proactive and talk to your leader about the situation as much as you feel comfortable. Even if your leader cannot help in the situation, they will be more understanding of how it can affect your performance for a period of time and may also be able to refer you to additional resources.

- Seek assistance or coaching if you are over your head with a project or with your current position responsibilities.

Resources

Books

Blanchard, Ken. *The One Minute Manager Balances Work and Life*. New York: William Morrow, 1999.

Charlesworth, Edward and Ronald Nathan. *Stress Management: A Comprehensive Guide to Wellness*. New York: Ballantine, 2004.

Davis, Martha et al. *The Relaxation and Stress Reduction Workbook*. Oakland, CA: New Harbinger, 2008.

Eriksen, Jorgen Bonde. *Walking on Water: Intuitive Leadership: Creating a Life Without Stress*. Amazon, 2012.

Harvard Business Review on Work and Life Balance. Boston: Harvard Review Press, 2000.

Jefferson, D. *Stress Relief Today: Causes, Effects, and Management Techniques That can Improve Your Life*. Charleston, SC: CreateSpace, 2012.

Kelly, Mathew. *Off Balance: Getting Beyond the Work Life Balance Myth to Personal and Professional Satisfaction*. New York: Hudson Street Press, 2011.

Lee, Deborah. *Having it All, Having Enough: How to Create a Career/Family Balance that Works for You*. New York: AMACOM, 1997.

Maravelas, Anna. *How To Reduce Workplace Conflict and Stress*. Pompton Plains, NJ: Career Press, 2005.

Price, Graham. *Introducing Stress Management: A Practical Guide*. Icon, 2013.

Quik, James Campbell; et al. *Preventive Stress Management in Organizations*. Washington, DC: American Psychological Association, 2012.

Sawi, Beth. *Coming Up for Air: How to Build a Balanced Life in a Workaholic World*. New York: Hyperion, 2000.

Wheeler, Claire. *10 Simple Solutions to Stress: How to Tame Tension and Start Enjoying Your Life*. Oakland, CA: 2007.

Websites

Stress management is covered extensively by Wikipedia at
http://en.wikipedia.org/wiki/Stress_management.

Help Guide provides excellent stress management tips at:
http://www.helpguide.org/mental/stress_management_relief_coping.htm.

MedicineNet offers doctors' tips on how to control and manage stress at http://www.medicinenet.com/stress_management_techniques/article.htm.

Other Resources

The Mayo Clinic is an excellent resource on stress management. See http://www.mayoclinic.com/health/stress-management/MY00435.

Change – Stress Management

Instructions

Using the table below and on the next page, refer to the items you listed in the Reflect – Stress Management worksheet and identify specific actions you will take to improve your weaknesses or enhance your strengths in each area. Refer to the Develop and Renew section on the previous pages for action ideas, keeping in mind the needs of your current or aspired position.

You can have multiple actions for each item you intend to focus on. In the first section, list the actions that are specific to the items you listed in the Reflect – Stress Management section. On the following page, list any actions you will take that are general to this competency and are related to more than one scored item. Finally, prioritize your actions based on the need for your current or aspired position. These actions will become part of your Personal Development Plan (PDP) for this competency in Appendix C.

Actions to Improve Weakness or Enhance Strength	Priority

Continue on next page.

273

Change – Stress Management

Actions to Improve Weakness or Enhance Strength	Priority

Other Actions You Will Take Related to Stress Management (not related to the identified strongest or weakest items)	Priority

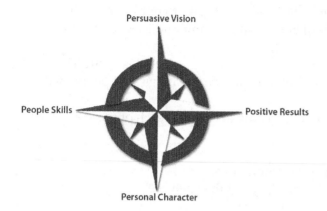

Persuasive Vision

People Skills — Positive Results

Personal Character

CHAPTER 25

Trust

(Personal Character)

"To be trusted is a greater compliment than being loved."

– George MacDonald

An important job of any leader is to trust others and be a leader who can be trusted. Trust is confidence borne of two dimensions: character and competence. Character includes your integrity, motive, and intent with people. Competence includes your capabilities, skills, results, and track record. Both dimensions are vital.

David Horsager defines trust as, "The confident belief in someone or something. To do what is right, to deliver what is promised, to be the same way every time, whatever the circumstances." (Horsager, 2012) People need to see and observe behavior before they trust because they bring their own history of trusting or mistrusting other leaders to the situation.

Stephen Covey describes trust as, "not some soft, illusive quality that you either have or don't have; rather, trust is a pragmatic, tangible, actionable asset that you can create…" (Covey, 2008) We strongly believe this and agree that trust can be created, MUST be created by any successful leader. Once trust is established, it can be very fragile and the leader must be constantly on guard to not damage the trusting relationship. If you want to be trusted, simply be trust<u>worthy</u>. The pressures are sometimes great to act otherwise. If you succumb, you will lose the trust of others and may never get it back.

Tell the truth. This is the first maxim of building and maintaining trust. It is not as easy as it may seem, however. Trust can easily be damaged when people discover you have been dishonest with them; they conclude your words cannot be trusted in the future.

There may be times when you cannot be totally honest. Sometimes you are legally bound to remain silent (Why was Joe fired last week?). Sometimes you are negotiating and cannot reveal your position. In those cases, consider saying, "I can't discuss that at this time." People may not like it, but they will not feel betrayed when the outcome is revealed. Most people will respect that you maintain confidence.

Keep your promises and commitments. If you say you will do something, do it. If you promise to show up, be there. If you say you will deliver high quality, do not skimp.

Another way to maintain trust is to put the interests of others ahead of your own. When people know you are looking out for them, they will believe in your intentions even when you have hard news to deliver or need them to put in extra effort.

Always behave ethically. People trust you when they know you are safe to deal with. They observe how you treat them and others. Do the right thing in all your dealings, and people will get it. They will know you are trustworthy.

David Horsager (2012) describes eight pillars of trust. Think about how each of these attributes applies to your situation:

1. Clarity – People trust the clear and mistrust the ambiguous.
2. Compassion – People put faith in those who care beyond themselves.
3. Character – People notice who does what is right over what is easy.
4. Competency – Knowing what you are doing gives people confidence.
5. Commitment – People believe in those who stand through adversity.
6. Connection – People want to follow, buy from, and be around friends.
7. Contribution – People respond to results.
8. Consistency – People like to know what they are getting in a leader.

To summarize, trust should be of paramount concern to every leader. Without it, you are viewed with suspicion. Trust is earned, and it is not always easy. A recent study found that only 51% of employees have trust and confidence in their leadership. In addition and more profoundly, only 36% of employees believe their leaders act with honesty and integrity, two key ingredients of a trusting relationship.

The bar is set high. We encourage you to focus on developing and maintaining trust in those around you.

Red Flag Behaviors

- You do not treat people fairly.
- You overlook misconduct of others, including those on your team.
- You avoid building relationships with others.
- You make decisions or take actions based on your self interest.
- You gossip about other people, including your leaders.
- You blame others for your mistakes.
- You do not tell the truth about situations or other people.

Case in Point

Paul's team needed to trust each other. Each person's work depended on the other's performance. If one person did not trust another, the whole process could fall apart. As the leader of the mountain community's search-and-rescue unit, the team was on call for any lost hiker or accident in the mountains. They often had to climb to precarious ledges to rescue injured people.

When the team first assembled two years ago (prior to this it was a volunteer organization with no leader, just people who wanted to help), Paul understood the importance of trust in this dangerous work. He started training by putting each team member into difficult situations where the help of their teammates was required.

To further the trust level, he provided opportunities for the team to socialize and get to know each other. He wanted them to bond like brothers and sisters. He also developed a code of conduct for the team. With input from the team, the code clearly stated the elements of trust. Team members would always be honest and respectful. They would be mission focused, but not put each other into dangerous positions without thinking things through. If there were issues between any team members they had a responsibility to immediately come to Paul for resolution. Any team member who did not live up to the code of conduct would be dismissed.

Practice and socializing were key to the team's success. Rarely did they encounter a situation they had not practiced. They knew what needed to be done in almost every situation and had the confidence they could trust each other, even in the most difficult or dangerous situations.

Notes for the Aspiring Leader

Focus on developing trust with others. More than any other competency, this one is essential. Get to know others and build relationships. Always be truthful. Always have pure motives and intentions. Develop habits now that reinforce that you can be trusted.

Assess Your Current Location – Trust

(Personal Character)

Instructions: Read each of the skills and behaviors below. As objectively as possible, score yourself for each according to the following scale: 1 = strongly disagree; 2 = disagree; 3 = agree; 4 = strongly agree. If a behavior is not appropriate for your current or aspired position, check the N/A column.

SKILL OR BEHAVIOR	1	2	3	4	N/A
I consistently tell the truth or, when unable to do so for legal or confidentiality reasons, explain that it cannot be discussed.					
I treat people with respect and dignity.					
I do not tolerate misconduct in the organization.					
I put the interests of others ahead of my own.					
I do what is right over what is easiest.					
I strive to always acknowledge the contributions of others.					
I strive to bring clarity to ambiguous situations.					
I disclose personal information as part of dialog with others, as appropriate.					
My actions cause people to have confidence in me.					
My motives are clear to others and they are right for the situation.					
I keep track of and fulfill commitments.					
I do not participate in or tolerate gossip and personally damaging conversations.					
I hold others accountable for their mistakes.					

Continue on next page.

Assess Your Current Location – Trust
(Personal Character)

SKILL OR BEHAVIOR	1	2	3	4	N/A
I admit mistakes.					
SCORES FOR TRUST (Total check marks in each column and multiply by the heading for the column. Record your scores here.)					

TOTAL SCORE FOR TRUST: _____

(Add scores from Columns 1, 2, 3, and 4. Record the total above and on the Master Score Sheet in Appendix A. Also, count the number of N/As and record on the Master Score Sheet.)

Reflect – Trust

Scoring Analysis

List Your Four Highest Scored Items (Strengths)

Note: If you have multiple items with the same high score, choose the four items that are most related to your current or aspired position.

Item	Score

List Your Four Lowest Scored Items (Weaknesses)

Note: If you have multiple items with the same low score, choose the four items that are most related to your current or aspired position.

Item	Score

Reflect – Trust Questions

Think about the following questions about trust:

- Think of some people you do not trust. Why? How could each restore your trust if given the opportunity?

- What kind of behaviors could a person demonstrate that would damage your trust in them?

- If a leader is not trusted by his/her direct reports, what are some of the consequences?

- How important is it for leaders to know what information can be shared and what cannot be shared with others?

- What does it mean to be authentic?

Develop – Trust

Develop and Renew

Consider the following development tactics to help improve your skills and behaviors that engender trust. Identify which tactics would be valuable to include in your Personal Development Plan (PDP) if you choose to improve in this competency.

- Be a model in telling the truth. If someone tries to get you to not tell the truth (to a customer or employee), do not become a part of it. It is one thing to not be able to disclose something; it is another to tell a lie.

- Keep track of your commitments. Not fulfilling a commitment, even if it is trivial, can damage a trusting relationship. At a minimum, get back to the person to ensure that they know you are aware of the commitment and will get to it as soon as possible. Remember, what may be trivial to you may be very important to the other person.

- As a leader, you should not participate in gossip, whether about other employees or customers. Be sure that, if you hear gossip, you take steps to point out this is poor behavior on anyone's part and that you will not tolerate it in your organization. If you participate in gossip, you give license to others to do the same, and the entire organization may be tainted.

- Sustain trust by putting the interests of others before your own. When people know you are looking out for them, they will believe your intentions even when you have hard news to deliver or need them to put in extra efforts.

- Be authentic. If people know you are consistent and what they see is what they get, people will develop trust. Be clear about your intentions and motives. If people sense that you are being ambiguous, they will question your intentions and motives.

- Do not tolerate misconduct in your team or your organization. We like to think that we do not tolerate bad behaviors, but in reality we often look the other way. Remember, when there is bad or unethical behavior, the leader's response is what many people are observing.

- Businesses often lose trust, just by not doing the right things. For example, when leaders get bonuses during a time when the messaging to employees is to cut costs, the organization damages trust with employees. Watch out for inadvertent actions that damage trust.

- Treat people with dignity and respect. Even if you are angry with someone and need to give them a difficult message regarding their performance, still treat them with dignity and respect.

- Trust is also the foundation of a collaborative culture. Leaders cannot expect teams to collaborate well to solve problems or achieve goals if the individuals that make up the team do not trust each other.

- Be accountable and hold others accountable. If you make a mistake, admit the mistake and move forward. If others make mistakes, hold them accountable. This doesn't mean that you blow things out of proportion and embarrass them in front of others. Accountability may be as simple as privately pointing out the mistake to them.

- To develop trust, you need to disclose information about yourself; then you can expect reciprocity from others. Share information, but be careful because sharing too much private information can be harmful.

- Strive to always acknowledge the contributions of others.

Resources

Books

Boverie, Patricia and Michael Kroth. *Transforming Work: The Five Keys to Achieving Trust, Commitment & Passion in the Workplace.* Cambridge, MA: Perseus Publishing, 2001.

Covey, Stephen. *The Speed of Trust: The One thing That Changes Everything.* New York: The Free Press, 2008.

Deems, Richard and Terri Deems. *Leading in Tough Times: The Manager's Guide to Responsibility, Trust, and Motivation.* Amherst, MA: HRD Press, 2003.

Feltman, Charles and Sue Hammond. *The Thin Book of Trust; An Essential Primer for Building Trust at Work.* Bend, OR: Thin Book Publishing, 2008.

Golin, Al. *Trust or Consequences: Build Trust Today Or Lose Your Market Tomorrow.* New York: AMACOM, 2006.

Hall, Vanessa. *The Truth About Trust in Business: How to Enrich the Bottom Line, Improve Retention, and Build Valuable Relationships for Success.* Austin, TX: Emerald, 2009.

Hayes, Merwyn and Michael Coner. *Start with Humility: Lessons From America's Quiet CEOs on How to Build Truest and Inspire Followers.* The Greenleaf Center for Servant Growth, 2010.

Horsager, David. *The Trust Edge: How Top Leaders Gain Faster Results, Deeper Relationships and a Stronger Bottom Line.* New York: Free Press, 2012.

Hurley, Robert. *The Decision to Trust: How Leaders Create High-Trust Organizations*. San Francisco: Jossey-Bass, 2011.

Morgan, Nick. *Trust Me: Four Steps to Authenticity and Charisma*. San Francisco: Jossey-Bass, 2008.

Peppers, Don and Martha Rogers. *Extreme Trust: Honesty as a Competitive Advantage*. New York: Portfolio Hardcover, 2012.

Reina, Dennis and Michelle Reina. *Rebuilding Trust in the Workplace: Seven Steps to Renew Confidence, Commitment and Energy*. Berrett Koehler, 2010.

Ryan, Kathleen and Daniel Oestreich. *Driving Fear Out of the Workplace: Creating the High-Trust, High Performance Organization*. San Francisco: Jossey-Bass, 1998.

Tracy, Diane and William Morin. *Truth, Trust, and the Bottom Line*. Chicago: Dearborn Trade Publishing, 2001.

Websites

An interesting concept document on The Trust Barometer can be found at http://www.edelman.com/trust/2011/.

Other Resources

An excellent article on building trust by the late Stephen Covey is located at http://www.leadershipnow.com/CoveyOnTrust.html.

This site offers numerous articles on trust at http://trustedadvisor.com/articles/trust-in-business-the-core-concepts.

See Horsager's website at: http://www.theTrustEdge.com.

Change – Trust

Instructions

Using the table below and on the next page, refer to the items you listed in the Reflect – Trust worksheet and identify specific actions you will take to improve your weaknesses or enhance your strengths in each area. Refer to the Develop and Renew section on the previous pages for action ideas, keeping in mind the needs of your current or aspired position.

You can have multiple actions for each item you intend to focus on. In the first section, list the actions that are specific to the items you listed in the Reflect – Trust section. On the following page, list any actions you will take that are general to this competency and are related to more than one scored item. Finally, prioritize your actions based on the need for your current or aspired position. These actions will become part of your Personal Development Plan (PDP) for this competency in Appendix C.

Actions to Improve Weakness or Enhance Strength	Priority

Continue on next page.

Change – Trust

Actions to Improve Weakness or Enhance Strength	Priority

Other Actions You Will Take Related to Trust (not related to the identified strongest or weakest items)	Priority

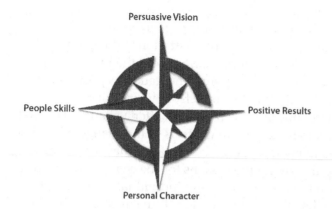

Persuasive Vision

People Skills — Positive Results

Personal Character

CHAPTER 26

Change Leadership

(People Skills)

"The rate of change is not going to slow down anytime soon. If anything, competition in most industries will probably speed up even more in the next few decades."

– John Kotter

Change is a constant in many organizations and affects leaders. However, leaders often distinguish themselves by being the initiators and implementers of change. We coach a significant number of people through change, either as the subject of a change or as the implementer of a change. It is important that people recognize changes that they go through or are tasked to lead others through.

Change leadership must be implemented on two levels. First, the leader must determine if a change is appropriate, what the change will be, how and when it will be put into place, and the desired effects of the change. At the second level, the leader must know how to implement the change and lead through the *transition*. The transition is what happens after the change is initiated. In other words, change is often instantaneous when it is announced. At that point the transition begins. People will either embrace the change and adapt to it or they will resist it, either overtly or covertly.

There should always be a good business case for a change, although sometimes it is based on a reaction to outside factors such as the economy. Too often in our coaching practice, we find leaders who do not think through a proposed change or understand how to implement it to achieve the desired results. Planning for change is critical. For significant changes - such as reorganization - developing a change plan is important if only to cause the leader to think through all the options and effects of the change. Change planning is often difficult because it must be kept confidential.

Leaders should also develop and communicate a strategy and vision for the change. The vision should be simple, easily understood by different audiences, and delivered in multiple formats.

When change comes from elsewhere, such as higher up the corporate chain, it is even more critical for leaders to quickly understand its effects on their part of the organization. If the leader is not part of the change-planning process, it is tempting to display frustration and negativity. Be careful not to do this. You should focus your attention on getting clarity about the purpose and goals for the change, along with as much of the detail regarding implementation as possible, so you have answers to the many questions that will undoubtedly come from your team.

It is the leader's responsibility to guide the team through the transition after a change. The first step is to thoroughly plan the change and consider all the potential effects of the change. Planning for change cannot be underestimated; if it is, too many unanticipated obstacles may arise. The next step is to communicate the change thoroughly, giving the reasons for the change, the process of implementation, and the anticipated effects on the organization and individuals. The leader should then answer any questions the team may have about the change. To be most effective, be prepared to answer any questions that may arise.

Finally, monitor the change through the transition. Is the change having the desired effects? How are people reacting to the change? Who is embracing the change and doing their best to implement it? Who is not supporting the change? What are the obstacles that are presented that were not anticipated? Closely monitor the team and help those who are having difficulty to be successful through the transition.

Change is a fact of everyday life in organizations, and leaders must be adept at all phases of change leadership. Change is usually positive and a process to help the organization survive and thrive in a competitive and demanding environment. If change is not managed effectively, people likely will feel insecure, conflict may arise, and team dynamics may be affected. Therefore, it is important that leaders understand the change process and aid their teams through the transition.

Red Flag Behaviors

- You complain about changes that come from the leadership of your organization.
- When you are thinking about making a change, you discuss it with others on your team, even if it involves other people on the team. You are not discreet.
- You get frustrated when others on your team do not adjust immediately to changes.
- You do not explain the rationale for a change when announcing it to your team.
- You make changes quickly, and often based on emotion and not thorough thought or consideration.

Case in Point

Sarah left the Senior Leadership Retreat with a hundred thoughts running through her head. The reorganization made sense, and no jobs would be eliminated, but it would cause a lot of turmoil in her department. Three of her best technicians would move to the quality department, and she would get twelve new engineers suited for the upcoming project. The reorganization would be announced in two days, so she had her work cut out for her.

First, she reviewed her entire staff and thought about how she would announce the reorganization with the least impact. Next, she developed a plan to move the three technicians. She wanted to have a staff party to give them a good farewell, along with welcoming the new engineers. She also wanted to meet with each of the departing and arriving team members in one-on-one sessions in the first week.

Logistics was an issue. Since her staff was growing, she needed to figure out where everyone would be located. Her solution was to delegate the problem to a small team that would provide recommendations to her.

She anticipated questions and concerns that would come up during the announcement. On the morning of the meeting, she spent some quiet time gathering her thoughts. The announcement went well, and she had anticipated and had answers to all but two questions; those she promised to get an answer within the next 24 hours.

Over the coming weeks, there were some hiccups, but because she had planned well the moves went smoothly. She focused on getting to know the new engineers and worked hard to identify anyone who was having difficulty with the transition.

Two of the engineers were having difficulty through the transition. One had interpersonal issues with some of the other team members, and conflict was building beneath the surface. Sarah recognized this and worked with the person to build new relationships. The other engineer did not believe the change was in the best interests of the organization and continually complained to team members. Sarah was a bit more harsh in this instance. After three warnings (and detailed discussions about the change), the person continued to complain. At that point, Sarah negotiated with his previous manager to take him back and provide another engineer.

Notes for the Aspiring Leader

Get used to change. It is a staple of any organization, and leaders not only adapt to it, they lead others through it. Focus your attention on how you and others are led through change. Learn about transitions and how they help you and others support and grow from change.

Assess Your Current Location – Change Leadership

(People Skills)

Instructions: Read each of the skills and behaviors below. As objectively as possible, score yourself for each according to the following scale: 1 = strongly disagree; 2 = disagree; 3 = agree; 4 = strongly agree. If a behavior is not appropriate for your current or aspired position, check the N/A column.

SKILL OR BEHAVIOR	1	2	3	4	N/A
I understand that change affects many things, including processes, people, and outcomes.					
I effectively plan the implementation of changes that come from other sources.					
I effectively plan self-initiated changes.					
I effectively communicate the vision and strategy of a change to team members and other stakeholders, including reason, expectations, and anticipated results.					
I display a positive attitude toward change when communicating with the team and other stakeholders.					
I work to lead team members successfully through each phase of the transition.					
I clearly answer questions about change from team members and stakeholders.					
I maintain discretion regarding potential changes, as appropriate.					
I coach team members who are having difficulty through a transition.					
I evaluate the business case for a change prior to planning and implementing.					

Continue on next page.

Assess Your Current Location – Change Leadership

(People Skills)

SKILL OR BEHAVIOR	1	2	3	4	N/A
I work to gain clarity on changes driven from higher or external sources.					
SCORES FOR CHANGE LEADERSHIP (Total check marks in each column and multiply by the heading for the column. Record your scores here.)					

TOTAL SCORE FOR CHANGE LEADERSHIP: _____

(Add scores from Columns 1, 2, 3, and 4. Record the total above and on the Master Score Sheet in Appendix A. Also, count the number of N/As and record on the Master Score Sheet.)

Reflect – Change Leadership

Scoring Analysis

List Your Four Highest Scored Items (Strengths)

Note: If you have multiple items with the same high score, choose the four items that are most related to your current or aspired position.

Item	Score

List Your Four Lowest Scored Items (Weaknesses)

Note: If you have multiple items with the same low score, choose the four items that are most related to your current or aspired position.

Item	Score

Reflect – Change Leadership Questions

Think about the following questions about change leadership:

- How do you feel when changes are made that you think are wrong?

- As a leader, what role do you have in supporting changes that come down from above?

- What could a leader do to make a change easier for a team?

- How do you get clarity about a change that comes from above?

- Do you make spur-of-the-moment changes or do you think them through? How do you communicate changes to your team?

Develop – Change Leadership

Develop and Renew

Consider the following development tactics to help improve your skills and behaviors in change leadership. Identify which tactics would be valuable to include in your Personal Development Plan (PDP) if you choose to improve in this competency.

- A business case for change should be developed and assessed before planning and implementing a change. Don't change just for change's sake; build a business case for the change and get other trusted opinions. The business case should evaluate the effects of the change in both the short term and long term. If a change does not make business sense, don't make the change and look for other solutions.

- Change planning is critical to the success of a change. As coaches, we have seen many changes have a negative impact because they were not planned in detail. When planning for a change, explore all the ramifications that the change will have on people, processes, and outcomes. Change planning also involves planning how people will be led through the transition and how you and other leaders will lead the change initiative. Be as detailed as possible in your change planning.

- Change is instant. Transition takes time and effort. As a leader, your most difficult work will be leading people through the transition. Some people may have difficulty getting through the transition and need coaching or other assistance. Effective leaders monitor the progress of people through each part of the transition and step in with coaching when needed.

- Some people cannot get through the transition and may self select out of the change. Understand that some people will long for the old way of doing things and not be able to adapt to the new methods. Provide them every opportunity to succeed through the transition – coaching, mentoring, and opportunities to talk with you and others about their feelings. However, if someone opts out of the change because of difficulties getting through the transition, enable them to move to another part of the organization or out of the organization without embarrassment.

- Whether the change comes from higher or external sources, leaders should support the change as much as possible. Leaders do not speak negatively to their team about a change. If the leader has misgivings about a change, it is their responsibility to go to the source of the change to gain a better understanding of the reasons for the change. In our coaching practice, we are often a safe venue for a leader to vent their opposition to a change from above. After venting their anger or disagreement, we then work with the person to build their support for the change. In some cases, our coachee sees the change differently and knows that it will not

294

work for the benefit of the organization. We must often encourage and help frame a leader's conversation with the source of the change to either modify or stop it from occurring.

- Sometimes discretion about the details of a change is required. Leaders must use discretion and only disclose what they have been given authorization to disclose. This is especially difficult to do if you object to the change because your urge is to begin building a case against it. However, you must follow the rules and voice your opposition only to those that are part of the change leadership team.

- Develop a communication plan to prepare for announcing a change. Who needs to speak? What is the message to be given? Who should receive the message? Think through how, what, when, and to whom the change message is to be given. In our coaching practice, we often work with leaders to develop these messages. The communication plan should not be done in isolation; others can provide feedback and ideas on how to overcome any potential obstacles.

Resources

Books

Aitkin, Paul and Malcolm Higgs. *Developing Change Leaders: The Principles and Practices of Change Leadership Development.* Oxford: Butterworth-Heinemann, 2009.

Anderson, Dean. *Beyond Change Management: How to Achieve Breakthrough Results Through Conscious Change Leadership.* New York: Pfeiffer, 2010.

Baca, Claudia. *Project Manager's Spotlight on Change Management.* San Francisco: Jossey-Bass, 2005.

Bridges, William. *Managing Transitions: Making the Most of Change.* Cambridge: Da Capo Lifelong Books, 2009.

Duncan, Rodger Dean. *Change-Friendly Leadership: How to Transform Good Intentions into Great Performance,* Carmichael, CA: Maxwell, 2012.

Fullan, Michael. *Motion Leadership: The Skinny on Becoming Change Savvy.* Corwin, 2009.

_____. *Change Leader: Learning to Do What Matters Most.* San Francisco: Jossey-Bass, 2011.

_____. *The Six Secrets of Change: What the Best Leaders Do to Help Their Organizations Survive and Thrive.* San Francisco: Jossey-Bass, 2011.

Harvard Business Review. *HBR's 10 Must Reads on Change Management.* Boston: Harvard Business Review Press, 2011.

Herold, David and Donald Fedor. *Change the Way You Lead Change: Leadership Strategies that REALLY Work.* Palo Alto: Stanford Business, 2010.

Hesselbein, Frances. and Rob Johnston. *On Leading Change: A Leader to Leader Guide.* San Francisco: Jossey-Bass, 2002.

Joiner, William. and Stephen Josephs. *Leadership Agility: Five Levels of Mastery for Anticipating and Initiating Change.* San Francisco: Jossey-Bass, 2006.

Kotter, John. *Leading Change.* Cambridge: Harvard Business School Press, 1996.

Pearce, Terry. *Leading Out Loud: Inspiring Change Through Authentic Communications.* San Francisco: Jossey-Bass, 2003.

Rowland, Deborah. and Malcolm Higgs. *Sustaining Change: Leadership that Works.* New York: Wiley, 2008.

Tozer, Jeremy. *Leading Through Leaders: Driving Strategy, Execution, and Change.* London: Kogan Page, 2012.

Websites

Excellent articles can be found at http://changeleadership.com/.

Other Resources

Benchmark Learning International offers a 1-day Change Leadership workshop for your company or organization. For more information, contact us at +1 (208) 433-9093 or at ben.m@benchmarkli.com.

The following is an excellent article on effective change:
http://www.innovationexcellence.com/blog/2010/08/20/six-characteristics-of-highly-effective-change-leaders/

Change – Change Leadership

Instructions

Using the table below and on the next page, refer to the items you listed in the Reflect – Change Leadership worksheet and identify specific actions you will take to improve your weaknesses or enhance your strengths in each area. Refer to the Develop and Renew section on the previous pages for action ideas, keeping in mind the needs of your current or aspired position.

You can have multiple actions for each item you intend to focus on. In the first section, list the actions that are specific to the items you listed in the Reflect – Change Leadership section. On the following page, list any actions you will take that are general to this competency and are related to more than one scored item. Finally, prioritize your actions based on the need for your current or aspired position. These actions will become part of your Personal Development Plan (PDP) for this competency in Appendix C.

Actions to Improve Weakness or Enhance Strength	Priority

Continue on next page.

Change – Change Leadership

Actions to Improve Weakness or Enhance Strength	Priority

Other Actions You Will Take Related to Change Leadership (not related to the identified strongest or weakest items)	Priority

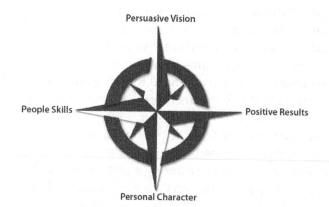

Persuasive Vision

People Skills — Positive Results

Personal Character

CHAPTER 27

Commitment to

Diversity

(People Skills)

"Strength lies in differences, not in similarities."

– Stephen Covey

Diversity is about empowering people to be exactly who they were created to be. An organization capitalizes on the strengths of each employee. Leaders must display equal respect to individuals regardless of race, age, culture, gender – and many other differences for that matter. The world is diverse and the workplace is a reflection of that diversity. We have a responsibility to understand those who are different from us. In addition to the commonly understood diversity issues mentioned above, leaders should also take steps to learn the differences individuals have in body language, communication styles, work styles, problem solving, and thought processes.

To obtain a competitive edge, leaders need to mold their workforce into teams that use the full potential of every individual. Failing to accept the diversity of others often keeps group members from achieving team goals. Embracing diversity is the first step toward building a great team.

Most organizations have clear policies regarding equal and fair treatment of their workers. It is the leader's responsibility to understand these policies, support them, and enforce a zero tolerance toward any infractions of these policies. Leaders are responsible for fostering a fair treatment environment throughout the organization. It is not only your responsibility to ensure that you are treating everyone fairly, but also to monitor the other leaders of your organization and be courageous enough to confront unfair treatment, regardless of its source in the organization.

Leaders must respect the diversity of ideas presented by others and recognize the benefits this diversity brings to the organization. In fact, the most successful leaders are those who encourage a diversity of ideas that expand the options available for decisions or actions. Team members should feel comfortable presenting ideas, objections and alternatives without fear of reprisal.

One area that is often overlooked concerning diversity is the differences in approach to problems or situations based on age and experience. The effective leader takes advantage of the experience older employees bring to the table and also the fresh, often creative approach of younger workers. Also, research has shown that gender-diverse teams are more creative and innovative. Consider your own stereotypes in these situations. Do you need to change how you assemble teams to gain greater creativity? Do you need to develop a mentoring program so that older and younger employees can learn more from each other?

Commitment to diversity goes beyond adhering to written policies or programs. Simply enforcing government or corporate regulations will not get you the best results. People need to see that the leader bases fairness on a personal commitment. Simply offering a class on diversity does not erase biases. Unfairness, in any form, is not acceptable and can be a glaring blemish on your leadership performance. Try to see people as individuals and not as members of a specific group. Get out of your comfort zone, and think about your own subtle biases and how they affect how you treat people. Consciously spend more of your time with people around you who are different. Solicit the points of view of each person.

Red Flag Behaviors

- You do not treat people fairly.
- You have personal biases and prejudices that impact your decisions.
- You do not learn and appreciate the backgrounds of others.
- You create divisiveness between people and teams.
- You do not think diversity of backgrounds or ideas contributes to success.
- You do not address biases of others or unfair practices.

Case in Point

Larry owned a small business known for its commitment to diversity. He actively reached out to all communities in his area to seek the best employees. He personally interviewed each person to determine not only their technical skills, but what else they could bring to his business.

His company policy was to hire the best and use each employee in the best way possible – for the benefit of his business and the individual. His policy also included a statement that no one would be discriminated against in hiring, promotion, or other opportunity due to any reason other than qualifications and performance. He did not tolerate any deviation from his policies on diversity.

His policy wasn't simply a statement, it was enforced. Just last year Larry observed one of his sales team members treating a female customer rudely. On investigation, he learned that this was a pattern with the sales person. He immediately fired the person and held a company meeting to explain what happened and to reiterate his policy.

In particular, Larry sought out those who brought creativity to his business. Selling home furnishings was a competitive industry, and he felt strongly that creative employees would come up with ideas to differentiate his business. He was proven right by the results of some of the sales campaigns suggested by his team. Even in accounting, he assigned a creative person to review the business processes and his company benefitted from their recommendations.

Over time, his sales record underscored his commitment to diversity. Not only did he sell furniture to those in the immediate area, but word spread and shoppers from diverse communities some distance away traveled to his store to purchase, simply because they knew they were welcome in his store.

Notes for the Aspiring Leader

Focus on the benefits of diversity in a team. It is this diversity of backgrounds, culture, and ideas that give life to exciting initiatives. Learn about others and their background. Seek out others who may think differently to provide feedback about your project and infuse ideas that can make a difference.

Assess Your Current Location – Commitment to Diversity

(People Skills)

Instructions: Read each of the skills and behaviors below. As objectively as possible, score yourself for each according to the following scale: 1 = strongly disagree; 2 = disagree; 3 = agree; 4 = strongly agree. If a behavior is not appropriate for your current or aspired position, check the N/A column.

SKILL OR BEHAVIOR	1	2	3	4	N/A
I display equal respect to individuals regardless of age, race, culture, or gender.					
I foster a fair treatment environment across the organization.					
I promote a one-team culture in the organization.					
I support diversity-awareness programs within the organization.					
I recognize the talent and unique contributions of every individual despite differences.					
I recognize and work to overcome any personal biases or prejudices.					
I hold zero tolerance for others displaying bias or prejudice in the workplace.					
I actively seek to understand the backgrounds of those from a different culture.					
I work to create an inclusive team spirit where every member feels a part of the team.					
I seek to attract those from a variety of backgrounds to the organization or team.					

Continue on next page.

Assess Your Current Location – Commitment to Diversity
(People Skills)

SKILL OR BEHAVIOR	1	2	3	4	N/A
I strive to understand cultural differences in body language, communication, work style, problem solving, and thought process.					
SCORES FOR COMMITMENT TO DIVERSITY (Total check marks in each column and multiply by the heading for the column. Record your scores here.)					

TOTAL SCORE FOR COMMITMENT TO DIVERSITY: _____

(Add scores from Columns 1, 2, 3, and 4. Record the total above and on the Master Score Sheet in Appendix A. Also, count the number of N/As and record on the Master Score Sheet.)

Reflect – Commitment to Diversity

Scoring Analysis

List Your Four Highest Scored Items (Strengths)

Note: If you have multiple items with the same high score, choose the four items that are most related to your current or aspired position.

Item	Score

List Your Four Lowest Scored Items (Weaknesses)

Note: If you have multiple items with the same low score, choose the four items that are most related to your current or aspired position.

Item	Score

Reflect – Commitment to Diversity Questions

Think about the following questions about commitment to diversity:

- What is meant by a diversity of ideas?

- Does everyone have biases of some sort? If so, what are yours? Are you biased toward or away from a particular group of people?

- Does commitment to diversity mean that you treat everyone exactly the same?

- Think about the various people on your team or your peers. What makes each different from the others? What are the strengths and weaknesses of each?

- If you observe someone being treated unfairly, what do you do?

- How does commitment to diversity help an organization?

Develop – Commitment to Diversity

Develop and Renew

Consider the following development tactics to help improve in your commitment to diversity. Identify which tactics would be valuable to include in your Personal Development Plan (PDP) if you choose to improve in this competency.

- Learn about your organization's diversity-awareness programs and be proactive in your support. If you feel the organization is weak in its diversity-support programs, bring to the attention of leadership.

- Consider your response when you see unequal treatment of individuals in your organization because of age, race, culture, or gender. How do you react? What steps could you take to create a culture that does not tolerate unequal respect and treatment?

- Identify some individuals in your work group. What are their strengths and unique contributions?

- In what ways could you communicate your commitment to diversity to others?

- In the future, when a project is completed or an initiative accomplished, take the time to think about the diversity of cultures, viewpoints, and behavioral styles that contributed to the success. Then compliment those involved, regardless of their culture, viewpoint, or behavioral style.

- Does your organization simply state its commitment to diversity or do you have programs that proactively ensure that diversity is a true commitment? If you simply state you are committed to diversity, consider how you could lead the effort to have a valid, proactive diversity program.

- Are there peer leaders in your organization who are divisive? If so, consider how you can mentor them to become more supportive of the team, whether it is the leadership team or project teams.

- Moving forward, speak of your work group as a team. Using team language builds team identity. Encourage others to think in terms of being a part of the team.

Resources

Books

Anderson, Redia and Lenora Billings-Harris. *Trailblazers: How Top Business Leaders are Accelerating Results through Inclusion and Diversity*. New York: Wiley, 2010.

Bell, Myrtle P. *Diversity in Organizations*. Cincinnati: South-Western, 2011.

Bucher, Richard and Patricia Bucher. *Diversity Consciousness: Opening our Minds to People, Cultures, and Opportunities*. New York: Prentice Hall, 2003.

Canas, Kathryn and Harris Sondak. *Opportunities and Challenges of Workplace Diversity*. New York: Prentice Hall, 2010.

Esty, Katherine. *Workplace Diversity: A Manager's Guide to Solving Problems and Turning Diversity Into a Competitive Advantage*. Adams Media Corporation, 1997.

Greer, Charles and W. Richard Plunkett. *Supervision: Diversity and Teams in the Workplace*. Upper Saddle River, NJ: Prentice Hall, 2002.

Harvard Business School Press. *Harvard Business Review on Managing Diversity*. Cambridge: Harvard Business Review, 2002.

Harvey, Carol and M. June Allard: *Understanding and Managing Diversity: Readings, Cases, and Exercises*. Upper Saddle River, NJ: Prentice Hall, 2011.

Hubbard, Edward. *The Manager's Pocket Guide to Diversity Management*. Amherst, MA: HRD Press, 2003.

Jacob, Nina. *Intercultural Management*. London: Kogan Page, 2003.

Lambert, Jonamay and Selma Myers. *The Diversity Training Activity Book: 50 Activities for Promoting Communication and Understanding at Work*. New York: AMACOM, 2009.

Lancaster, Lynne, et al. *When Generations Collide: Who They Are, Why They Clash, and How to Solve the Generational Puzzle at Work*. New York: Harper Collins, 2002.

Liswood, Laura. *The Loudest Duck: Moving Beyond Diversity while Embracing Differences to Achieve Success At Work*. New York: Wiley, 2009.

Livers, Ancella and Keith Caver. *Leading in Black and White: Working Across the Racial Divide in Corporate America*. San Francisco: Jossey-Bass, 2003.

Loden, Marilyn. *Implementing Diversity*. New York: McGraw-Hill, 1995.

Lustig, Myron and Jolene Koester: *Intercultural Competence: Interpersonal Communication Across Cultures.* Boston: Allyn & Bacon, 2002.

Ross, Howard J. *Reinventing Diversity: Transforming Organizational Community to Strengthen People, Purpose, and Performance.* Lanham, MD: Rowman, 2011.

Sonnenschein, William. *The Diversity Toolkit: How You Can Build and Benefit from a Diverse Workforce.* New York: McGraw-Hill, 1999.

_____. *The Practical Executive and Workforce Diversity.* New York: NTC Business Books.

Thiederman, Sondra. *Making Diversity Work: 7 Steps to Defeating Bias in the Workplace.* Kaplan Publishing, 2008.

Thomas, R. Roosevelt; et al. *Harvard Business Review on Managing Diversity.* Cambridge, MA: Harvard Business School Press, 2002.

Zemke, Ron and Claire Raines. *Generations at Work: Managing the Clash of Veterans, Boomers, Xers, and Nexters in Your Workplace.* New York: AMACOM, 1999.

Websites

Workplace fairness is described at http://www.workplacefairness.org.

The following site describes best practices: http://www.diversitybestpractices.com/events/top-five-ways-ceos-show-commitment-diversity.

Other Resources

The following government site provides much information on diversity practices: http://govinfo.library.unt.edu/npr/library/workforce-diversity.pdf.

Change – Commitment to Diversity

Instructions

Using the table below and on the next page, refer to the items you listed in the Reflect – Commitment to Diversity worksheet and identify specific actions you will take to improve your weaknesses or enhance your strengths in each area. Refer to the Develop and Renew section on the previous pages for action ideas, keeping in mind the needs of your current or aspired position.

You can have multiple actions for each item you intend to focus on. In the first section, list the actions that are specific to the items you listed in the Reflect – Commitment to Diversity section. On the following page, list any actions you will take that are general to this competency and are related to more than one scored item. Finally, prioritize your actions based on the need for your current or aspired position. These actions will become part of your Personal Development Plan (PDP) for this competency in Appendix C.

Actions to Improve Weakness or Enhance Strength	Priority

Continue on next page.

Change – Commitment to Diversity

Actions to Improve Weakness or Enhance Strength	Priority

Other Actions You Will Take Related to Commitment to Diversity (not related to the identified strongest or weakest items)	Priority

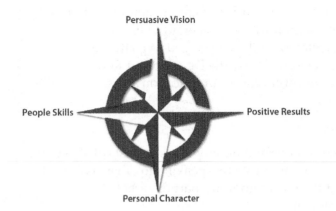

Persuasive Vision

People Skills

Positive Results

Personal Character

CHAPTER 28

Communication

(People Skills)

"The single biggest problem in communication is the illusion that it has taken place."

– George Bernard Shaw

Being an ineffective communicator can be a show-stopper for any leader or manager. We communicate on many different levels every day – e-mail, reports, feedback sessions, meetings, one-on-one, presentations, customer meetings, idle chit chat. Many are good at some communication and not others; few excel at all methods. This is one of the competencies in which everyone can improve.

For every communication, there is a communicator and those receiving the communication. Unfortunately, they may not always agree on what was said or written. Listening is also part of communication, a part that we do not often consider. A large part of the leader's time is spent listening and it is important for the leader to demonstrate that listening is taking place through body language and responses to the speaker.

For communication to be successful, the communicator must be sending a message and the receiver(s) must get the message and understand it the way the communicator intended. That does not happen all the time. Poor communication is the cause of many conflict situations.

Leaders should assess their ability to communicate in all different methods – oral, written, presentations, listening. Miscommunication can be very risky and sometimes harmful to operations, quality, and relationships. In addition, communications are sometimes rushed and not well thought out, leading to the potential for embarrassing or negative consequences. By the same token, excellent communicators can mask their weaknesses in other competencies.

Think about your style of communicating and that of others you regularly interact with. How do you communicate during meetings? How do you communicate one on one in a difficult conversation? How well do you communicate in written documents? How strong are your presentation skills?

This introduction and the self assessment will focus on four key areas of communication skills and behaviors – verbal communications, written communications, listening skills, and presentation skills. Communication is a key competency, and we urge you to go through the recommendations after your self assessment very closely. Using the Develop and Renew recommendations, develop a plan to improve in your weakest communication areas.

Verbal Communications

Speaking to others in meetings, one-on-one conversations and other venues consists of 35% of our communication time. Learning how to effectively communicate by speaking to others is critical to leaders (Burley-Allen, 1995). We have found that the most important part of verbal communications is preparation. Consider the following:

- Never go into a meeting without preparing. Know what the agenda is and how you will respond to each topic.
- Think before you speak. Often, things we say to someone else without thinking can damage trust and credibility.
- Prepare for difficult conversations. Many times we avoid preparing for a difficult conversation and when it is over, we wonder why the conversation went so poorly. What are the objectives of the conversation? What will be the reaction of the recipient? How will you approach the topic? What questions do you anticipate?

Written Communications

Many leaders are poor writers. After all, we typically don't become leaders because of our writing ability. However, poor writing skills can have a negative effect on the leader's credibility. Writing is a critical means of communicating. Think of the reports, proposals, memoranda, and e-mails that you must write. We strongly recommend that if written communications is a weakness, you immediately seek help through seminars or tutoring by a specialist.

Writing weaknesses are usually in one of three areas: grammar, punctuation, and usage. These are areas in which we can all improve, but if you are weak in them, get help to develop your skills. We also recommend using a professional editor for key documents and reports.

Good writing can be described by the following:

- It has a clear purpose.
- It is audience focused.
- It is grammatically correct.
- It states the key message clearly.
- It stays on the intended topic.
- It observes economy of words.
- It uses simple sentences.

Listening Skills

We spend 40% of our communication time listening (Burley-Allen, 1995). Active listening not only enables us to clearly hear the intended message from the speaker, but also serves to instill trust. If your actions and body language indicate you are truly listening, the speaker develops trust in your level of concern for them and their viewpoints.

But, many of us are poor listeners. The most common practice when listening is to think about what you will say in response to the person talking. We may even demonstrate good listening body language (nods, attentive posture), but still do not really hear what the person is saying.

Good listening skills take practice. One method to adopt is to focus on replaying what the person has said to ensure that you understood the points of the message. Another tactic is to ask questions. This not only demonstrates you are listening, but also serves to clear up any ambiguity in the conversation.

Listening takes focus and attention. You are required to put your agenda aside when the other person is speaking. This is difficult because our native reaction is to state our position, give our points, and even to debate the person. Thinking about how we will respond is not listening.

Presentation Skills

Leaders often give presentations to more senior leaders and to customers. Developing excellent presentation skills takes time, effort, and often training. If presentation skills are a weakness, our recommendations include getting training, practicing your presentations, and getting feedback from others.

There are many excuses given for not preparing for a presentation. A few that we have heard include:

- "I don't have enough time to rehearse."
- "I've given presentations thousands of times, no sweat."
- "I know this customer, and whatever we do will go over fine."

Nancy Duarte made an excellent point when she wrote, "The amount of time required to develop a presentation is directly proportional to how high the stakes are (Duarte, 2008)." We totally agree and have worked with some excellent clients who realize this. In particular, presentations to customers to win new business require the most preparation and rehearsal. We have worked with some clients who create teams to prepare the presentation over a week's time and then repeatedly practice and revise for another week.

Duarte (2012) gives some excellent tips regarding presentations you may be required to give to senior leaders or customers. They include:

- Get to the point – be succinct. A model to use is: Findings, Conclusions, Recommendations, and Call for Action.
- Give them what they asked for – stay on topic.
- Set expectations – tell them what you will tell them.

- Create executive summary style slides.
- Make an impact.
- Rehearse!

In summary, communicating is a key part of every leader's life. Communication is a competency that should be a life-long learning activity. The most effective leaders write well, speak well, listen well, and present well.

Red Flag Behaviors

- When listening to others, you think about other things and demonstrate through your body language that you are not listening.
- You don't prepare for presentations, feeling that you either don't have enough time or you are overconfident and do not need to prepare.
- When writing memos, e-mails, or reports, you make it a point to say your message over and over with slightly different terms so everyone will understand you.
- You aren't concerned about using correct grammar in your writing.
- You fail to seek feedback about your communication skills, especially your presentation performance.
- You avoid eye contact when speaking to others.

Case in Point

Shelby worked with enough people over her career who did not communicate well that she knew the importance of effectively communicating. She experienced the consequences of poor communications. She strived to be concise and impactful in her conversations. She developed good listening habits and frequently asked for feedback regarding her communication style.

She responded to e-mails within 24 hours and was concise and to the point in each, yet she also was kind in her responses. Shelby reviewed each e-mail before hitting Send to ensure that her point was made and there were no mistakes in the mail. She did not send e-mails unless needed and clearly indicated to recipients whether she needed a reply or not. Her written communications in letters and reports were also well-delivered. It was not easy sometimes; she needed to use a dictionary and thesaurus at times to be exact in her word usage. Before sending or submitting any letter or report, she carefully proofread the document to insure there were no errors. Because she was skilled in this area, she was able to coach her team in how to communicate better. One way she did this was to conduct brown bag sessions at lunch time once a week to cover topics such as writing clearly and concisely, outlining, editing, and writing to standard business formats.

Her weakness, however, was in delivering presentations. It was a requirement of her leadership role to present during company meetings and, most importantly, to potential and existing customers. To improve in this important area, she sought out training in presentation skills. This intensive training did a lot to boost her confidence. After the training, she ensured that she practiced important presentations beforehand and sought out peers to observe and provide her with valuable feedback. She also sought coaching by the Vice President of Sales and Marketing, who was an excellent presenter. He was able to help Shelby develop more customer-focused presentations and suggest language to her that would clearly demonstrate benefits to the potential customer without being "too sales-y."

Notes for the Aspiring Leader

Make it a point to constantly improve your communication skills. Be an excellent listener. Learn how to use language to impress and influence people. Observe every presenter to learn behaviors you can model and those you should avoid.

Assess Your Current Location – Communication

(People Skills)

Instructions: Read each of the skills and behaviors below. As objectively as possible, score yourself for each according to the following scale: 1 = strongly disagree; 2 = disagree; 3 = agree; 4 = strongly agree. If a behavior is not appropriate for your current or aspired position, check the N/A column.

SKILL OR BEHAVIOR	1	2	3	4	N/A
Verbal Communications					
My verbal communications are concise and to the point.					
I think before speaking to ensure that no one is offended.					
My body language demonstrates that I listen to others.					
When someone is speaking, I ask clarifying questions to ensure that I have understood them.					
I consider the audience for my verbal communications and use the best tactics for them to understand my message.					
I make direct eye contact with those to whom I am speaking.					
I prepare for difficult conversations by determining my desired outcomes.					
When preparing for a difficult conversation, I anticipate questions the other person may ask.					
SUBTOTAL SCORE – VERBAL COMMUNICATIONS					

Continue on next page.

Assess Your Current Location – Communication

(People Skills)

SKILL OR BEHAVIOR *Written Communications*	1	2	3	4	N/A
My e-mail communications are concise.					
I outline written communications to ensure that key messages are clear and highlighted.					
I develop drafts of important written communications and review and get feedback if appropriate.					
My key written documents are edited and proofread to insure accuracy.					
I use graphics and diagrams in written communications as appropriate.					
I use the appropriate delivery method for written communications (e-mail, report, memo, etc.).					
I understand the needs of the audience when I develop written communications.					
I work to improve my grammar and general writing skills.					
I emphasize the importance of excellent written communications to my team.					
SUBTOTAL SCORE – WRITTEN COMMUNICATIONS					

Continue on next page.

Assess Your Current Location – Communication
(People Skills)

SKILL OR BEHAVIOR *Presentation Skills*	1	2	3	4	N/A
I prepare for presentations to ensure that customer or audience key issues are addressed.					
I prepare presentations with sufficient time to review with others.					
I practice my presentations and receive feedback from others.					
I open presentations with a dynamic introduction.					
I use body movements to emphasize major points and add interest.					
I use voice and tone to add variety to my presentations and to emphasize points.					
My slides use phrases, bullets and no more than six lines of text.					
My slides represent an executive summary of my presentation.					
My slide graphics are simple and easy to understand, while clearly emphasizing a major point.					
I respond concisely to audience questions.					
I close my presentations with a dynamic synthesis of key messages.					
SUBTOTAL SCORE – PRESENTATION SKILLS					

Continue on next page.

Assess Your Current Location – Communication

(People Skills)

Communication (Verbal, Written, Presentation Skills)	1	2	3	4	N/A
SCORES FOR COMMUNICATION (Total check marks in each column and multiply by the heading for the column. Record your scores here.)					

TOTAL SCORE FOR COMMUNICATION: _____

(Add scores from Columns 1, 2, 3, and 4. Record the total above and on the Master Score Sheet in Appendix A. Also, count the number of N/As and record on the Master Score Sheet.)

Reflect – Communication

Scoring Analysis

List Your Four Highest Scored Items (Strengths)

Note: If you have multiple items with the same high score, choose the four items that are most related to your current or aspired position.

Item	Score

List Your Four Lowest Scored Items (Weaknesses)

Note: If you have multiple items with the same low score, choose the four items that are most related to your current or aspired position.

Item	Score

Reflect – Communication Questions

Think about the following questions about communication:

- What type of communications do you most rely on with your team and peers?

- Think about your listening skills. When someone else is speaking, what are you thinking about? What does your body language say to the speaker?

- What makes a presenter effective?

- Think about the e-mails that you receive each day. Are most written in a concise manner to convey the intended message? How could you improve your e-mail communications?

- Why should a communicator consider the audience for their message?

- Have you ever worked for a leader who did not communicate enough? What was the result?

Develop – Communication

Develop and Renew

Consider the following development tactics to help improve in your communication skills and behaviors. Identify which tactics would be valuable to include in your Personal Development Plan (PDP) if you choose to improve in this competency.

- After a conversation with a trusted colleague, ask them what indicators you gave that demonstrated to them you were listening. If you do this with a few colleagues, what patterns exist that indicate how you demonstrate you are listening?

- Identify barriers to effective listening that may affect you and your team. These may include noise in the work area, language or accent variations, attention span, interruptions, biases, etc. Talk with your team about how these barriers to effective listening can be eliminated or dealt with by the team.

- Are you easily distracted? Do you tune out speakers because you are bored? Do you tend to argue with speakers? Do you tend to finish the speaker's sentences? Do you acknowledge the speaker's emotional state and commitment to their position? Answering these questions will help you understand your listening style.

- Are you argumentative with others? Think about the language you use when communicating with others. Do you use respectful language? Do you speak around difficult topics or are you direct? Do you immediately judge what others are saying and express your judgment immediately? Remember, you are in the conversation to not only express your views and provide information, but to also learn what the speaker has to say.

- As a leader, it is not only important that you set the example regarding direct and respectful language, but also that you ensure others follow suit. If you see someone being disrespectful in their communication, point out that this is destructive behavior and cannot continue.

- Think about a recent discussion you had with a co-worker. What clarifying questions could you have asked? Think about why you may not have asked clarifying questions. Were you in a hurry to get the conversation over? Think about your listening skills. Were you an active listener?

- Talk with some trusted colleagues to determine if they think your messages could be more concise. Do they feel you repeat yourself (possibly delivering the message in a few different ways)?

- Take steps to understand where your weaknesses in written communications are and how you can improve. One way is to show samples of your writing to someone who is a good writer or a writing instructor. Have them evaluate how you can improve.

- It will help you to have an objective critique of a presentation you are delivering. Arrange for a trusted, objective team member to evaluate your next presentation. Have them evaluate your materials, structure of the presentation, and your delivery style. From this critique, develop a plan to improve using the resources recommended in this report.

- What is your communication style in meetings? Do you dominate the conversation? Do you not communicate, keeping your thoughts to yourself and then bring them up to others after the meeting? Do you interrupt others? Are you disrespectful to others who speak in a meeting who present things you disagree with?

Resources

Books

Abel, Alicia. *Business Grammar, Style & Usage: The Most Used Desk Reference for Articulate and Polished Business Writing and Speaking by Executives Worldwide.* Aspatore Books, 2003.

Bailey, Edward. *Writing and Speaking at Work.* Upper Saddle River, NJ: Prentice Hall, 2001.

Baldoni, John. *Great Communication Secrets of Great Leaders.* New York: McGraw-Hill, 2003.

Becker, Ethan and Jon Wortmann. *Mastering Communications at Work: How to Lead, Manage and Influence.* New York: McGraw-Hill, 2009.

Bly, Robert. *Persuasive Presentations for Business.* New York: McGraw-Hill, 2008.

Bonet, Diana. *The Business of Listening: A Practical Guide to Effective Listening.* Crisp Learning, 2001.

Booher, Dianna. *Speak With Confidence: Powerful Presentations That Inform, Inspire, and Persuade.* New York: McGraw-Hill, 2002.

_____, *The Voice of Authority: 10 Communication Strategies Every Leader Needs to Know.* New York: McGraw-Hill, 2007.

_____. *Booher's Rules of Business Grammar.* New York: McGraw-Hill, 2008.

Booth, David, et al. *Own the Room: Business Presentations That Persuade, Engage, and Get Results.* New York: McGraw-Hill, 2006.

Burley-Allen, Madelyn. *Listening: The Forgotten Skill: A Self-Teaching Guide.* San Francisco: Wiley, 1995.

Campbell, Michael. *Communication Skills for Project Managers.* New York: AMACOM, 2009.

Carroll, Nannette. *The Communication Problem Solver.* New York: AMACOM, 2009.

Cunningham, Helen and Brenda Greene. *The Business Style Handbook: An A-to-Z Guide for Writing on the Job With Tips From Communications Experts at the Fortune 500.* Chicago: McGraw-Hill.

Duarte, Nancy. *slide:ology: The Art and Science of Creating Great Presentations.* O'Reilly Media, 2008.

_____. *Harvard Business Review Guide to Persuasive Presentations.* Harvard Business Review Press, 2012.

Ferrari, Bernard. *Power Listening: Mastering the Most Critical Business Skill of All.* Portfolio Hardcover, 2012.

Goulston, Mark. *Just Listen: Discover the Secret to Getting Through to Absolutely Anyone.* New York: AMACOM, 2009.

Green, Thad and Jay Knippen. *Breaking the Barrier to Upward Communication: Strategies and Skills for Employees, Managers, and HR Specialists.* New York: Praeger, 1999.

Guffy, Mary Ellen and Dana Loewy. *Business Communication: Process and Product.* Cincinnati: South-Western, 2010.

Hardman, Emilia. *Active Listening 101: How to Turn Down Your Volume to Turn Up Your Communication Skills.* Amazon Digital Services, 2012.

Harvard Business School Press. *Giving Presentations: Expert Solutions to Everyday Challenges.* New York: Pocket Mentor Series, 2007.

Harvard Business Essentials. *Business Communication.* (Harvard Business Essentials). Cambridge: Harvard Business School Press, 2003.

Holtz, Shel. *Corporate Communications: A Guide to Crafting Effective and Appropriate Internal Communications.* New York: AMACOM, 2003.

Iacone, Salvatore. *Write to the Point: How to Communicate in Business With Style and Purpose.* Franklin Lakes, NJ: Career Press, 2003.

Koegel, Timothy. *The Exceptional Presenter: A Proven Formula to Open Up and Own the Room.* Greenleaf Book Group Press, 2007.

Kaye, Ellen. *Maximize Your Presentation Skills: How to Look, Speak, and Act on Your Way to the Top.* New York: Prima Lifestyles, 2002.

Lauchman, Richard. *Punctuation at Work.* New York: AMACOM, 2010.

Locker, Kitty and Stephen Kaczmarek. *Business Communication: Building Critical Skills.* New York: McGraw, 2010.

Mai, Robert and Alan Akerson. *The Leader as Communicator: Strategies and Tactics to Build Loyalty, Focus Effort, and Spark Creativity.* New York: AMACOM, 2003.

Monarth, Harrison. *The Confident Speaker: Beat Your Nerves and Communicate at Your Best in Any Situation.* New York: McGraw-Hill, 2007.

Newman, Amy and Scot Ober. *Business Communication: In Person, In Print, Online.* South-Western College Publications, 2012.

O'Hair, Dan; et al. *Strategic Communication in Business and the Professions.* Boston: Allyn & Bacon, 2010.

Roman, Kenneth. and Joel. Raphaelson. *Writing That Works: How to Communicate Effectively in Business.* New York: Harper Collins, 2000.

Ryan, Kevin. *Write Up the Corporate Ladder: Successful Writers Reveal the Techniques That Help You Write With Ease and Get Ahead.* New York: AMACOM, 2003.

Steele, William. *Presentation Skills 201: How to Take it to the Next Level as a Confident, Engaging Presenter.* Outskirts Press, 2009.

Thill, John V. and Courtland Bovee. *Excellence in Business Communication.* New York: Prentice Hall, 2010.

Tracy, Brian. *Speak to Win.* New York: AMACOM, 2008.

Wilson, Kevin and Jennifer Wauson. *The AMA Handbook of Business Documents.* New York: AMACOM, 2011.

_____. *The AMA Handbook of Business Writing.* New York: AMACOM, 2010.

Websites

Wikipedia offers an excellent overview of communication theory at http://en.wikipedia.org/wiki/Communication.

This site provides resources on listening skills: http://www.studygs.net/listening.htm.

Other Resources

An excellent article can be found at http://www.noupe.com/how-tos/12-secrets-of-effective-business-communication.html.

This article describes the various types of business communication: http://www.rizwanashraf.com/2008/02/04/business-communication-and-its-types/.

Change – Communication

Instructions

Using the table below and on the next page, refer to the items you listed in the Reflect – Communication worksheet and identify specific actions you will take to improve your weaknesses or enhance your strengths in each area. Refer to the Develop and Renew section on the previous pages for action ideas, keeping in mind the needs of your current or aspired position.

You can have multiple actions for each item you intend to focus on. In the first section, list the actions that are specific to the items you listed in the Reflect – Communication section. On the following page, list any actions you will take that are general to this competency and are related to more than one scored item. Finally, prioritize your actions based on the need for your current or aspired position. These actions will become part of your Personal Development Plan (PDP) for this competency in Appendix C.

Actions to Improve Weakness or Enhance Strength	Priority

Continue on next page.

Change – Communication

Actions to Improve Weakness or Enhance Strength	Priority

Other Actions You Will Take Related to Communications (not related to the identified strongest or weakest items)	Priority

327

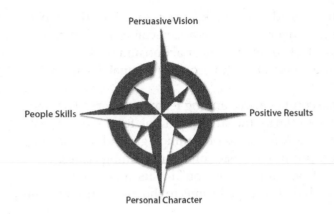

Persuasive Vision

People Skills — Positive Results

Personal Character

CHAPTER 29

Conflict Management

(People Skills)

"Dialogue is the most effective way of resolving conflict."

– Tenzin Gyatso, The 14th Dalai Lama

Leaders often encounter conflict situations in their position. In fact, it sometimes seems that conflict in the workplace is a way of life. Regardless whether the leader is part of the conflict or it is among team members or peers, the leader needs to have tools to manage the conflict.

Our coaching practice is largely focused on how to manage conflict. Many people need help walking through it to get the best outcome. Conflict not only wastes time and money, but can be emotionally destructive to those participating, and even to those observing the conflict. Sometimes you may lose good people simply because they do not want to be in an environment where there is substantial conflict. Even if they aren't one of the participants, they can still feel the pain.

One of the most difficult conflicts sometimes occurs between a leader and their boss. This type of conflict is never fun and always difficult to deal with. But conflict can occur between team members and departments, and with customers. There are many causes of conflict that go beyond a current situation or problem. People are different and sometimes personalities clash. We can all think of two (or more) people we have known who just don't get along. There may be philosophical or ideological differences. A commitment to diversity of ideas and personalities can go a long way toward avoiding these types of personal conflict, but rarely can they be totally avoided. People carry baggage. For example, a person may not like someone and create conflict with them for the simple reason that the other person looks similar to their ex-spouse.

There is such a thing as a healthy level of conflict. In fact, conflict may be needed in an organization to help address problems that exist beneath the surface. It helps people learn how to recognize their differences and benefit from them. The leader, however, must take care to ensure that a small level of conflict is not generating larger issues that can come to the surface in a situation.

It is when the conflict becomes unhealthy that a leader must take action to reduce the level of discord. Bear in mind that emotional disagreement over a policy or action can be healthy to an organization. It forces leadership to look at the effects of the policy or action and make modifications if necessary. However, if the conflict persists or it becomes personal, it can be detrimental to the organization.

So what does the leader do when destructive conflict arises among team members? The first step is to listen to both parties and ask questions to clarify the situation. Look for the root causes of the conflict. Then broaden the perspective and look for areas of common ground. If you can get the parties to agree on parts of the problem, compromise is easier on the remaining issues. Finally, try to change the framing of the conflict from "me versus you" to "us versus the problem." Also, invite the parties to come up with their own solutions to the problem. Get them talking constructively.

Debates over policy or actions should not become personal and cause attacks between people. When this occurs, the leader must step in and defuse the situation using conflict management techniques. Sometimes the conflict is personal and involves transgressions that go beyond the workplace. In this type of instance, we recommend getting the involvement of a professional, such as your human resources department. It is not in your interest to solve deep personal issues such as someone having an affair with a co-worker's spouse. This type of conflict is beyond most leaders' scope and responsibility; thus, the recommendation for extended involvement. Regardless, something major would need to occur in this type of situation to enable the parties to continue working together.

Most of the conflicts leaders deal with are not as dramatic as just described. Most can be resolved by the parties talking through the issues, finding common ground, and compromising. You may recommend some relationship-building actions such as weekly coffee time together to help keep the conflict under control, but you must consider the right timing for healing to begin. Often, the leader is best served when the conflict is resolved and relationship building takes place naturally.

Red Flag Behaviors

- You avoid addressing conflict – both when it involves you or when it is between team members.
- You keep subordinates at arm's length and do not build any relationship with them.
- When resolving conflict among team members, your response is, "Work it out and fast."
- You complain to your team when you have a conflict with a peer or senior leader.
- You display anger and become irrational when engaged in a conflict.

Case in Point

The pressure in John's department was tremendous – tight deadlines, need for perfection, and a lot of overtime hours during the wonderful summer. Everyone was on edge, and there were almost daily outbursts and verbal fights among the team. John realized that the conflict was getting out of control and he needed to do something.

John understood the sources of the conflict, but there wasn't much he could do about the deadlines and need for quality. After thinking about it and having a discussion with his Human Resources Manager, he came up with some ideas.

First, he held a team meeting (with Krispy Kreme donuts!) and acknowledged the difficult circumstances for the team. He assured them that it would not last longer than two more months. He stressed the importance of the projects to the overall health of the company and that their contributions would not be forgotten.

Next, he set up a few mechanisms to handle conflicts. He encouraged those who felt under extreme pressure during the day to take a quick break and take a walk outside to clear their mind. Second, he made it clear that if two or more people were in a conflict situation, they had a responsibility to bring it to him to resolve. He would listen and if a decision needed to be made, he would make it. He would keep the people in conflict in his office until the situation was resolved and agreed that the conflict would not be held against anyone. He emphasized that the sooner the conflicts could be identified and brought to his attention, the sooner everyone could get back to work.

John also set aside a room where two people could discuss issues in private. Finally, he told them that he would do everything possible to give each person extra time off at least once a month to relax. He could not promise that it would happen with everyone and it was dependent on a number of factors, but he said he would do his best.

John then opened the meeting to any suggestions that the team members had to prevent or resolve conflict. Several were presented, such as flexible time so that team members could enjoy at least two evenings each week at home. John thought this was a good idea, and he promised to review the schedule and do what he could to make it happen.

Notes for the Aspiring Leader

Do not be discouraged when you see conflict in your team or organization. It is systemic to any organization. Acquire the right skills and attitudes to effectively deal with conflict when it occurs on your team or among your peers.

Assess Your Current Location – Conflict Management

(People Skills)

Instructions: Read each of the skills and behaviors below. As objectively as possible, score yourself for each according to the following scale: 1 = strongly disagree; 2 = disagree; 3 = agree; 4 = strongly agree. If a behavior is not appropriate for your current or aspired position, check the N/A column.

SKILL OR BEHAVIOR	1	2	3	4	N/A
I understand that a level of conflict in an organization can be a good thing.					
I proactively build relationships with subordinates.					
I have and use a core process to handle excessive and/or destructive conflict within the team.					
I effectively manage conflict in meetings.					
When I have a conflict with another leader, I do not discuss the conflict with others.					
When dealing with personal conflict, I remove emotion and anger from my personal thought process to consider solutions.					
I try to understand other people's needs.					
I involve team members in making decisions when appropriate.					
I take action when it is apparent there is destructive conflict within the team.					
I proactively try to smooth things over before conflict arises.					
I consider all reasonable alternatives when seeking a method to resolve team conflict.					
I recognize when conflict is caused by my actions and proactively address it					

Continue on next page.

Assess Your Current Location – Conflict Management

(People Skills)

SKILL OR BEHAVIOR	1	2	3	4	N/A
I recognize when conflict is a personality, ideological, or philosophical difference and handle accordingly.					
I know when to refer a conflict situation to other professionals, such as Human Resources.					
I am alert to conflict patterns and take necessary actions to address and resolve.					
SCORES FOR CONFLICT MANAGEMENT (Total check marks in each column and multiply by the heading for the column. Record your scores here.)					

TOTAL SCORE FOR CONFLICT MANAGEMENT: _____

(Add scores from Columns 1, 2, 3, and 4. Record the total above and on the Master Score Sheet in Appendix A. Also, count the number of N/As and record on the Master Score Sheet.)

Reflect – Conflict Management

Scoring Analysis

List Your Four Highest Scored Items (Strengths)

Note: If you have multiple items with the same high score, choose the four items that are most related to your current or aspired position.

Item	Score

List Your Four Lowest Scored Items (Weaknesses)

Note: If you have multiple items with the same low score, choose the four items that are most related to your current or aspired position.

Item	Score

Reflect – Conflict Management Questions

Think about the following questions about conflict management:

- Have you ever seen conflict between individuals grow to be destructive to the team or organization?

- Who has the responsibility to resolve conflict situations in an organization?

- Have you ever been in a conflict situation with others and not taken steps to resolve it? What were the effects?

- What are some techniques to help resolve conflict in an organization? What about between two individuals on your team?

- What happens if conflict is not addressed?

Develop – Conflict Management

Develop and Renew

Consider the following development tactics to help improve in conflict management. Identify which tactics would be valuable to include in your Personal Development Plan (PDP) if you choose to improve in this competency.

- A level of conflict in an organization can be a good thing. Do not try to be the cure all and search out all conflict situations and try to address them. It is important to know when to get involved in resolving a conflict. Be judicious and don't overstep your boundaries if the conflict should be the responsibility of another leader. You may consult with another leader about a conflict within their purview and work with them to help resolve it if necessary.

- Leaders should proactively build relationships with all subordinates. Get to know them. Ask them about their accomplishments, challenges, and issues. This helps to build trust, and people will feel comfortable bringing conflict to you before it gets out of hand. You should also take steps to help your team members get to know each other and build trust among the group.

- Get team members involved in making decisions. You may have the final decision, but participation in the process is the key to reducing unnecessary conflict. Usually your team members look at situations differently from you, and it is important to hear their perspective.

- If conflict is widespread across your team and is having a negative effect on people or productivity, take action. Do not pretend that it will go away. Consider all your alternatives – team meetings, one-on-one discussions, negotiations, or an offsite team retreat complete with teambuilding.

- Have a core process for solving conflict. Adopt this process as your standard. Communicate this strategy to your team members and colleagues. If team members are having a conflict, recommend that they use your conflict resolution process before they bring it to you for resolution.

- If conflict flares up during a meeting or conversation, do your best to calm things down, remove the emotion, and set steps to resolve the issue offline. If you allow conflict to escalate during a meeting, it will be counterproductive. Simply say, "This is an important issue and there are different viewpoints so let's take it offline and we can discuss after this meeting."

- When negotiating conflict between two people, look for areas of agreement. Use these areas as anchors to return to when the situation gets more difficult.

- Develop a culture of collaboration that encourages people to work together. Recognize that some people cannot work well with others. Avoid setting up a conflict situation by forcing two people to work closely who have substantial differences. However, you should also be taking steps to work with the individuals to resolve their differences so that they can work together in the future.

- For personal conflict (conflict where you are one of the principals), do your best to accommodate it. Work to ensure that it does not affect your performance or the perceptions of others. Compromise where you can to get past the issue and move forward. Do not dwell on personal conflict. Resolve it and move on to be productive.

- When dealing with personal conflict, discuss with a trusted adviser to gain a fresh perspective. Try to remove the emotion and biases from the situation. Consider that you may be tired or angry at something else.

- For personal conflict, identify all potential courses of action. Then, list the pros and cons of each. Pick the alternative that will not hurt or be the least hurtful to yourself and others.

- Leaders must rise above conflict and manage it well, whether a personal conflict or a conflict within their organization or team. You should be concerned about your skill in managing conflict and take the necessary steps to learn better techniques.

- Choose your battles. You should intervene when conflict becomes damaging to individuals or the organization. However, you need to be adept at resolving and managing conflict before jumping into the conflict situation.

- Read the book by Runde and Flanigan, *Developing Your Conflict Competence*. As you read it, consider your situation and how you currently handle conflict. Open yourself to new ideas and how you can become more effective.

- Observe how other leaders handle conflict. What do they do that is successful in removing the emotion from the conflict? What do they do that gains resolution? Talk to leaders who are excellent at handling conflict and gain their ideas on tactics you can use effectively.

- Do you have difficulty removing emotion when dealing with your personal conflict? If so, consider that emotion only makes it more difficult to reach resolution and serves to increase the emotion in the other party. Work to remove emotion from your conflict before you attempt to resolve with the other party.

- If you have a personal conflict with another individual, do not surface the conflict with others. The only exception is if you are talking with a respected and trusted colleague to gain advice on how to resolve the conflict.

- If your team is mired in conflict, you have a responsibility to work with them to resolve it before it becomes destructive to the team. This may require a lot of planning and time on your part. Do not take sides initially; rather, listen to each person, defuse the emotion, and have them participate in finding a solution.

Resources

Books

Blackard, Kirk and James Gibson. *Capitalizing on Conflict: Strategies and Practices for Turning Conflict into Synergy in Organizations*. Palo Alto, CA: Davies-Black Publishing, 2002.

Budjac, Barbara. *Conflict Management: A Practical Guide to Developing Negotiation Strategies*. New York: Prentice Hall, 2006.

Cartwright, Talula. *Managing Conflict with Peers*. Greensboro, NC: Center for Creative Leadership, 2003.

Cloke, Ken and Joan Goldsmith. *Resolving Conflicts at Work: A Complete Guide for Everyone on the Job*. San Francisco: Jossey-Bass, 2000.

Crawley, John and Katherine Graham. *Mediation for Managers: Resolving Conflict and Rebuilding Relationships at Work*. Yarmouth, ME: Nicholas Brealey Publishing, 2002.

Dana, Daniel. *Conflict Resolution*. New York: McGraw-Hill, 2000.

Deutsch, Morton and Peter Coleman. *The Handbook of Conflict Resolution: Theory and Practice*. San Francisco: Jossey-Bass, 2000.

Digerty, Nora and Marcelas Guyler. *The Essential Guide to Workplace Mediation and Conflict Resolution: Rebuilding Working Relationships*. London: Kogan Page, 2008.

Eunson, Baden. *Conflict Management*. Wrightbooks, 2011.

Furlong, Gary. *The Conflict Resolution Toolbox: Models and Maps for Analyzing, Diagnosing and Resolving Conflict*. New York: Wiley, 2005.

Jones, Tricia and Ross Brinkert. *Conflict Coaching: Conflict Management Strategies and Skills for the Individual*. Thousand Oaks, CA: Sage, 2007.

Kriesberg, Louis. *Constructive Conflicts: From Escalation to Resolution*. Lanham, MD: Rowman and Littlefield Publishers, 2006.

Liptak, John and Ester Leutenberg. *The Conflict Management Skills Workbook*. Duluth, MN: Whole Person Assoc, 2010.

338

Maravelas, Anna. *How to Reduce Workplace Conflict and Stress: How Leaders and Their Employers Can Protect their Sanity and Productivity From Tension and Turf Wars.* Career Press, 2005.

Masters, Marick and Robert Albright. *The Complete Guide to Conflict Resolution in the Workplace.* New York: AMACOM, 2002

McConnon, Shay and Margaret McConnon. *How to Manage Disagreements and Develop Trust and Understanding.* Oxford, UK: How To Books, 2010.

Perlow, Leslie. *When You Say Yes but Mean No: How Silencing Conflict Wrecks Relationships and Companies...And What You Can Do About It.* New York: Crown Publishing, 2003.

Runde, Craig E. and Tim Flanagan. *Developing Your Conflict Competence: A Hands-On Guide for Leaders, Managers, Facilitators, and Teams.* San Francisco: Jossey-Bass, 2010.

Shearous, Susan. *Conflict 101: A Managers Guide to Resolving Problems So Everyone Can Get Back to Work.* New York: Amacom, 2011.

Van Slyke, Erik. *Listening to Conflict.* New York: AMACOM, 1999.

Weeks, Dudley. *The Eight Essential Steps to Conflict Resolution.* Los Angeles: Tarcher, 1994.

Websites

Wikipedia provides an excellent description of conflict management at http://en.wikipedia.org/wiki/Conflict_management.

Mind Tools offers a description of conflict management and various methods of dealing with conflict at http://www.mindtools.com/pages/article/newLDR_81.htm.

Other Resources

This article from HelpGuide describes steps for conflict resolution: http://www.helpguide.org/mental/eq8_conflict_resolution.htm.

The following article is an excellent resource for developing conflict management strategies: http://www.wright.edu/~scott.williams/LeaderLetter/conflict.htm.

More information on dealing with conflict can be found at http://www.nsba.org/sbot/toolkit/Conflict.html.

Change –   Conflict Management

Instructions

Using the table below and on the next page, refer to the items you listed in the Reflect – Conflict Management worksheet and identify specific actions you will take to improve your weaknesses or enhance your strengths in each area. Refer to the Develop and Renew section on the previous pages for action ideas, keeping in mind the needs of your current or aspired position.

You can have multiple actions for each item you intend to focus on. In the first section, list the actions that are specific to the items you listed in the Reflect – Conflict Management section. On the following page, list any actions you will take that are general to this competency and are related to more than one scored item. Finally, prioritize your actions based on the need for your current or aspired position. These actions will become part of your Personal Development Plan (PDP) for this competency in Appendix C.

Actions to Improve Weakness or Enhance Strength	Priority

Continue on next page.

Change – Conflict Management

Actions to Improve Weakness or Enhance Strength	Priority

Other Actions You Will Take Related to Conflict Management (not related to the identified strongest or weakest items)	Priority

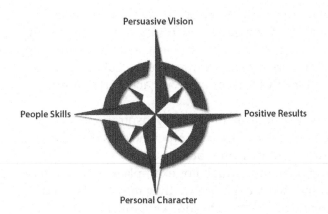

Persuasive Vision

People Skills — Positive Results

Personal Character

CHAPTER 30

Interpersonal Skills

(People Skills)

"No matter how busy you are, you must take time to make the other person feel important."

- Mary Kay Ash

Interpersonal skills are all the behaviors and feelings that exist within us that influence our interactions with others. We commonly think of interpersonal skills as soft skills – behaviors that encompass personal and social communication and self management. Hard skills, on the other hand, are the technical abilities and factual knowledge needed to do your job.

Everyone is different; thus, interactions between people are different. Poor interpersonal skills have been career limiting for many people. Yes, many leaders and senior managers have gotten to their position despite poor interpersonal skills. However, for the most part, having poor interpersonal skills can keep someone from being promoted to a position of more responsibility. At a minimum, poor interpersonal skills have a negative effect on both individual and organizational performance. This is particularly true in today's environment in which leaders must manage employees who may be younger, come from different cultures, and have different values than they do.

If there were no need for interaction and communication, interpersonal skills would not be very important. However, interaction and communication are at the heart of any business or organization. Leaders must set the example, be as open as possible in their communication, and hone their skills so that people receive and understand their messages. However, interpersonal skills go beyond simply the message; they involve attitude and body language between the leader and the person or group.

Interpersonal skills also determine how we handle conflict and influence others. There is less conflict in an organization that is staffed with leaders who have good interpersonal skills. This is because people like them and understand them. Leaders with excellent interpersonal skills are less self-centered and have greater success influencing others to do things or agree with their position.

Leaders must be authentic in their interpersonal skills. Others can easily detect when a leader is not being authentic and honest in their relationships. Being authentic means you are sincere in what you say to those with whom you communicate. Many workplaces have an active culture of politics in which communication between team members is disingenuous and calculated to produce a desired result. Leaders should watch out for this type of behavior and curtail it in the organization as much as possible.

Other competencies directly related to interpersonal skills include Trust, Inspiration, Teamwork, Communication, and Talent Management. Each of these competencies is directly affected by the quality of interpersonal relationships that the leader builds.

Interpersonal skills often reflect the background of an individual. For example, if a person has had a challenging background in their family or other work experiences, they may be reserved, untrusting, or perhaps negative in their interactions with others. This does not mean that every person who has had challenges exhibits these behaviors, simply that the leader must be patient and aware that interpersonal behaviors are learned over a long period of time and, of course, take a long time to change. Poor interpersonal behaviors can dampen team spirits and productivity. It is the leader's responsibility to set the example and coach team members in developing better interpersonal skills if needed.

Red Flag Behaviors

- You avoid building professional relationships with others.
- You show favoritism.
- You take the credit for good things that happen and do not credit your team.
- You often tell jokes that offend others.
- You insulate your team from others in the organization.
- You fail to encourage others; rather, you look for ways to criticize others.
- You feel and communicate that you, and only you, have the right answer to problems or issues.

Case in Point

Brittni was happy with her team. Everyone got along and had a good time at work. But when Cory transferred into her division from the Fairmount office, things went south. Cory was very difficult to work with, did not communicate well, and seemed to strive to cause as much divisiveness and conflict as possible.

At first, Brittni did not do anything about it. When three of her team members asked for a meeting and told her they were considering leaving the division because of Cory, she knew she needed to get to the bottom of things. She promised them she would take action.

Brittni's first step was to meet with Cory. It was a tough meeting but after about an hour of his rants, he broke down into tears. He felt that no one was giving him a chance. He thought that no one on the team wanted to get to know him, and he felt like an outsider. He admitted that he could be hard to get along with, but promised to meet others halfway if they would give him a chance. He disclosed that he had a rough background and had difficulty trusting people because of his parent's tumultuous divorce some years before.

Brittni thought about her conversation and took two actions. First, she started having a morning coffee/tea time once a week, and she provided the donuts. The rule was that there would be no talking about work. It would be all learning about each other. In fact, she used ice breaker exercises the first few sessions to get things moving.

Second, she met with Joseph, Carolyn, and Cindy, the three team members who met with her earlier. She challenged them to get to know Cory better and reach out to him while keeping his confidence. She suggested they all go to lunch at least once a month and just have some fun together. She told them that Cory promised to meet others halfway and encouraged them to take the first step.

Over time, things worked out well. Cory could still be difficult at times, but trust and respect grew slowly. The lunches were successful, and Cory soon felt part of the team.

Notes for the Aspiring Leader

Do your best to develop relationships at all levels of the organization, not just with those whom you think will contribute to your career. Be authentic and learn about others as people. Strong relationships can not only make the present workplace more enjoyable to work in, but also turn into long-term relationships with great benefits down the road.

Assess Your Current Location – Interpersonal Skills

(People Skills)

Instructions: Read each of the skills and behaviors below. As objectively as possible, score yourself for each according to the following scale: 1 = strongly disagree; 2 = disagree; 3 = agree; 4 = strongly agree. If a behavior is not appropriate for your current or aspired position, check the N/A column.

SKILL OR BEHAVIOR	1	2	3	4	N/A
I collaborate effectively across organizational boundaries.					
I consider the needs, feelings, and capabilities of others and respond appropriately.					
I demonstrate an appropriate sense of humor.					
I demonstrate sincere concern for others.					
I am authentic in personal interactions.					
I do not show favoritism or bias.					
I maintain a check on my emotions when dealing with others.					
I practice encouraging behavior with others.					
I proactively try to solicit and understand the viewpoints of others.					
I am willing to admit mistakes.					
I treat others with respect, regardless of their position.					
I value individuals and their contributions.					
I seek out others to establish relationships.					

Continue on next page.

Assess Your Current Location – Interpersonal Skills

(People Skills)

	1	2	3	4	N/A
SCORES FOR INTERPERSONAL SKILLS (Total check marks in each column and multiply by the heading for the column. Record your scores here.)					

TOTAL SCORE FOR INTERPERSONAL SKILLS: _____

(Add scores from Columns 1, 2, 3, and 4. Record the total above and on the Master Score Sheet in Appendix A. Also, count the number of N/As and record on the Master Score Sheet.)

Reflect –   Interpersonal Skills

Scoring Analysis

List Your Four Highest Scored Items (Strengths)

Note: If you have multiple items with the same high score, choose the four items that are most related to your current or aspired position.

Item	Score

List Your Four Lowest Scored Items (Weaknesses)

Note: If you have multiple items with the same low score, choose the four items that are most related to your current or aspired position.

Item	Score

348

Reflect – Interpersonal Skills Questions

Think about the following questions about interpersonal skills:

- Why do you think interpersonal skills are important in your job?

- What role do you see body language in your interpersonal skills?

- How important is it for your peers and team members to like you?

- What does it mean to be authentic in your interactions with others?

- Do interpersonal skills have a relation to influencing others?

- Why do you think those who have excellent interpersonal skills succeed more often than those who do not?

- How do interpersonal skills relate to developing trust?

Develop – Interpersonal Skills

Develop and Renew

Consider the following development tactics to help improve your interpersonal skills. Identify which tactics would be valuable to include in your Personal Development Plan (PDP) if you choose to improve in this competency.

- Leaders should strive to create a culture that nurtures compassion and understanding of others. The culture should also be one that encourages people to listen to others empathetically and to respect the capabilities of each team member. If this is lacking in your organization, work with your peer leaders to understand the cause and effect change.

- Think of instances when you have shown disrespect to others. Why did you behave in this manner? Was outside stress the cause of your disrespectful behavior? If so, make sure you refrain from allowing outside circumstances to negatively influence your behavior. Identify three behaviors to change that would demonstrate respectful behavior to others. Implement steps to incorporate these new behaviors into your interactions with others.

- Examine your behavior toward others. Do you make decisions based on what is best for the organization or based on whom you like or dislike? Identify three behaviors you will change that will demonstrate that you do not show favoritism or bias. Next, implement these behaviors as part of your daily routine.

- Being honest and straightforward is a two-way street. If you are not truthful and candid with others, they will hesitate to be transparent with you. Although you must safeguard confidential or sensitive information, you should strive to be as open and transparent with others as you can be in every situation.

- Consider having either one-on-one or open feedback sessions with team members and customers. Express your desire to receive valuable, helpful feedback about you and the organization. Get back to each individual or customer regarding the results of your feedback sessions and the actions you will be taking in response.

- How do you give feedback? Do you meet with team members regularly to give them feedback on their performance? Or do you give them on-the-spot feedback? Seek new methods of giving feedback, and continue to be proactive and constructive in your feedback.

- Consider how seeking the viewpoint of others and seeking out additional information will improve your decision making. You will receive the benefit of this information and opinion. You, of course, have the right to ignore bad information or what you may consider invalid viewpoints of others. However, seeking out and listening to others will typically provide

350

valuable information and approaches in dealing with an issue or decision, along with building relationships.

- As a leader, you must not only keep your own emotions in check but coach others to control themselves as well. If you observe an explosive situation where anger is driving a conversation, don't hesitate to intervene and calm the situation. If you know a peer who has difficulty controlling their emotions, volunteer to coach them to achieve better control.

Resources

Books

Alessandra, Tody. *The 10 Qualities of Charismatic People: Secrets of Personal Magnetism.* Chicago: Nightingale Conant, 2002.

Autry, James. *Love and Profit: The Art of Caring Leadership.* New York: Morrow, 1991.

Benton, D. *Executive Charisma: Six Steps to Mastering the Art of Leadership.* New York: McGraw-Hill, 2003.

Bolton, Robert and Dorothy Grover Bolton. *People Styles at Work: Making Bad Relationships Good and Good Relationships Better.* New York: AMACOM, 1996.

Brinkman, Rick. *Dealing with Difficult People: 24 Lessons for Bringing Out the Best in Everyone.* New York: McGraw-Hill, 2003.

Brooks, Michael. *Instant Rapport.* New York: Warner Books, 1989.

Cava, Roberta. *Dealing with Difficult People: How to Deal with Nasty Customers, Demanding Bosses, and Annoying Co-workers.* Tonawanda, NY: Firefly Press, 2004.

DuBrin, Andrew J. *Human Relations: Interpersonal Job-Oriented Skills.* New York: Prentice, 2011.

De Janasz, Suzanne; et al. *Interpersonal Skills in Organizations.* New York: McGraw, 2011.

Folkman, Joseph R. and John Zenger. *The Power of Feedback: 35 Principles for Turning Feedback from Others into Personal and Professional Change.* New York: Wiley, 2006.

Fritz, Susan, et al. *Interpersonal Skills for Leadership.* New York: Prentice-Hall, 2004.

Hayes, John. *Interpersonal Skills at Work.* New York: Routledge, 2002.

Klaus, Peggy. *The Hard Truth About Soft Skills: Workplace Lessons Smart People Wish They'd Learned Sooner.* NY: Harper Business, 2008.

Robbins, Stephen P. and Phillip Hunsaker. *Training in Interpersonal Skills: Tips for Managing People at Work.* New York: Prentice Hall, 2011.

Websites

For an excellent resource for articles about interpersonal skills, see: http://www.skillsyouneed.co.uk/interpersonal_skills.html.

Other Resources

This AllBusiness article includes steps to improve interpersonal communications: http://www.allbusiness.com/improve-interpersonal-skills/15606969-1.html#axzz24wXBnLxB.

This article focuses on the effect of interpersonal skills and career advancement: http://teresacoppens.hubpages.com/hub/Interpersonal-Skills-to-Boost-Your-Career.

Hurley, Robert F.; Galford, Robert; Drapeau, Anne Seibold; Kim, W. Chan; and Mauborqne, Renee. "Winning Your Employees' Trust." Harvard Business Review. September 1, 2006.

Change – Interpersonal Skills

Instructions

Using the table below and on the next page, refer to the items you listed in the Reflect – Interpersonal Skills worksheet and identify specific actions you will take to improve your weaknesses or enhance your strengths in each area. Refer to the Develop and Renew section on the previous pages for action ideas, keeping in mind the needs of your current or aspired position.

You can have multiple actions for each item you intend to focus on. In the first section, list the actions that are specific to the items you listed in the Reflect – Interpersonal Skills section. On the following page, list any actions you will take that are general to this competency and are related to more than one scored item. Finally, prioritize your actions based on the need for your current or aspired position. These actions will become part of your Personal Development Plan (PDP) for this competency in Appendix C.

Actions to Improve Weakness or Enhance Strength	Priority

Continue on next page.

Change – Interpersonal Skills

Actions to Improve Weakness or Enhance Strength	Priority

Other Actions You Will Take Related to Interpersonal Skills (not related to the identified strongest or weakest items)	Priority

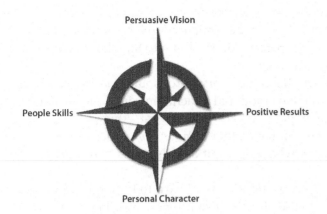

Persuasive Vision

People Skills

Positive Results

Personal Character

CHAPTER 31

Negotiation

(People Skills)

"The most important trip you may take in life is meeting people half way."

– Henry Boyle

Negotiation is an interactive process between two or more parties on an issue or issues of mutual interest or dispute. Typically the parties seek to make or find a mutually acceptable agreement that all concerned will honor. Negotiation tactics are the detailed methods employed by negotiators to gain an advantage over other parties.

We negotiate every day – from negotiating for time off to difficult and complex contract negotiations. Think for a moment about how you make important decisions in your life – the decisions that have the greatest impact on your performance at work and your satisfaction at home. How many of those decisions can you make unilaterally, and how many do you have to reach with others through negotiation? Negotiation is the pre-eminent form of reaching agreement in personal and professional life.

We may all be negotiators, yet many of us don't like to negotiate. We see negotiations as stressful confrontations. We see ourselves faced with an unpleasant choice. If we are soft in order to preserve the relationship, we end up giving up our position. If we are hard in order to win our position, we risk straining the relationship or even losing it altogether.

The alternative is joint problem solving, or adaptive negotiation. It is neither exclusively soft nor hard, but a combination of each. It is soft on the people, hard on the problem. Instead of attacking each other, you jointly attack the problem. Instead of looking angrily across the table, you sit next to each other and problem solve. Joint problem solving revolves around interests instead of positions.

Excellent leaders always negotiate with integrity. However, some people view negotiations as a situation to get as much as possible from the opponent. This is certainly not the case in most negotiations. Leaders must not only use ethical negotiation tactics but also must know how to handle opponents who do not operate ethically. Never be afraid to leave the table if the opponent is not operating ethically or is not negotiating in good faith with the goal of reaching an agreement.

The first key to success in negotiations is preparation. Always prepare more than the other party. Knowledge is power at the negotiation table. Being better prepared gives you more confidence, which improves your negotiation results. Before you sit down to talk, know your goals and understand your limits on all aspects of the deal.

Excellent negotiators know when to walk away. This can be very hard; sometimes we convince ourselves that we want the deal so much we even have emotional attachments to it. Nevertheless, learning to walk away is sometimes the only way to get what you really want. Always have viable alternatives and be ready to walk. Knowing you have other options gives you power over the other party. If the negotiation is not going to get what you want or falls out of your budget, simply walk away.

At some point in a negotiation, it is best to keep your mouth shut. Learn to keep quiet and hear what the other party has to offer. Make it a point to use effective listening skills. When you hear something that you really like, you can express interest in the offer by probing more.

Always have the right people involved in a negotiation. You will never know everything, no matter how prepared you are or how good you think you are. Your team will determine the success of your negotiation. Make sure your team is better prepared than the other party.

As you grow in your leadership career, you will participate in more negotiations and in those that are even more critical to the organization. Learn as much as possible about negotiation tactics and strive to turn each negotiation into a joint problem-solving session.

Red Flag Behaviors

- You pride yourself on being a tough negotiator who never gives in to the opponent.
- You prefer to go to a negotiation with a minimal number of people since you want to be in control.
- You try to learn dirt on the opponent to use in the negotiation.
- You often lie during a negotiation to better position yourself.
- You do not prepare for a negotiation.

Case in Point

Kelcie's company had just won a long-term contract with Hudson Industries. It would be the company's bread and butter for the next three years. All that remained was negotiating the final terms of the agreement. There were some sticky points, such as frequency of site visits and payment terms. But Kelcie felt she was in a good position with each of the obstacles.

Her first step was to outline her position on each issue and get the support of her leadership. At that time, she also got their agreement of any fall-back positions if the customer was adamant.

Next, she selected her team to attend the negotiations. She thought about each issue and selected the person best suited to represent the company. She then reviewed her positions and established the ground rules for the negotiation. She would be the leader and direct questions or openings to the other team members when appropriate. Otherwise, the team members were not to speak or add on to anything she said. This gave her control over her own team and enabled her to direct issues to the person most suited to answer.

Finally, she assembled a team to practice the negotiation. They included people who knew the customer and were familiar with the issues. Her team did well during the practices, and it gave them confidence in their upcoming negotiation.

Just prior to the negotiation she reviewed her positions and the ground rules with the team. In the actual negotiation, things went very well. She established rapport with her counterpart and reached agreement and common ground on the minor issues. When the major issues were discussed, she closely monitored her counterpart. When things were beginning to get heated, she called for a break. During that time she socialized with the other team. After that, things went well, and Kelcie got a very favorable agreement.

Notes for the Aspiring Leader

Learn negotiation tactics from a leader who excels in creating an environment that leads to success for both sides. Think about how often you negotiate in your personal life and consider what works and what does not work.

Assess Your Current Location – Negotiation

(People Skills)

Instructions: Read each of the skills and behaviors below. As objectively as possible, score yourself for each according to the following scale: 1 = strongly disagree; 2 = disagree; 3 = agree; 4 = strongly agree. If a behavior is not appropriate for your current or aspired position, check the N/A column.

SKILL OR BEHAVIOR	1	2	3	4	N/A
I understand the importance of negotiating with others regarding differences in issues.					
I approach negotiations with the goal of establishing a win-win result.					
I know when to say no during a negotiation.					
I prepare for negotiations by analyzing the negotiation environment.					
I prepare for negotiations by identifying all alternatives.					
I enter negotiations with the right team in place to negotiate.					
I understand that ongoing relationships are important in negotiations.					
I approach negotiations with a clear understanding of the big picture.					
I effectively handle unethical negotiation tactics.					
I negotiate with integrity.					
SCORES FOR NEGOTIATION (Total check marks in each column and multiply by the heading for the column. Record your scores here.)					

TOTAL SCORE FOR NEGOTIATION: _____

(Add scores from Columns 1, 2, 3, and 4. Record the total above and on the Master Score Sheet in Appendix A. Also, count the number of N/As and record on the Master Score Sheet.)

Reflect - Negotiation

Scoring Analysis

List Your Four Highest Scored Items (Strengths)

Note: If you have multiple items with the same high score, choose the four items that are most related to your current or aspired position.

Item	Score

List Your Four Lowest Scored Items (Weaknesses)

Note: If you have multiple items with the same low score, choose the four items that are most related to your current or aspired position.

Item	Score

Reflect – Negotiation Questions

Think about the following questions about Negotiation:

- Think of someone who demonstrates excellent negotiation skills. What do they do that makes them successful?

- How often do you participate in a negotiation? Include daily negotiation opportunities, not just formal negotiations.

- Why is it important that a negotiator prepare for a formal negotiation?

- Why is it important to know when to walk away from a negotiation? Have you ever not walked away at the appropriate time and ended up on the short end of the negotiation?

- What is the role of listening in negotiation?

Develop – Negotiation

Develop and Renew

Consider the following development tactics to help improve in your negotiation skills and behaviors. Identify which tactics would be valuable to include in your Personal Development Plan (PDP) if you choose to improve in this competency.

- Recognize when you are faced with a negotiation. This enables you to prepare. Too often, we get into a negotiation without preparation and end up on the losing end of things because the other party is much more prepared.

- Understand that you are faced with negotiating circumstances throughout a day. What may appear minor may have long-term effects.

- If you are uncomfortable entering an unexpected negotiation, always ask for more time. Use this time to prepare your position.

- Go into a negotiation knowing your BATNA – the Best Alternative to a Negotiated Agreement. This is the route you will take if agreement can't be reached. The BATNA gives you confidence that if everything fails you have a course of action. You will be much less prone to accepting a result that is not in your interest or the interest of your organization.

- Actively listen to the other party. Find common ground in objectives and purposes.

- Always be prepared to say no if the negotiation is not going well and the other party is obstinate and not willing to compromise or seek other solutions. Don't feel you must come away with a solution even if it is not one that is in your favor.

- Strive to look at things from the other party's point of view. This is not to help you move to their position, but rather to help you understand their motivators and how to respond to them in the most effective way.

- Think of an upcoming negotiation. How can you turn it into a joint problem-solving session instead of a hard negotiation?

Resources

Books

Babcock, Linda and Sara Laschever. *Women Don't Ask: Negotiation and the Gender Divide*. Princeton, NJ: Princeton University Press, 2003.

Bazerman, Max and Deepak Malhotra. *Negotiating Genius: How to Overcome Obstacles and Achieve Brilliant Results at the Bargaining Table*. New York: Bantam, 2008.

Bazerman, Max and Margaret Neale. *Negotiating Rationally*. New York: Free Press, 1994.

Camp, Jim. *Start with NO: The Negotiating Tools That the Pros Don't Want You to Know*. New York: Crown Publishing, 2002.

Dawson, Roger. *Secrets of Power Negotiating: Inside Secrets From a Master Negotiator*. Franklin Lakes, NJ: Career Press, 2010.

Diamond, Stuart. *Getting More: How You Can Negotiate to Succeed in Work and Life*. Three Rivers Press, 2012.

Donaldson, Michael. *Fearless Negotiating: The Wish, Want, Walk Method To Reaching Solutions*. New York: McGraw-Hill, 2007.

Fisher, Roger; et al. *Getting to Yes: Negotiation Agreement Without Giving In*. New York: Penguin, 2011.

Lax, David A. and James Sebenium. *3-D Negotiation: Powerful Tools to Change the Game in Your Most Important Deals*. Cambridge: Harvard Business, 2006.

Lee, Michael and Sensei Tabuchi. *Black Belt Negotiating*. New York: AMACOM, 2007.

Lewicki, Roy; et al. *Essentials of Negotiation*. New York: McGraw, 2010.

_____. *Think Before You Speak: A Complete Guide to Strategic Negotiation*. New York: Wiley, 1996.

Luecke, Richard and James Patterson. *How to Become a Successful Negotiator*. New York: AMACOM, 2008.

Miller, Lee and Jessica Miller. *A Woman's Guide to Successful Negotiating: How to Convince, Collaborate, & Create Your Way to Agreement*. New York: McGraw-Hill, 2002.

Mnookin, Robert. *Beyond Winning: Negotiating to Create Value in Deals and Disputes*. Cambridge, MA: Belknap Press, 2004.

Oliver, David. *How to Negotiate Effectively*. London: Kogan Page, 2003.

Shell, Richard. *Bargaining for Advantage: Negotiation Strategies for Reasonable People*. New York: Penguin, 2006.

Ury, William. *Getting Past No: Negotiating in Difficult Situations.* New York: Bantam, 1993.

Watkins, Michael. *Breakthrough Business Negotiation.* San Francisco: Jossey-Bass, 2002.

Websites

See articles on negotiation at www.work911.com/articles/negotiate.htm.

Wikipedia provides extensive material on negotiation strategies and tactics at http://en.wikipedia.org/wiki/Negotiation .

An excellent blog resource is http://wwwthenegotiationblog.com

Review the following blog about mediation: http://www.stevemehta.wordpress.com.

Other Resources

A critical article on negotiation tactics can be found at http://www.csoonline.com/article/595564/7-essential-business-negotiation-tactics.

Negotiation tactics for small businesses can be found at http://smallbusiness.chron.com/10-recommendations-effective-negotiation-business-relationships-20352.html.

Harvard University maintains and excellent LinkedIn Group – See The Program on Negotiation

Change – Negotiation

Instructions

Using the table below and on the next page, refer to the items you listed in the Reflect – Negotiation worksheet and identify specific actions you will take to improve your weaknesses or enhance your strengths in each area. Refer to the Develop and Renew section on the previous pages for action ideas, keeping in mind the needs of your current or aspired position.

You can have multiple actions for each item you intend to focus on. In the first section, list the actions that are specific to the items you listed in the Reflect – Negotiation section. On the following page, list any actions you will take that are general to this competency and are related to more than one scored item. Finally, prioritize your actions based on the need for your current or aspired position. These actions will become part of your Personal Development Plan (PDP) for this competency in Appendix C.

Actions to Improve Weakness or Enhance Strength	Priority

Continue on next page.

Change – Negotiation

Actions to Improve Weakness or Enhance Strength	Priority

Other Actions You Will Take Related to Negotiation (not related to the identified strongest or weakest items)	Priority

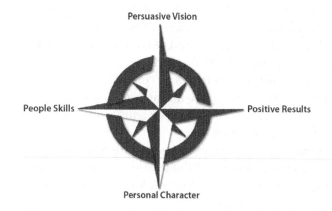

Persuasive Vision

People Skills — Positive Results

Personal Character

CHAPTER 32

Problem Solving

(People Skills)

"A problem clearly stated is a problem half solved."

– Dorothea Brande

We expect leaders to solve problems and most of the day that is exactly what they do. Successful leaders, however, use intelligent problem-solving techniques. Methodically solving problems leads to much better solutions. All too often, people jump from a problem to a solution, without any thought involved. Problem solving occurs at all levels of an organization. Problems are normal and part of everyday life. The types of problems may be different, but everyone should address the problems at their level; it is part of everyone's job.

There are two levels of problems that leaders must deal with. First, the daily, minor problems that don't require much effort to resolve. Don't be fooled, however. Information must still be gathered and considered before finding the right solution. But for the most part, leaders can easily become adept at handling easy problems on the spot.

Major, and more long-term problems, require more time and effort to solve. As a leader, you may be dealing with multiple major problems that require a well-thought out process and a good dose of patience to solve.

The best companies and the best leaders look on problems as opportunities to make things better, and successful organizations develop a culture where people view problems as opportunities.

The first step is to *recognize that there is a problem*. Sometimes leaders do not recognize a problem when others do. Leaders must listen to others and learn where problems are arising and be proactive in identifying them.

Next, the *problem needs to be defined*. This may involve collecting data, interviewing others, or just thinking about what the problem is, its effects, and who is impacted. Analyze and define the problem as specifically as possible. Get others' perspectives as well; they may see an aspect of the problem you do not see.

The leader should next *determine the root cause of the problem*. Some models use diagramming to help the problem solver get beyond the defined problem to the root cause. Regardless, something is causing the problem. It may be simple or complex, but the root cause needs to be determined and addressed. If not, the problem will arise again.

The next step is to *determine the alternatives available or solutions to consider*. It often benefits the leader to brainstorm this step with others who may have an interest in solving the problem. After a set of alternatives or solutions is established, the leader or team must look at the viability, effectiveness, risk, and cost of each alternative or solution.

Once this is done, the leader can *choose the most appropriate solution* that fits the strategy, goals, and objectives of the organization. Consider that at this point the leader may need to justify or build support for the chosen solution. Resources are often needed to implement the solution. Without support for the solution, this may be difficult.

The final step is to *implement the solution* and measure the result to determine if it is the right solution. If it can be quickly determined that the solution will not be successful, there may be an opportunity to reassess the problem and choose a different solution. Most likely, however, the original solution found through the above process will be the correct one.

Just as with decision making, ineffective leaders often delay in solving problems, thinking they may simply go away. Typically, this is not the case and it is important that leaders be proactive in facing and solving problems. A leader must also demonstrate patience in solving problems. It may take time to get the necessary information that leads to the right solution. During that time, the leader should not show frustration, especially with the problem-solving process.

Because problem solving is critical to every leader's success, it pays to follow a problem-solving process. Leaders should not feel they must solve every problem in isolation. A team approach helps to more clearly define the problem and identify the best solution.

Red Flag Behaviors

- You solve problems without collecting the necessary information and exploring all the alternatives.
- You delay solving problems because you are always looking for the right solution.
- You shirk responsibility by passing problems on to others to solve.
- You prefer to solve problems in isolation and not collaboration.
- You do not care what caused a problem, only the solution.

Case in Point

Kass had a difficult problem. His company manufactured widgets for NASA, and there seemed to be a quality problem because the NASA engineers were rejecting an increasing number of widgets. Not only was this damaging his company's reputation, but it was also becoming very costly. He knew that if he didn't solve the problem, his contract may be cancelled.

First, he wrote the problem on his white board and listed the effects. To more clearly define the problem, he called in his Chief Designer and Manager of Production. Together they defined the problem as being defective sensors in the widgets. They were not clear on what was causing the sensors to go bad, but they were confident they had defined the problem.

The team next investigated to determine the root cause of the problem. They talked to their engineers and quality control teams. Numerous possibilities were brought forward, and Kass assigned a testing team to examine the sensors more closely.

After a week of testing, the team brought their results to Kass. It seemed that there was a machine used in the production that was malfunctioning on an irregular basis. Kass questioned the team and it seemed that simply replacing the machine was one alternative, albeit an expensive one. They discussed other alternatives. Cindy, one of the lead engineers, said that she faced this problem before and solved it by replacing a head on one of the grinders. It was very inexpensive to do this, but would require the machine to be offline for two days. This was acceptable to Kass and he reviewed the plan with the Chief Designer and Manager of Production. They agreed and the problem was solved.

Notes for the Aspiring Leader

Learn a comfortable problem-solving model and use it for both personal and professional problems. Do not be afraid to solve problem. While it may seem difficult at first, the more success you have in readily solving problems, the more comfortable you will become with the process.

Assess Your Current Location – Problem Solving

(People Skills)

Instructions: Read each of the skills and behaviors below. As objectively as possible, score yourself for each according to the following scale: 1 = strongly disagree; 2 = disagree; 3 = agree; 4 = strongly agree. If a behavior is not appropriate for your current or aspired position, check the N/A column.

SKILL OR BEHAVIOR	1	2	3	4	N/A
I collaborate with others as appropriate to solve problems.					
I delegate authority to individuals or teams to solve problems as appropriate.					
I demonstrate a positive attitude toward problem solving.					
I am willing to change my position or decision when provided with new information.					
I evaluate problems from various perspectives to formulate an approach.					
I identify all reasonable alternatives when analyzing a problem.					
I identify and collect information relevant to problems.					
I present problems beyond my responsibility to the appropriate person(s).					
I prioritize problems and address them according to their importance.					
I demonstrate patience during the problem-solving process.					
I set an example in proactively addressing problems.					
I use brainstorming techniques when appropriate to understand and solve problems.					

Continue on next page.

Assess Your Current Location – Problem Solving

(People Skills)

SKILL OR BEHAVIOR	1	2	3	4	N/A
I use questioning techniques to learn causes of problems and potential solutions from a variety of sources.					
I use risk-assessment techniques to evaluate possible solutions to problems.					
SCORES FOR PROBLEM SOLVING (Total check marks in each column and multiply by the heading for the column. Record your scores here.)					

TOTAL SCORE FOR PROBLEM SOLVING: _____

(Add scores from Columns 1, 2, 3, and 4. Record the total above and on the Master Score Sheet in Appendix A. Also, count the number of N/As and record on the Master Score Sheet.)

Reflect – Problem Solving

Scoring Analysis

List Your Four Highest Scored Items (Strengths)

Note: If you have multiple items with the same high score, choose the four items that are most related to your current or aspired position.

Item	Score

List Your Four Lowest Scored Items (Weaknesses)

Note: If you have multiple items with the same low score, choose the four items that are most related to your current or aspired position.

Item	Score

Reflect – Problem Solving Questions

Think about the following questions about Problem Solving:

• How often do you have to solve problems? Do you have a system to consider all possible solutions or alternatives?

• What are the impacts of not reaching a timely solution for a problem?

• Why do team members respect a leader who has excellent problem-solving skills?

• What does it mean to have a positive problem-solving attitude? What behaviors demonstrate this attitude?

• What is the role of risk analysis in solving problems?

• Do you know others who seem to never be able to recognize a problem?

Develop – Problem Solving

Develop and Renew

Consider the following development tactics to help improve in your problem solving skills and behaviors. Identify which tactics would be valuable to include in your Personal Development Plan (PDP) if you choose to improve in this competency.

- Consider the attitude you present when faced with a problem. Do you complain about the problem? Do you avoid facing problems? List three behaviors you could change that would improve your attitude toward problems and problem solving. Take steps to improve these behaviors.

- Think of a recent problem you needed to solve. Did you seek out a sufficient amount of information to make an informed decision? Before solving your next problem, list the information necessary to make your decision. Also, identify what information would be nice to have when considering your alternatives?

- Identify peer leaders or direct reports who have difficulty identifying and considering reasonable alternatives when analyzing a problem. Meet with each and evaluate their strategies for problem solving. Develop a plan with each to improve their skills in identifying reasonable alternatives.

- Think of a recent problem you needed to solve. Build a decision tree that has each reasonable alternative as a separate limb. Can you think of alternatives now that you didn't consider during the process? In the future, use a similar decision tree to help identify and consider all reasonable alternatives.

- When you are faced with your next problem to be solved, take the time to list the questions you need to ask to learn the cause of the problem. Contact those who may have the answers and discuss with them.

- Identify a problem that you need to address. Is it appropriate that you collaborate with others to find the best solution for this problem? If so, list who you will seek out as a resource for helping to solve the problem. Why is each person appropriate for this problem? What information do they provide?

- For the next problem you need to solve, consider brainstorming with colleagues to explore possible solutions. Who are the appropriate people to include in the brainstorming session? Whose input would you most respect and value?

- List the problems and issues you currently face. Prioritize them into categories - most critical, critical, important, and less important. Let your list sit for a day. Then review the list and validate how well you prioritized the items. Continue to maintain this list and check the priorities regularly.

- Consider mapping a problem by outlining all the stakeholders and their view of the problem and possible solutions. What would be the best possible outcome for each stakeholder? What would be the best outcome for the organization? Collaborate with others when developing your problem map to get additional ideas or input.

Resources

Books

Adair, John. *Decision Making and Problem Solving Strategies*. Philadelphia: Kogan, 2012.

Bazerman, Max. *Judgment in Managerial Decision Making*. New York: Wiley, 2002.

Ben, David. *Advantage Play: The Manager's Guide to Creative Problem Solving*. Toronto: Key Porter Books, 2002.

Fanning, Patrick and Matthew McKay. *Successful Problem Solving: A Workbook to Overcome the Four Core Beliefs That Keep You Stuck*. Oakland, CA: New Harbinger Publications, 2002.

Firestine, Roger. *Leading on the Creative Edge: Gaining Competitive Advantage Through the Power of Creative Problem Solving*. Colorado Springs, CO: Pinon Press, 1996.

Higgins, James M. *101 Creative Problem Solving Techniques: The Handbook of New Ideas for Business*. Winter Park, FL: New Management Publishing Company, 2005.

Hoch, Stephen et al. *Wharton on Making Decisions*. New York: Wiley, 2001.

Jones, Morgan D. *The Thinker's Toolkit: 14 Powerful Techniques for Problem Solving*. New York: Three Rivers Press, 2008.

Nadler, Gerald and Shozo Hibino. *Breakthrough Thinking: The Seven Principles of Creative Problem Solving*. Rocklin, CA: Prima Publishing, 1998.

Okes, Duke. *Root Cause Analysis: The Core of Problem Solving and Corrective Action*. ASQ, 2009.

Proctor, Tony. *Creative Problem Solving for Managers: Developing Skills for Decision Making and Innovation*. New York: Routledge, 2010.

Watanabe, Ken. *Problem Solving 101: A Simple Book for Smart People.* Portfolio Hardcover, 2009.

Welch, David. *Decisions, Decisions: The Art of Effective Decision Making.* Amherst, NY: Prometheus Books, 2001.

Zeitz, Paul. *The Art and Craft of Problem Solving.* New York: Wiley, 2006.

Websites

MindTools.com http://www.mindtools.com/pages/main/newMN_TMC.htm Many articles and helpful problem solving tools.

Many resources on problem solving can be found at http://powerful-problem-solving.com/.

Other Resources

The following is an excellent article describing 9 steps to aid in problem solving: http://articles.businessinsider.com/2011-07-19/strategy/30065949_1_problem-solution-entrepreneurs.

Hammond, John S.; Keeney, Ralph L.; and Raiffa, Howard. "The Hidden Traps in Decision Making." Harvard Business Review. January 1, 2006.

Change – Problem Solving

Instructions

Using the table below and on the next page, refer to the items you listed in the Reflect – Problem Solving worksheet and identify specific actions you will take to improve your weaknesses or enhance your strengths in each area. Refer to the Develop and Renew section on the previous pages for action ideas, keeping in mind the needs of your current or aspired position.

You can have multiple actions for each item you intend to focus on. In the first section, list the actions that are specific to the items you listed in the Reflect – Problem Solving section. On the following page, list any actions you will take that are general to this competency and are related to more than one scored item. Finally, prioritize your actions based on the need for your current or aspired position. These actions will become part of your Personal Development Plan (PDP) for this competency in Appendix C.

Actions to Improve Weakness or Enhance Strength	Priority

Continue on next page.

Change – Problem Solving

Actions to Improve Weakness or Enhance Strength	Priority

Other Actions You Will Take Related to Problem Solving (not related to the identified strongest or weakest items)	Priority

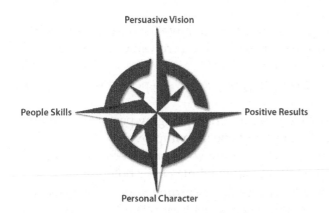

Persuasive Vision

People Skills

Positive Results

Personal Character

CHAPTER 33

Talent Management

(People Skills)

"My main job was developing talent. I was a gardener providing water and other nourishment to our top 750 people. Of course, I had to pull out some weeds, too."
– Jack Welch

Every organization can gain by having the right people doing the right jobs. And, people need a path to build on their talent and experience to grow in the company or organization. Talent management is a widely used term to refer to the overall human resources strategy in the workplace. Talent management is a key component of an organization's business strategy to differentiate themselves from the competition and achieve desired goals. Often what gives a competitive edge to a company is its people – who they are, what they know, how they behave, and how they interact with each other and customers. Your talent creates your products and services, serves your customers, and manages the important daily administration of your organization. Talk about an important component to an organization's success!

Talent management has become even more important because of employee churn – people are simply not as loyal to their organization as in past generations. External talent management (finding and recruiting the best people) has become critical.

Internal talent management must work well in order to retain the best people. If you are not developing your staff to be the future leaders, they will soon find an organization that does emphasize employee growth and reward.

One component of talent management is leadership development. The best organizations have an active leadership pipeline to provide the best talent where needed internally. High-potential people are identified and groomed to move up in the organization. They are assessed and provided opportunities to develop their skills and behaviors, leading to advancement in the organization.

Many leaders have difficulty managing others. They would rather just focus on doing their job. Who has time for feedback sessions, career counseling, training, mentoring, and discipline? The most effective leaders know that they are only as good as the people in their charge, and they go to great effort to do all those things that help every individual succeed.

Talent management consists of seven areas:

- **Corporate identity** – Who are you as an organization? Do you have the desired culture? Do all of your employees understand your mission, vision, and core values? Are you known as a company that values its employees and leaders?
- **Recruitment and selection** – How do you select the right people? Do people want to work for your organization?
- **Performance management and coaching** – Are you properly managing performance and providing the kind of feedback and coaching employees need to improve?
- **Employee development and training** – Are you developing your employees? Are you helping them create a plan to improve their skill set and maximize their potential?
- **Compensation, rewards, and benefits** – Are you properly rewarding your employees? Do you have the proper structures to assure your employees meet their needs?
- **Succession planning and leadership development** – Do you have a plan in the event a key person leaves the organization? How are you creating tomorrow's leaders?
- **Compliance, policy, and procedures** – Do you have procedures and policies in place to give employees a structure? Are you meeting your legal requirements?

Talent management is one of the most important leadership competencies because it involves people. Without motivated, skilled people, a business or organization will not succeed. Surprisingly, however, in our experience of assessing hundreds of leaders across many organizations, talent management is the lowest-scored competency on our leadership assessments. A deeper analysis of this has shown that the actual management of people - including coaching, mentoring, and providing feedback - are the weakest behaviors. People are not systematically trained to fulfill these critical leadership roles and it shows when people are asked to assess their leaders.

Red Flag Behaviors

- You do not give feedback to others (positive or negative).
- You do not feel it is your responsibility to develop your team members.
- You do not reward those who do an excellent job or perform beyond expectations.
- You overlook disciplinary problems with members of your team.
- You do not coach or mentor your team members.
- When hiring, you seek the best bargain and hire people who may not be the best qualified but who ask for the least compensation.
- You do not set expectations for those on your team.

Case in Point

When Tara was at Blu Designs, she was very impressed with the talent management programs that were an integral part of the company's culture. When she was recruited by USCCA, she told them how committed she was to talent management, especially coaching and mentoring. They agreed that she could implement these programs at USCCA, and she readily accepted her new position.

At USCCA, Tara had four direct reports and a total of 37 employees in her department. After she got to know each and explained her expectations, she initiated a coaching and mentoring program. Her four managers were given an external coach to insure confidentiality and objectivity. The program was designed to develop them to become better leaders. To initiate the program, each manager underwent a 360-degree leadership assessment to determine their strengths and weaknesses. They then underwent weekly training for six months. Along with the coaching, each manager created a development plan, approved by their coach, to improve their leadership skills over the next year.

The managers were tasked with mentoring their direct reports. This program was more skill related to ensure that each staff member was able to grow in their position. Each person created a development plan to improve their skill level over the next year.

Most staff members were appreciative of the opportunity, although a few were skeptical that it would work. Over the first few months, Tara could see noticeable improvement in both managers and staff. Her attention then began to focus on specific topics she could mentor her managers in, such as interviewing, conflict management, and presentation skills.

Notes for the Aspiring Leader

Take every opportunity to learn how to find the best people for your team. Focus on empowering them to do their best job, and reward them accordingly. Take the time and effort to develop a relationship with them, coach them, and give feedback to help them improve. Their development and success is your responsibility.

Assess Your Current Location – Talent Management

(People Skills)

Instructions: Read each of the skills and behaviors below. As objectively as possible, score yourself for each according to the following scale: 1 = strongly disagree; 2 = disagree; 3 = agree; 4 = strongly agree. If a behavior is not appropriate for your current or aspired position, check the N/A column.

SKILL OR BEHAVIOR	1	2	3	4	N/A
I assign tasks according to skills and knowledge of others.					
I challenge others to achieve their maximum potential.					
I demonstrate actions to retain the best talent in the organization.					
I establish and clarify expectations in others.					
I follow appropriate organization disciplinary procedures.					
I identify high potential individuals and groom them for promotion.					
I identify opportunities to coach/mentor others.					
I manage an effective and fair promotion process.					
I recognize technical strengths and weaknesses in others.					
I seek development opportunities for others.					
I proactively take steps to attract the best talent to the organization.					
I recognize and reward talent according to my organization's policies.					

Continue on next page.

Assess Your Current Location – Talent Management
(People Skills)

SKILL OR BEHAVIOR	1	2	3	4	N/A
I am proactive in my professional development efforts and model the importance to others.					
SCORES FOR TALENT MANAGEMENT (Total check marks in each column and multiply by the heading for the column. Record your scores here.)					

TOTAL SCORE FOR TALENT MANAGEMENT: _____

(Add scores from Columns 1, 2, 3, and 4. Record the total above and on the Master Score Sheet in Appendix A. Also, count the number of N/As and record on the Master Score Sheet.)

Reflect – Talent Management

Scoring Analysis

List Your Four Highest Scored Items (Strengths)

Note: If you have multiple items with the same high score, choose the four items that are most related to your current or aspired position.

Item	Score

List Your Four Lowest Scored Items (Weaknesses)

Note: If you have multiple items with the same low score, choose the four items that are most related to your current or aspired position.

Item	Score

Reflect – Talent Management Questions

Think about the following questions about talent management:

- Talent management is typically the lowest-scored competency for leaders. Why do you think that is the case?

- Have you ever had a leadership or executive coach? If so, what value did they bring to you?

- How do you like to receive feedback from your leadership?

- Why is it important for leaders to develop their team members?

- Why is it important to communicate your expectations to your team members?

- What does it mean to groom someone for a higher position?

Develop – Talent Management

Develop and Renew

Consider the following development tactics to help improve in talent management. Identify which tactics would be valuable to include in your Personal Development Plan (PDP) if you choose to improve in this competency.

- What are your organization's processes for attracting talent? Could they be improved? If so, discuss with your peer leaders to find a solution. The best organizations are those staffed with the best talent. If there are obstacles to this in your organization, take steps to overcome them.

- Think about your participation in the talent acquisition process. What areas are your weak points? What behaviors could you change to improve in these areas? Identify three areas for change and implement them immediately.

- High performers are often ignored because leaders spend an inordinate amount of time dealing with problem situations and people. Talk with your peer leaders and consider how you can recognize the achievements and efforts of high performers. Identify high-potential people for further development.

- An organization's policies for recognition and reward are put in place to insure fairness. Be careful that you are fair in how you recognize and reward individuals who excel. Stay within the boundaries of the organization's policies. If you don't, you may leave yourself open to accusations of being unfair or showing favoritism.

- Consider meeting with each team member regarding your expectations. Ask them to state what they feel are your expectations of them. Is there alignment between your perception and theirs? If not, take the time to clarify any expectations that are in question. Be sure that your expectations are consistent with the abilities of the team and each team member. It is unfair to have expectations that cannot be met with the skill level of an individual unless you provide developmental opportunities or mentoring. Encourage team members to bring any expectations to your attention that are beyond their capabilities.

- List your team members and identify the strengths and weaknesses of each. Do you assign tasks accordingly? What developmental opportunities do you provide to each to mitigate their weaknesses and enhance their skills? Identify behaviors you can change in this area to more appropriately assign tasks based on the skills and knowledge of team members.

- If you are not currently mentoring any team members, consider doing so. What are each team member's weaknesses? In which weak areas is it most appropriate for you to help? What are your strengths? Use your strengths to mentor a team member with a weakness in that area.

386

For other team members, consider pairing them with a more senior person or a peer leader who has strength in an area of the person's weakness.

- Set a regular time each month to meet with each team member and provide him or her with feedback. Assign developmental activities for them to accomplish between sessions, and check on progress throughout the month. Ensure that team members view these meetings as developmental and balance both positive and constructive feedback.

- Don't hesitate to give on-the-spot feedback to correct someone or to praise their performance. However, be very careful of who else is in the area and can hear your feedback. Feedback - whether positive or negative - is normally a private matter. There is a place for positive recognition in public, but even this type of feedback should be carefully constructed to not embarrass the recipient or offend someone else. Additionally, feedback should be based on observation and results, not hearsay.

- Who are the high-potential members of your team? How can you help develop them to be leaders? Even if your organization does not have a formal succession plan, you should consider who you would mentor to take your position if needed.

- Are you fully aware of your organization's disciplinary policies? If not, meet with the appropriate human resources professional to learn the proper procedures to follow. Are there other leaders who are hesitant to discipline when appropriate? If so, consider discussing with them and coaching them through their situations.

Resources

Books

Autry, James. *Love and Profit: The Art of Caring Leadership*. New York: Morrow, 1991.

Becker, Brian E.; et al. *The HR Scorecard: Linking People, Strategy and Performance*. Cambridge: Harvard Business School Press, 2005.

Bell, Chip. *Managers As Mentors: Building Partnerships for Learning*. San Francisco: Berrett-Koehler, 2002.

Berger, Lance and Dorothy Berger. *The Talent Management Handbook: Creating a Sustainable Competitive Advantage by Selecting, Developing, and Promoting the Best People*. New York: McGraw-Hill, 2010.

Bernardin, John. *Human Resources Management*. New York: McGraw-Hill, 2012.

Byham, William C.; et al. *Grow Your Own Leaders: How to Identify, Develop and Retain Leadership Talent*. New York: Prentice Hall, 2002.

Charan, Ram. *Leaders at All Levels: Deepening Your Talent Pool to Solve the Succession Crisis.* San Francisco: Jossey-Bass, 2007.

Conety, Bill and Ram Charan. *The Talent Masters: Why Smart Leaders Put People Before Numbers.* New York: Crown Business, 2010.

DeLong, David and Steve Trautman. *The Executive Guide to High-Impact Talent Management: Powerful Tools for Leveraging a Changing Workforce.* New York: McGraw-Hill, 2010.

Effron, Marc and Ort, Miriam. *One Page Talent Management: Eliminating Complexity, Adding Value.* Cambridge: Harvard Business, 2010.

Falcone, Paul. *The Hiring and Firing Question and Answer Book.* New York: AMACOM, 2002.

Fields, Martha. *Indispensable Employees: How to Hire Them, How to Keep Them.* Franklin Lakes, NJ, 2001.

Flaherty, James. *Coaching: Evoking Excellence in Others.* Butterworth-Heinemann, 2010.

Fulmer, Robert and Jay Conger. *Growing Your Company's Leaders.* New York: AMACOM, 2004.

Grote, Dick. *Discipline Without Punishment.* New York: AMACOM, 1995.

Harvard Business School Press. *Coaching People* (Pocket Mentor Series). Cambridge: Harvard Business School Press, 2006.

Harvard Business School Press. *Retaining Your Best People: The Results-Driven Manager.* Cambridge: Harvard Business School Press, 2005.

Harvard Business School Press. *Giving Feedback* (Pocket Mentor Series). Cambridge: Harvard Business School Press, 2007.

Kouzes, James and Barry Posner. *Encouraging the Heart: A Leader's Guide to Rewarding and Recognizing Others.* San Francisco: Jossey-Bass, 2003.

Oakes, Kevin and Pat Galagan. *The Executive Guide to Integrated Talent Management.* American Society for Training & Development, 2011.

O'Neil, Mary Beth. *Executive Coaching with Backbone and Heart: A Systems Approach to Engage in Leaders with Their Challenges.* San Francisco: Jossey-Bass, 2007.

Schiemann, William and Susan Messinger. *Reinventing Talent Management: How to Maximize Performance in the New Marketplace.* New York: Wiley, 2009.

Sims, Doris, *The 30-Minute Guide to Talent and Succession Management: A Quick Reference Guide for Business Leaders.* AuthorHouse, 2011.

_____. *Building Tomorrow's Talent: A Practitioner's Guide to Talent Management and Succession Planning.* AuthorHouse, 2007.

Stone, Florence. *Coaching, Counseling and Mentoring.* New York: AMACOM, 1999.

White, Daniel and Marshall Goldsmith. *Coaching Leaders: Guiding People Who Guide Others.* San Francisco: Jossey-Bass, 2005.

Websites

Wikipedia provides an excellent overview of talent management at http://en.wikipedia.org/wiki/Talent_management.

Workforce offers numerous blogs about talent management at http://www.workforce.com/.

Other Resources

Talent Management magazine is an excellent resource. Their site also provides articles and white papers about talent management. Go to http://talentmgt.com/.

An excellent article focusing on succession planning: http://humanresources.about.com/od/successionplanning/g/talent-management.htm.

Change – Talent Management

Instructions

Using the table below and on the next page, refer to the items you listed in the Reflect – Talent Management worksheet and identify specific actions you will take to improve your weaknesses or enhance your strengths in each area. Refer to the Develop and Renew section on the previous pages for action ideas, keeping in mind the needs of your current or aspired position.

You can have multiple actions for each item you intend to focus on. In the first section, list the actions that are specific to the items you listed in the Reflect – Talent Management section. On the following page, list any actions you will take that are general to this competency and are related to more than one scored item. Finally, prioritize your actions based on the need for your current or aspired position. These actions will become part of your Personal Development Plan (PDP) for this competency in Appendix C.

Actions to Improve Weakness or Enhance Strength	Priority

Continue on next page.

Change – Talent Management

Actions to Improve Weakness or Enhance Strength	Priority

Other Actions You Will Take Related to Talent Management (not related to the identified strongest or weakest items)	Priority

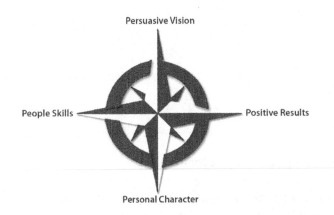

Persuasive Vision

People Skills — Positive Results

Personal Character

CHAPTER 34

Teamwork

(People Skills)

"Coming together is a beginning. Keeping together is progress. Working together is success."
– Henry Ford

Leaders either lead teams or are part of a team; thus, teams are a central part of the leader's role. Leaders need to be aware of their skills and behaviors in managing work teams, but they must also be aware of their skills and behaviors when they are functioning as part of a team. Teams must work together with other teams and with organizational systems and processes to achieve goals and overcome the challenges that are faced.

Michael West (2012) has studied a massive amount of research on teams. In particular, he focuses on what characterizes an effective team and what he describes as a dream team. An effective team is the right size, is relatively stable in membership, and is working on a task that legitimately requires teamwork. The team must have an overall purpose that adds value and is translated into clear, challenging team objectives. The team needs the right people as team members with the required skills in the right roles. They must be enablers, not derailers – people who support effective teams, not people who sabotage, undermine or obstruct team functioning.

Dream teams are characterized by transformational leadership that reinforces an inspiring and motivating team purpose. The purpose is sharply focused on the needs of the team's stakeholders. It encourages all team members to value the diversity of its membership. Dream teams have a high level of positivity, characterized by optimism and a healthy balance of positive and negative interactions. Members are open, appreciative, kind, and genuine in their interactions with each other and eager to learn from each other. They believe in the team's ability to be successful and effective in their work. They are secure in their team membership and attached to the team because of the level of trust and support they encounter.

When leading a team, the leader needs to be aware of their attitude toward and understanding of team processes that make the difference between a team that goes through the motions and one that thrives.

A leader of strong teams:

- Helps team members achieve success.
- Creates team cohesion.
- Cares about the well-being of team members.
- Creates a positive, inspiring atmosphere.
- Respects every member of a team.
- Shares credit and shoulders responsibility.
- Gives team members the skills to succeed, then steps back to let them thrive.

Strong team leaders align themselves with their teams and the goals and objectives of the team. They consider themselves part of the team, not leaders walking out ahead. They encourage and take pride in the success of the team and its individual members. Effective team leaders communicate with clarity and conciseness. Team leaders do not need to have all the right answers; they only need to ask the right questions.

John Maxwell has also written substantially about teams. One interesting list he has developed is what an effective team does for the leader (2009):

- It makes you better than you are.
- It multiplies your value to others.
- It enables you to do what you do best.
- It allows you to help others do their best.
- It gives you more time.
- It provides you with companionship.
- It helps you fulfill the desires of your heart.
- It makes everyone on the team a winner.

The strongest companies and organizations are those that focus on developing teamwork. Teams can accomplish much more than any individuals working separately. But the teams must be strong and function well to gain the best results. It is the leader's responsibility to ensure that every team is working at its best.

Red Flag Behaviors

- You do not see the value of a team; you would rather work alone even if it means you must contribute more time and effort.
- You play one member against another in your team.
- You do not set expectations for your team members.
- You do not motivate your team members to do their best.
- You do not set a team vision or establish team goals.
- You do not build relationships with your team members.

Case in Point

Blake was excited about his new assignment as head of the proposal team. He had a great background in proposals and was sure that the team would be successful. He needed to quickly ramp them up for a big opportunity. His first order of business was to get to know the team better and identify their strengths and weaknesses.

Next, he focused on identifying any conflict the team had, either internally or with external departments. In a team meeting, he expressed his expectation that any difficulties or conflicts within the group or with external departments should be brought to his attention. When working on proposals, there was not time or energy to devote to conflict. During this team meeting he also set his goals. He got feedback from the team on the realism of the goals and gained their buy-in on his strategy to achieve the goals.

When Blake met one-on-one with his team members, he was clear on his expectations. But he also asked each what they expected of him. He took notes and promised he would do his best. If a person's expectations were unrealistic, he discussed with them and negotiated a better approach.

To build team unity, Blake scheduled one night each month to get together for a fun activity. He asked the team to come up with a schedule for the year and identify each month's activity. In addition, he asked them to give him three suggestions each on how the proposal processes could be improved.

Moving forward, things were not perfect because of the stress of the job, but the team worked well together, made adjustments, and learned to trust and respect each other.

Notes for the Aspiring Leader

Seek to understand the dynamics of teams you are a part of. Coach your team members. Strive to infuse team spirit and reach for success as a team, not as individuals. Help develop your team to be the best it can be.

Assess Your Current Location – Teamwork

(People Skills)

Instructions: Read each of the skills and behaviors below. As objectively as possible, score yourself for each according to the following scale: 1 = strongly disagree; 2 = disagree; 3 = agree; 4 = strongly agree. If a behavior is not appropriate for your current or aspired position, check the N/A column.

SKILL OR BEHAVIOR	1	2	3	4	N/A
I actively build alignment toward shared outcomes.					
I administer reward systems that encourage teamwork and cooperation.					
I build a sense of team ownership and pride.					
I instill a sense of purpose in other members of my team.					
I effectively build teams when necessary to complete projects.					
I facilitate cooperation between others.					
I forge consensus when appropriate.					
I motivate others to work as a team.					
I proactively work collaboratively with others.					
I use influencing skills appropriately to gain alliances on positions.					
I value cooperation.					
I recognize the importance of teamwork to accomplish organizational goals.					

Continue on next page.

Assess Your Current Location – Teamwork

(People Skills)

	1	2	3	4	N/A
SCORES FOR TEAMWORK (Total check marks in each column and multiply by the heading for the column. Record your scores here.)					

TOTAL SCORE FOR TEAMWORK: _____

(Add scores from Columns 1, 2, 3, and 4. Record the total above and on the Master Score Sheet in Appendix A. Also, count the number of N/As and record on the Master Score Sheet.)

Reflect - Teamwork

Scoring Analysis

List Your Four Highest Scored Items (Strengths)

Note: If you have multiple items with the same high score, choose the four items that are most related to your current or aspired position.

Item	Score

List Your Four Lowest Scored Items (Weaknesses)

Note: If you have multiple items with the same low score, choose the four items that are most related to your current or aspired position.

Item	Score

Reflect – Teamwork Questions

Think about the following questions about teamwork:

- What is a leader's role in selecting a team for a project or initiative?

- What is the importance of setting team goals? What happens if the team does not have clearly defined goals?

- What role do interpersonal skills play in leading a team?

- How does a leader build a cohesive team?

- Are you a member of multiple teams? What do you do if the goals of teams conflict?

- How does the effectiveness of teams contribute to the success or failure of an organization?

Develop – Teamwork

Develop and Renew

Consider the following development tactics to help improve in your teamwork skills and behaviors. Identify which tactics would be valuable to include in your Personal Development Plan (PDP) if you choose to improve in this competency.

- Consider an initiative you plan to begin or have recently begun. Who are the stakeholders for this initiative? What steps can you take to build alignment toward a shared outcome?

- Although you need to be concerned about what motivates each team member, it is also important to develop a unified purpose for the team. When motivating a team to accomplish an initiative, clearly describe the benefits to the organization and the team.

- Collaboration does not mean everyone is happy all the time. There is even room for conflict between individuals or teams who are working collaboratively. The difference is that disagreements are presented and resolved and the team moves forward. The conflict does not remain to inhibit progress.

- For each future initiative, develop a purpose statement that clearly communicates to stakeholders and team members the importance of the tasks and their role in its success.

- Everyone has an influencing style. Those who work on improving their influencing style get more cooperation from stakeholders and team members. The strategies for influencing others should be dependent on the style by which each person is more readily influenced, whether logic, emotion, facts, or authority.

- As a team leader, you are responsible for the professional development of each person. Take steps to learn the strengths and weaknesses of each and help them create a personal development plan to guide their efforts.

- You may not always be successful in building team ownership and pride. Sometimes, renegade team members pursue their own goals and objectives that interfere with your ability to build team pride. How can you handle this situation? Consider the different avenues available to you, and discuss with your human resources professional.

- Have a team meeting to establish team norms. These norms help guide your team, provide consistency, and help keep everyone on the same page.

Resources

Books

Avery, Christopher; et al. *Teamwork is an Individual Skill: Getting Your Work Done When Sharing Responsibility.* San Francisco: Berrett-Koehler Publishers, 2001.

Barna, George: *The Power of Team Leadership: Achieving Success Through Shared Responsibility.* WaterBrook Press, 2001.

Carter, Carol, Bishop; et al. *Keys to Success: Teamwork and Leadership.* New York: Prentice Hall, 2012.

Chang, Richard Y. and Curtin, Mark J. *Succeeding as a Self-Managed Team: A Practical Guide to Operating as a Self-Managed Work Team.* New York: Pfeiffer, 1999.

Deeprose, Donna. *Making Teams Work: How to Form, Measure, and Transition Today's Teams.* New York: AMACOM, 2001.

Hackman, Richard. *Leading Teams: Setting the Stage for Great Performances.* Boston, Harvard Business School Press, 2002.

Harvard Business School Press. *Leading Teams* (Pocket Mentor Series). Cambridge: Harvard Business School Press, 2006.

Harvard Business Essentials. *Creating Teams With an Edge.* Boston: Harvard Business School, 2004.

Jones, Steven and Don Schilling. *Measuring Team Performance: A Step-By-Step, Customizable Approach for Managers, Facilitators and Team Leaders.* San Francisco: Jossey-Bass, 2000.

Katzenbach, Jon and Douglas Smith. *The Wisdom of Teams: Creating the High-Performance Organization.* New York: Harper Business, 2003.

Lencioni, Patrick. *The Five Dysfunctions of a Team: A Leadership Fable.* San Francisco: Jossey-Bass, 2002.

_____. *Overcoming the Five Dysfunctions of a Team: A Field Guide for Leaders, Managers, and Facilitators.* New York: Wiley, 2005.

Maxwell, John. *The 17 Indisputable Laws of Teamwork: Embrace Them and Empower Your Team.* Nashville, TN: Thomas Nelson, 2001.

_____. *Teamwork Makes the Dream Work.* Nashville, TN: Thomas Nelson, 2002.

_____. *The 17 Essential Qualities of a Team Player.* Nashville, TN: Thomas Nelson, 2006.

_____. *Teamwork 101: What Every Leader Needs to Know.* Nashville, TN: Thomas Nelson, 2009.

Miller, Brian. *Nice Teams Finish Last*. New York: AMACOM, 2010.

Parker, Glenn M.; et al. *Rewarding Teams: Lessons From the Trenches*. San Francisco: Jossey-Bass, 2000.

_____. *Cross-Functional Teams: Working with Allies, Enemies, and Other Strangers*. San Francisco: Jossey-Bass, 2002.

_____. *Team Players and Teamwork: New Strategies for Developing Successful Collaboration*. San Francisco: Jossey-Bass, 2008.

Robbins, Harvey and Michael Finley. *The New Why Teams Don't Work: What Goes Wrong and How to Make it Right*. San Francisco: Berrett-Koehler, 2000.

Robustelli, Bob. *TeamWork*. Charleston, SC: CreateSpace, 2011.

West, Michael A. *Effective Teamwork: Practical Lessons from Organizational Research (Psychology of Work and Organizations)*. New York: Wiley, 2012.

Wysocki, Robert. *Building Effective Project Teams*. New York: Wiley, 2001.

Websites

Wikipedia explores various aspects of teamwork at http://en.wikipedia.org/wiki/Teamwork.

The College of Executive Coaching offers numerous articles regarding teamwork at: http://www.executivecoachcollege.com/teamwork_in_management.htm.

Other Resources

The following Hub Pages article provides excellent resources on teamwork: http://cmoe.hubpages.com/hub/businessteamwork.

An excellent article on how teamwork makes a difference can be found at http://smallbusiness.chron.com/teamwork-difference-business-12085.html.

Change – Teamwork

Instructions

Using the table below and on the next page, refer to the items you listed in the Reflect – Teamwork worksheet and identify specific actions you will take to improve your weaknesses or enhance your strengths in each area. Refer to the Develop and Renew section on the previous pages for action ideas, keeping in mind the needs of your current or aspired position.

You can have multiple actions for each item you intend to focus on. In the first section, list the actions that are specific to the items you listed in the Reflect – Teamwork section. On the following page, list any actions you will take that are general to this competency and are related to more than one scored item. Finally, prioritize your actions based on the need for your current or aspired position. These actions will become part of your Personal Development Plan (PDP) for this competency in Appendix C.

Actions to Improve Weakness or Enhance Strength	Priority

Continue on next page.

Change – Teamwork

Actions to Improve Weakness or Enhance Strength	Priority

Other Actions You Will Take Related to Teamwork (not related to the identified strongest or weakest items)	Priority

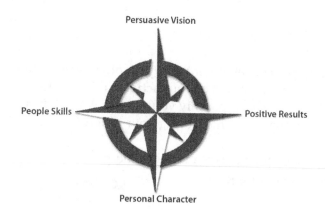

Persuasive Vision

People Skills

Positive Results

Personal Character

CHAPTER 35
Creating Long-Term Change

"Destiny is not a matter of chance; it is a matter of choice. It is not a thing to be waited for; it is a thing to be achieved."

– William Jennings Bryan

Change takes place incrementally and over a period of time. It is also ongoing – nothing ever stays the same. We seldom see changes in behavior instantly; therefore, changing behavior, improving skills, and adapting new ways of thinking and doing things requires reflection, commitment, and motivation on the part of the individual to achieve change over time.

At first, implementing change may result in failures or awkward behavior until the new practiced behavior becomes a regular habit in your leadership thinking and activities. Therefore, it is important to have a mindset that is constantly thinking about the new behaviors needed, the specific actions to apply, and the enthusiasm to keep going despite imperfection. The development plan you have completed will help you stay motivated and on track, so refer to it often and enhance it when needed.

If you have followed the Leadership Compass development process as we have outlined and have reached this point, we commend your commitment and efforts. By now you have:

- Assessed your leadership competencies.
- Reflected on your self assessment results, including your strongest and weakest leadership competencies.
- Identified specific development actions you will take that will increase your effectiveness and success.
- Prioritized your development actions and set specific dates that you can accomplish improvements.

Measuring Change

To ensure that your hard work and effort in leadership development is paying off, it is important to measure your improvements. If you don't measure the results of your **actions,** it is easy to stagnate. You may find that it is harder to reach your goals, especially your stretch goals, which are usually the most difficult. Additionally, the very nature of measuring your progress stimulates internal motivation to keep going.

Remember, the whole process of leadership development takes initiative and personal responsibility, so set your **milestones** and commit to reaching them.

In addition to setting milestones, you can measure change by verifying that a specific development action produces a **desired outcome**. For instance, if your goal is to improve your presentations, ask a respected colleague who is good in this area to observe several presentations during the period you are implementing your development actions. This observer can provide you with feedback to further assist your improvement and indicate when you have achieved your desired outcome.

Finally, to ensure that the changes you are making in your leadership development are sticking and are now a part of your leadership behaviors and skill set, we recommend that you retake the self assessment every 24-36 months. This **review** of your leadership skills not only provides you with confidence that your development actions are working and improvement is actually taking place, but it also puts you in a more positive place in your current job position and for future opportunities. This increases the likelihood of greater overall career success.

As you embark on your leadership development journey, we want to leave you with some practical guidelines to increase your success in incorporating these new behaviors and skills into your day-to-day work.

- Stay focused. You will surely have distractions and frustrations along the way, so it is up to you to keep a strong commitment to see the results of improved effectiveness.

- Stay on schedule. Plan your ongoing development into your daily schedule.

- Seek the advice and feedback of a trusted colleague, mentor, or coach, especially in those areas that challenge you the most.

- Share your leadership development plan with your direct supervisor if you are comfortable doing so. This shows your level of commitment to professional development and may be another source of feedback.

- Review your entire development plan monthly to ensure that each action is relevant and prioritized for your current position and desired future goals. This will also help you stay on track.

- Encourage your organization or team to initiate professional development. This will motivate others to be their best, create a culture of continuous development and improvement, and most likely increase the overall success of the organization.

- Reward yourself after you have reached specific milestones, especially if those milestones have resulted in promotions or specific leadership successes.

Spread the Love

As coaches, we want to leave you with a few important thoughts. Leadership is not easy and takes a commitment to do the right thing even though it may not always be the easiest thing to do. Leaders are bombarded with pressures, and these pressures often place us in a position in which we need to choose how we will think and behave.

While our behavior may not always be perfect, even when we are trying to follow the Leadership Compass, we need to remember that our behavior influences others in the organization. For example, if we are frequently under stress, others will notice and unfortunately, many will mirror this same behavior. It is your responsibility to know and improve your weak areas and take responsibility to set an example that you wish others to follow. Your behavior does affect others either positively or negatively.

As a leader, it is your responsibility to not only have competency in the areas we have discussed in The Leadership Compass, but also to help others improve their skills and behaviors. This requires that you coach, mentor, and lead in these important areas. The more effective you are in growing others, the greater likelihood your organization will achieve its goals. After all, that is one of the important responsibilities that leaders have – organizational success.

While organizational success is often solely linked to financial success, financial success is best achieved when each person in the organization is performing at their best and contributes to a thriving organizational culture. Organizations can be likened to living organisms and similarly experience growth, change, and face difficulties in which each person is required to work, react and grow individually and corporately to achieve and maintain a thriving work environment.

The Leadership Compass competencies and development process are purposefully designed to assist leaders in setting an example that can ultimately help the organization become one that is highly functional and that provides a healthy culture in which individuals can succeed

In closing, we recommend you regularly visit the Renew Leadership Movement website at **www.renewleadership.com**. Here you will be able to read the latest blogs and news on leadership. We also encourage you to be active in the forums. Ask questions, give answers, discuss issues, and be a part of the Renew Leadership Movement.

APPENDICES

APPENDIX A

Master Score Sheet

On the following page is a scoring sheet for the 30 leadership competencies. As you complete the self assessment for each competency, enter your score in the Your Score column.

To determine your percentage for the competency, divide your score by the maximum possible score for the competency (indicated in the second column). Subtract 4 points for each N/A you selected for the competency. Here's an example:

COMPETENCY	MAXIMUM SCORE	YOUR SCORE	% Your Score/ Maximum Score	AREA TO FOCUS (Y or N)
Business Development	64	44	79% 44/64 – 8 (2 N/As)	N

In the Area to Focus column, identify those competencies that you wish to focus on improving. They may not always be your lowest scored competencies (by %). You should also take into consideration those that are most important in your current or aspired position. For example, if you scored 72% for decision making and 65% for strategic thinking, you may want to check decision making if you are required to make a lot of decisions in your position. You may choose not to check strategic thinking if it is not an important competency for your current position, even though your score is below 70%.

It is also important to assess your scores by P. Our competencies are grouped in these areas for a reason. If you score low in a particular P, it can be an indicator that you need to work on the competencies in that area. For example, if your score for Persuasive Vision is the lowest of the four areas, take a closer look at the competencies in this area and include steps in your Personal Development Plan to improve in this area, even if there are competencies in other areas that may individually be lower.

Use the worksheets in Appendix B to evaluate your scores by identifying the highest and lowest competencies, items, and P scores. Use this information as a guide to create your Personal Development Plan in Appendix C. For further information on how to create your Personal Development Plan, or PDP, refer to Chapter 3.

Master Score Sheet

COMPETENCY	MAXIMUM SCORE	YOUR SCORE	% Your Score / Maximum Score	AREA TO FOCUS (Y or N)
Persuasive Vision				
Creativity	52			
Influencing	56			
Inspiration	60			
Motivation	40			
Planning	64			
Strategic Thinking	80			
P Score	*340*			
Positive Results				
Business Development	64			
Commitment to Quality	72			
Customer Focus	44			
Decision Making	40			
Financial Management	44			
Focus on Results	80			
Technical Skills	40			
Time Management	120			
P Score	*504*			
Personal Character				
Courage	64			
Credibility	52			
Followership	48			
Initiative	60			
Integrity	60			
Stress Management	52			
Trust	56			
P Score	*392*			
People Skills				
Change Leadership	44			
Commitment to Diversity	44			
Communications	112			
Conflict Management	52			
Interpersonal Skills	52			
Negotiation	40			
Problem Solving	56			
Talent Management	52			
Teamwork	48			
P Score	*500*			

APPENDIX B

Personal Development Plan Worksheets

The following worksheets will help you determine what competencies you should focus on in your Personal Development Plan. Here are the instructions for each worksheet.

Worksheet 1 – Ranking of Competencies

Using this worksheet, rank your competency scores with the highest first, then moving toward the lowest. Use the information in Appendix A to complete this worksheet.

Worksheet 2 – Ranking of P Areas

Refer to the scores in Appendix A and list the P areas in order with the highest scored first.

APPENDIX B – WORKSHEET 1

COMPETENCY RANKING

RANK	COMPETENCY	SCORE	AREA OF FOCUS (√)
1			
2			
3			
4			
5			
6			
7			
8			
9			
10			
11			
12			
13			
14			
15			
16			
17			
18			
19			
20			
21			
22			
23			
24			
25			
26			
27			
28			
29			
30			

APPENDIX B – WORKSHEET 2

P RANKING

RANK	P AREA	SCORE	AREA OF FOCUS (√)
1			
2			
3			
4			

APPENDIX C

Personal Development Plan

To complete your Personal Development Plan (PDP), refer to the competencies you desire to develop and the information you identified in Appendices A and B. We strongly recommend that you re-read Chapter 3 and review the sample PDP prior to completing *your* PDP. If you need additional copies of PDP templates, visit *http://www.renewleadership.com* to print.

PERSONAL DEVELOPMENT PLAN (PDP)

Competency: **Score:**   %
                                                                     (from Appendix A)

General Steps for this Competency:

Actions (See Change Section)	Resources Needed	Date Compl.

Item-Related Steps:

Item (See Reflect Section)	Score	Actions (See Change Section)	Resources Needed	Date Compl.

PERSONAL DEVELOPMENT PLAN (PDP)

Competency:

Score: %
(from Appendix A)

General Steps for this Competency:

Actions (See Change Section)	Resources Needed	Date Compl.

Item-Related Steps:

Item (See Reflect Section)	Score	Actions (See Change Section)	Resources Needed	Date Compl.

PERSONAL DEVELOPMENT PLAN (PDP)

Competency: **Score:**   %
                                                             (from Appendix A)

General Steps for this Competency:

Actions (See Change Section)	Resources Needed	Date Compl.

Item-Related Steps:

Item (See Reflect Section)	Score	Actions (See Change Section)	Resources Needed	Date Compl.

About Benchmark Learning International and Renew Leadership

"Leadership is a journey and starts with you."
                                                    - Ben McDonald

Benchmark Learning International has worked with corporate and university leaders since 1999 and specializes in leadership assessments, executive coaching, and leadership training and retreats.

Corporate clients have included such companies as McDonnell Douglas, GTE, US West, KBR, Halliburton, CB&I, Lore International Institute, and others. Leading universities include Case Western Reserve University, Illinois Institute of Technology, Dartmouth College, Johns Hopkins Medical University, and The University of Chicago.

For more information about Benchmark Learning International, see http://www/benchmarkli.com.

Renew Leadership was launched in 2013 to support current and aspiring leaders in building a passion for leadership growth and provide a place for leadership development conversations and resources.

For more information about Renew Leadership, to participate in leadership discussions, and access additional resources, see http://www.renewleadership.com.

About the Authors

Everyone should care about leadership. If you are leading, you need to be your best because your actions affect others. If you are following, you seek confidence in your leaders because their actions affect you."

- Sidney McDonald

As leadership speakers, coaches, and authors, Ben McDonald and Sidney McDonald have worked with leaders of all levels and across a multitude of industries over the last three decades. As founders of Benchmark Learning International, they have helped leaders around the globe increase the effectiveness of their leadership skills and behaviors.

Both began their careers in modest beginnings. However, they each took the course of hard work with a zeal for continuous learning and an inner passion to help others succeed. After the twists and turns of education, corporate jobs, and gaining valuable experience in a variety of industries, they launched Benchmark Learning International to focus their efforts on bringing success to a wider audience.

Through their work at Benchmark Learning International they have gathered cumulative quantitative and qualitative leadership data. Much of the information presented in *The Leadership Compass: Mapping Your Leadership Direction* is taken from this data, and is combined with their success in helping people navigate the demanding journey of effectively leading others.

As parents and grandparents, Ben and Sidney value sharing time with their incredible family. They are also active in their Boise, Idaho community, serving others where they can. In their free time, they enjoy traveling, biking, hiking, and gardening.

CPSIA information can be obtained
at www.ICGtesting.com
Printed in the USA
LVOW03s1747030216

473528LV00006B/243/P